ACRL MONOGRAPH NO. 31

The Undergraduate Library

Irene A. Braden

American Library Association

Chicago 1970

Standard Book Number 8389-3097-2 (1970)
The Library of Congress card number for
   the ACRL Monograph Series is 52-4228.
The card number of this title is 75-80834.
Copyright © 1970 by the American Library Association
All rights reserved
Printed in the United States of America

Cover: *Exterior view, Undergraduate Library and Academic Center Building,*
         University of Texas

Contents

	Tables	v
	Illustrations	vii
	Preface	ix
1.	Introduction	1
2.	Lamont Library, Harvard University	5
3.	The Undergraduate Library, The University of Michigan	29
4.	The Undergraduate Library, The University of South Carolina	63
5.	The Undergraduate Library, Indiana University	78
6.	Uris Library, Cornell University	93
7.	The Undergraduate Library, The University of Texas	116
8.	Conclusions	137
	Selected Bibliography	151
	Index	155

Tables

1. Capital Costs of the Lamont Library   7

2. Withdrawals from the Lamont Library Collection   16

3. Growth of the Book Collection, Lamont Library   17

4. Circulation Statistics (Two-Week Books), Lamont Library   23

5. Reserve Statistics, Lamont Library   24

6. Initial Budget for the Undergraduate Library, University of Michigan   31

7. Growth of the Book Collection, Undergraduate Library, University of Michigan   46

8. Books Found Missing in the Annual Inventory, Undergraduate Library, University of Michigan   47

9. New Titles and Volumes Purchased for Reserve, Undergraduate Library, University of Michigan   48

10. Reference Statistics, Undergraduate Library, University of Michigan   51

11. Comparison of Undergraduate and General Library Circulation, University of Michigan   56

12. Percentage of Circulation for Voluntary Reading, Undergraduate Library, University of Michigan   57

13. Home Circulation Statistics, Undergraduate Library, University of Michigan   57

14. Reserve Statistics, Undergraduate Library, University of Michigan   58

15. Percentage of Circulation by Level of User, Undergraduate Library, University of Michigan   58–59

16. Circulation Statistics, Undergraduate Library, University of South Carolina   75

17. Growth of the Book Collection, Undergraduate Library, University of South Carolina   75

18. Attendance Statistics, Undergraduate Library, University of South Carolina   76

19. Growth of the Book Collection, Undergraduate Library, Indiana University   85

20. Book Budget, Undergraduate Library, Indiana University   85

21. Circulation Statistics, Undergraduate Library, Indiana University   90

22. Circulation of Reserve Books, Undergraduate Library, Indiana University   90

23. Seating in the Uris Library   100

24. Growth of the Book Collection, Uris Library   103

25. Record of Inventories, Uris Library   104

26. Reference Statistics, Uris Library   106

27. Attendance in Olin and Uris Libraries, September 19–23, 1962   109

28. Circulation Statistics, Uris Library   110

29. Use of Home Circulation Books, Uris Library   110

30. Reserve Statistics, Uris Library   111

31. Seating Capacity in the Undergraduate Library, University of Texas 123

32. Growth of the Book Collection, Undergraduate Library, University of Texas 126

33. Reference Statistics, Undergraduate Library, University of Texas 128

34. Books Placed on Reserve, Undergraduate Library, University of Texas 129

35. Circulation Statistics, Undergraduate Library, University of Texas 132

36. Use of Reserve Books, Undergraduate Library, University of Texas 132

37. Audio Library Use, Undergraduate Library, University of Texas 133

38. Comparison of Circulation and Attendance, Undergraduate Library, University of Texas 134

39. Comparison of Enrollment, Total Book Use, and Attendance in the
Six Undergraduate Libraries Surveyed 146–47

Illustrations

FIGURES

1. Widener Stack, Lamont Library   8

2. Houghton Stack, Lamont Library   9

3. First Level, Lamont Library   10

4. Second Level, Lamont Library   11

5. Third Level, Lamont Library   12

6. Fifth Level, Lamont Library   13

7. Sixth Level, Lamont Library   13

8. Former Organization Chart of the Lamont Library   22

9. Organization Chart of the Lamont Library, 1965   22

10. Basement Floor, Undergraduate Library, University of Michigan (original plan)   33

11. First Floor, Undergraduate Library, University of Michigan (original plan)   34

12. Second Floor, Undergraduate Library, University of Michigan (original plan)   35

13. Third Floor, Undergraduate Library, University of Michigan (original plan)   36

14. Fourth Floor, Undergraduate Library, University of Michigan (original plan)   37

15. Basement Floor, Undergraduate Library, University of Michigan (revised plan)   39

16. First Floor, Undergraduate Library, University of Michigan (revised plan)   40

17. Second Floor, Undergraduate Library, University of Michigan (revised plan)   41

18. Third and Fourth Floors, Undergraduate Library, University of Michigan (revised plan)   42

19. Organization Chart, Undergraduate Library, University of Michigan   50–51

20. Ground Floor, Undergraduate Library, University of South Carolina   64

21. First Floor, Undergraduate Library, University of South Carolina   66

22. Mezzanine Floor, Undergraduate Library, University of South Carolina   67

23. Basement and Second Floors, Undergraduate Library, Indiana University   80

24. Main Floor, Undergraduate Library, Indiana University   81

25. Organization Chart, Undergraduate Library, Indiana University   89

26. First Floor, Uris Library   97

27. Lower Floor, Uris Library   98

28. Top Floor, Uris Library   99

29. Douglass Carrel   100

30. Organization Chart, Uris Library   109

31. First Floor, Undergraduate Library and Academic Center Building, University of Texas   118

32. Second Floor, Undergraduate Library and Academic Center Building, University of Texas   119

33. Third Floor, Undergraduate Library and Academic Center Building, University of Texas   120

34. Fourth Floor, Undergraduate Library and Academic Center Building, University of Texas   121

35. Basement Level, Undergraduate Library and Academic Center Building, University of Texas   122

36. Administrative Structure of the Undergraduate Library, University of Texas   131

PHOTOGRAPHS

Reading Area and Stack Area, First and Second Levels, Lamont Library   14

First Floor Reading Area, Undergraduate Library, University of Michigan   30

First Floor Reading Area, Undergraduate Library, University of South Carolina   68

First Floor Reading Room, West Wing, Undergraduate Library, Indiana University   82

Dean Reading Room, Uris Library   96

First Floor Reading Area, Undergraduate Library, University of Texas   123

Preface

The undergraduate library is one of the important academic library services to be developed in the last two decades. The present study is concerned with the emergence of the separately housed undergraduate library in the university context. It excludes undergraduate collections housed in the central library, as well as the libraries of four-year colleges whose enrollment consists mainly of undergraduates. The six separately housed undergraduate libraries described—Lamont Library, Harvard University; the Undergraduate Library, University of Michigan; the Undergraduate Library, University of South Carolina; the Undergraduate Library, Indiana University; Uris Library, Cornell University; and the Undergraduate Library, University of Texas—were in operation in September, 1965. Undergraduate collections (those housed in general library buildings) are excluded because they differ in scope of operation and type of service offered. Furthermore, such undergraduate collections are too many and varied to be covered in depth.

Descriptions of these six undergraduate libraries come from two main sources: personal interviews and office files. The major problem in approaching the study was the lack of published material. As a result, the only way to acquire the information was by visiting each of the six libraries, talking with the persons concerned and examining their files when possible. The data for this study were gathered during 1965/66 and cover operations in these six libraries only through 1964/65. Since then changes have occurred. Some significant ones have been noted, but, for the most part, the text reflects the 1964/65 situation.

For each of the libraries included, consideration is given to the background of the idea at that institution (who initiated it and why); development of the project; financing; the building (including physical descriptions of the arrangement, furniture, lighting, flooring, and special features); the book collection (means of acquiring, size, and scope); and staff. In addition, the operation of the library including public services (reference, reserve, circulation, and special services, such as audio facilities) and technical services is described. The discussion concludes with how and to what extent the library is used.

Time and space did not permit treating every aspect mentioned in full detail. On the other hand, as much detail as seemed feasible was included. It was felt that persons interested in specific topics would find this material useful.

I wish to express my thanks to all the librarians who gave so freely of their time: Billy Wilkinson, Stephen A. McCarthy, G. F. Shepherd, Keyes D. Metcalf, Theodore Alevizos, Edwin E. Williams, J. Mitchell Reames, Alfred H. Rawlinson, Imogene Thompson, Jean Cassel, Alexander Moffit, Fred Folmer, Frances Hudspeth, Robert A. Miller, Neil Boardman, Janet Horton, Rose-Grace Faucher, Rolland Stewart, Roberta Keniston, and Frederick Wagman. Their assistance and cooperation were invaluable.

This study was originally prepared as a doctoral dissertation at the University of Michigan. Dr. Wallace J. Bonk, as Chairman of my Doctoral Committee, was especially helpful in his guidance and counsel. To Dr. Joe Lee Davis, Dr. Anthony Kruzas, and Dr. Frederick Wagman, I also owe my appreciation.

Introduction

The development of the separately housed undergraduate library on the modern university campus is a recent innovation—so recent, in fact, that in September, 1965, there were only six such libraries in the United States.[1] The interest in effective undergraduate education which led to the creation of these libraries, however, is not of such recent origin. As early as 1608, when Thomas James was appointed to Bodley's Library, "he proposed the establishment of an undergraduate library to help the younger student. But Sir Thomas Bodley was opposed."[2] So it is to Harvard that we turn for an example of the protracted concern for the undergraduate's plight.

In 1765, there was acknowledgment of the needs of "younger students" at Harvard College by setting aside a "smaller library for the more common use of the College."[3] In 1815, Andrews Norton, Librarian of Harvard College, in a letter to John T. Kirkland, President of Harvard College, pointed out that undergraduates needed to use the books in the College Library and recommended a separate undergraduate library.[4] During the nineteenth century and early twentieth century, there was concern about the plight of the undergraduate in regard to library service, and partial answers were found in "subscription libraries managed by the students, and reserve books; later, classroom and laboratory libraries; and finally, Widener's great reading room, a separate library for freshmen, and the House libraries."[5]

Despite the concern voiced by these earlier writers, most universities and their libraries were relatively small until this century. More important, they were largely undergraduate institutions. The great expansion of graduate education is a twentieth-century phenomenon. The problems of the undergraduate in using university collections were greatly compounded by the striking growth in the size of collections and by an increasing emphasis on the acquisition of materials suitable for research.

The large university collections became increasingly difficult for the undergraduate to use. When he had to select his books from the card catalog and obtain them through paging in a closed-stack system, he might well abandon the attempt before finally locating a book which was not checked out, missing, or at the bindery—and which was suitable for his purposes. The university library was also difficult to use because it was crowded—study conditions were unsatisfactory and staff was insufficient to handle the volume of work.

Arthur McAnally summed up the difficulties facing the undergraduate in his attempts to use university collections: Books are not very accessible to the undergraduate and reserve room service, which was about all most of them got freely, was not very satisfactory educationally. Of course the enterprising undergraduate could surmount the obstacles of huge card catalogs, impersonal circulation desks, etc., but he was discouraged at every hand.[6]

At the same time that university libraries were becoming more difficult for the undergraduate to use successfully, new teaching methods sent him to the library with greater frequency. Wider independent reading was being encouraged as teachers moved away from the traditional textbook/reserved book reading pattern. Thus the undergraduate was trapped by this double development: increasing emphasis on the use of the library at a time when the library was becoming increasingly difficult to use.

The first response to this problem was the development of the undergraduate collection housed in the main library. The University of Chicago and Columbia University early founded undergraduate collections. Many other universities have since adopted what might be called the "undergraduate plan." Examples are (or in some cases were) found at the University of New Mexico, University of Cincinnati, University of Illinois, University of Tennessee, Duke University, University of Washington, University of California at Los Angeles, and Yale University. Many new libraries built in the past decade, those presently being built, and those in the planning stage incorporate the undergraduate plan in some form.

Most take the form of setting aside one or two floors or a new building for this purpose. Small institutions may only provide a large reading room. An undergraduate collection may be little more than a reserve collection for lower-division students; it may be a browsing collection of light fiction, periodicals, and noncourse-related materials; or it may be a "learning center"—a relatively small collection of books, some of which relate to the curriculum and some of which are of general interest.

With the constant growth of the central university collection, the increasing demand for service to graduate students and faculty, and the increasing inadequacy of the central library to handle these demands and resources, the undergraduate collection housed in the main building began to be viewed as an unsatisfactory solution to the undergraduate's problems, and the separately housed undergraduate library was advanced as a more satisfactory solution.

These separately housed libraries were to differ from the traditional university collection by:

> Providing open access to the collection to avoid the difficulties of the closed-stack system
>
> Centralizing and simplifying services to the undergraduate
>
> Providing a collection of carefully selected books, containing the titles all undergraduates should be exposed to for their liberal education, as well as incorporating the reserved-book collection
>
> Attempting to make the library an instructional tool by planning it as a center for instruction in library use, to prepare undergraduates for using larger collections, and by staffing it with librarians interested in teaching the undergraduate the resources of a library and the means of tapping those resources
>
> Providing services additional to those given by the research collection
>
> Constructing a building with the undergraduate's habits of use in mind.

The first of these changes—provision of open access to the collection (exclusive of some reserve books)—would allow the student to do his book selection directly from the shelves, rather than relying on the card catalog as his only approach to the collection. By surrounding the student with books—not separating him from them—it was hoped that he would be encouraged to read more than assigned titles. Open access was envisaged as one of the most important contributions of the undergraduate library.

Second, centralization of services was intended to remove the obstacles which impeded the undergraduate in his search for library materials, making the learning process easier and more satisfactory. The undergraduate library was to bring together in one place all aspects of library service relating to the undergraduate curriculum, thereby encouraging the student to learn. The undergraduate would no longer be faced by a system in which he had to go to one place to read reserve books, another to find materials for a term paper, a third to find avocational reading, and yet another to find a place to sit and read these materials. He would no longer face the dispersion of reserve materials among the main library and the several branch libraries, nor was he to be discouraged by being subjected to the idiosyncrasies of a treasure hunt to find the books he needs. The needs of undergraduates and graduate students, it was increasingly felt, were vastly different; the two did not mix well. The undergraduate library would try to furnish a kind of service that was not possible in the large university library, and it would provide one place in which the undergraduate could do most of his work.

In addition, these centralized services would be simplified. Because the collection would be relatively small, the catalog confronting the student would not be huge and forbidding. Likewise, there would not be so many books on any one subject that the student would become confused by the large array before him. The library staff would also be able to assist him more readily in his use of this smaller and more easily approachable collection.

Third, the undergraduate library was to house a carefully selected duplicate collection of books which would support the curriculum, but which would, in addition, attempt to reach beyond the curriculum to provide a selection of the best writings of all times and all peoples. It was to attempt to satisfy the instructional needs and general reading interests of the undergraduate. Besides providing the general collection, the undergraduate library was to include the reserve books which are a part of the curriculum. In no case was the undergraduate library thought of as satisfying only the needs of course-assigned reading. It was seen as an "educational breakthrough in our universities. . . . Its real strength is in its provision for individual differences, its balance of over-specialization and its creation of a true learning climate."[7] Keyes Metcalf saw Lamont Library's general collection as one of its greatest contributions.

Fourth, the undergraduate library was to serve as an instructional tool. It was envisaged as a workshop in which the undergraduate could learn on a relatively small scale those library skills which could later be applied to larger and more complex collections. The staff was seen as having a teaching function as one of its most important tasks. The library should be "staffed by a group of librarians who have a keen interest and an understanding of undergraduate education."[8]

The card catalog was to be a tool used in teaching the student how to approach the collection, as were the periodical indexes, the reference collection, and the vertical file, which were also to be used as sources of information. The book collection itself was to be used to help mold student reading habits. The collection was to be a tool used to supplement and to implement the instructional program of the university. Thus the librarians were not primarily to help the student do his work, but to teach him how to do it; to lay a foundation on which the student could build in the future.

Fifth, the undergraduate library was to embody something more than the traditional university library. Not only were there to be facilities for reading—books and chairs—but there were to be facilities for listening to recordings, for holding meetings and discussions, for viewing art exhibits, and for other activities. By combining various media from which to learn, the undergraduate library would afford the student a broader opportunity.

Sixth, the undergraduate library was to be designed and built with the express needs and habits of the undergraduate in mind. How, why, and when he uses the library were to dictate the character of the building. The building was to be conveniently located in terms of student habits. At some universities, this would be interpreted as on the central campus near an important student traffic route. At other places, it was thought best to locate it near the student living quarters. In the design of the building, simplicity of layout was considered desirable.

In the succeeding chapters, six undergraduate libraries will be examined (in the order of their creation) to see how each dealt with the six topics which have been presented in this chapter as the aims of the undergraduate library. An effort will be made to describe how closely each library adhered to these visions for planning, where divergences occurred and why, and what judgment has been about the success each library has had in carrying out its special program for undergraduate education. A final chapter will compare the major differences and similarities among the six libraries.

NOTES

[1] A new undergraduate library opened at Stanford University in September, 1966. Other new undergraduate libraries are under construction at the University of North Carolina, the University of Illinois, and elsewhere.

[2] Frederick H. Wagman, "Library Service to Undergraduate College Students: The Case for the Separate Undergraduate Library," *College and Research Libraries,* XVII (March, 1956), 150.

[3] Keyes D. Metcalf, "The Undergraduate and the Harvard Library, 1765–1877," *Harvard Library Bulletin,* I (Winter, 1947), 29–30.

[4] *Ibid.,* 35.

[5] Robert W. Lovett, "The Undergraduate and the Harvard Library, 1877–1937," *Harvard Library Bulletin,* I (Spring, 1947), 221.

[6] Arthur M. McAnally, "Library Service to Undergraduates: A Symposium—Introductory Remarks," *College and Research Libraries,* XIV (July, 1953), 266.

[7] Louis Shores, "The Undergraduate and His Library," in *University of Tennessee Library Lectures,* ed. by Lanelle Vandiver, No. 11 (Knoxville: Univ. of Tennessee, 1960), p. 33.

[8] Interview with Stephen A. McCarthy, Director of the University Libraries, Cornell University, Oct. 20, 1965. Mr. McCarthy is now Executive Director, Association for Research Libraries.

Lamont Library, Harvard University

In 1939, Harvard University Library was experiencing severe space shortages. Keyes Metcalf, Librarian of Harvard, prepared a series of reports delineating the space needs of the library system. He proposed a building program which would give priority to the construction of an undergraduate library. He argued that such a building would relieve the pressures on Widener, thus improving service to graduate students and faculty. He maintained that Widener could never be successfully adapted to provide undergraduate service, since it had been built as a research library and functioned best as such.[1]

Metcalf later outlined the difficulties the Harvard undergraduate faced in his efforts to use the collections. Books and services available to undergraduates were scattered, reducing the student's use of the library if for no other reason than the time involved in going from place to place. Second, the undergraduate student at Harvard did not have access to any extensive collection such as might be found at one of the better undergraduate colleges. Either he had to use the small House collections (which ranged in size from 10,000 to 13,000 volumes), the reserve collection, or the mammoth collection housed in Widener. Third, the problem of access was especially difficult in Widener. The only approach to the collection was a card catalog which contained approximately 5,000,000 cards in 1949. Fourth, the undergraduate student had to compete with graduate students and faculty for service and books. Because of the emphasis on research, it was usually the undergraduate who was slighted.[2]

Metcalf believed that improved service to the Harvard undergraduate would involve a separate library which should embody three general characteristics: (1) The library should be located for convenient access. (2) It should provide undergraduate students with library materials covering the whole range of knowledge, since most undergraduates work in many different fields simultaneously. (3) The library should be easy to use: — the catalog should be as intelligible as possible; the classification scheme should be easy to use; the charging system should be simple. Such a collection should be housed in surroundings that the student would find attractive.[3]

After the general program had been outlined and financing assured, the architects — Coolidge, Shepley, Bulfinch and Abbott, of Boston — began work on the plans for the building. The first decision confronting the librarian was the selection of a site for the building. Four sites were considered. The first was the area occupied by Boylston Hall near Widener Library, but it was too small without also demolishing Gray Hall and Weld Hall. Two sites on Mt. Auburn Street midway between the upperclass and freshmen dormitories were also considered. But since they were far from the central library and the classrooms, they were rejected. The last location was on the corner of Massachusetts and Quincy avenues at the southeast corner of the Harvard Yard.[4] There were two definite advantages in favor of this latter site. First, it was near the other library buildings and so would ease administrative problems. Second, the location was in the Yard near the freshmen dormitories and near the classroom facilities. The Yard location was the one decided upon after consultation with students, library staff, and the Harvard Corporation.[5] Five reasons were enumerated for the decision:

1. It was the only remaining available site in the Yard large enough for a building of the desired size. Its location in the Yard close to the two other central library buildings, Widener and Houghton, to which it could be connected by tunnel, was an important factor.
2. It was so placed that the freshmen passed its front entrance six times a day going to and from their meals in the Freshmen Union. It was near a main walk between the houses where the upperclassmen lived and the classrooms, and closer to the latter.
3. It had a long east-west axis, giving the desirable long north and south exposures for the reading areas.
4. The ground slope was such that two levels with windows below the main entrance, which was only one short step up, were possible, with two more without windows below them. It was possible to have above the entrance level a mezzanine, a full second floor, and a penthouse with a good deal of useful space in it, and still have the latter closer to the ground than the main reading room in Widener.
5. Policy decisions on the part of the university, limiting the number of undergraduate students, and on the part of the library authorities, limiting the size of the undergraduate book collection indicated that provision did not have to be made for a future extension.[6]

To make the building a success in the physical sense, the following features were important:

1. The efficiency of the ventilation system.
2. The lighting.
3. The sound absorption quality of the walls and ceiling.
4. The ease with which the students could find their books for assigned reading and obtain them.[7]

After the librarian and his staff formulated the basic concepts of an undergraduate library, they sought faculty and student opinion in planning it. The Dean of the Faculty of Arts and Sciences appointed a committee to advise in planning the undergraduate library, consisting of faculty members from various departments.[8] The faculty committee did not provide much help, but the faculty felt that they were being consulted, and, therefore, made no strong opposition to the project.[9]

In 1946, the Dean of Harvard College, Chester Hanford, appointed a student council committee on the undergraduate library, giving the students an opportunity to express their opinions on what they felt the undergraduate library should be.[10] The students provided help on two questions. It was their decision not to have a cloakroom and to limit smoking to certain areas of the building. It was also on student recommendations that 80 percent of the chairs were armchairs.[11]

One problem which faced Harvard in planning its undergraduate library is unique to its situation. Should Radcliffe girls be allowed into the Lamont Library? The decision made was negative for the following reasons:

1. Radcliffe maintains an undergraduate library of its own with a collection larger than the one now installed in Lamont and as large as the Lamont collection is expected to be in the future.
2. The money available would not provide for a building large enough to care for both the Harvard and Radcliffe undergraduates.
3. Experience here and elsewhere has shown that a library for men only or for women only can be administered with almost no supervision in the reading rooms, but that a coeducational library requires supervision if reasonable quiet is to be preserved. In order to achieve most efficiently its primary aims, Lamont has been designed in such a way that the staff would have to be doubled if adequate reading room supervision were to be provided on a coeducational basis.[12]

FINANCING

To make the building a reality at Harvard, Mr. Thomas W. Lamont, Harvard Class of 1892, gave a timely and generous gift of $1,500,000 in 1945. Mr. Metcalf first mentioned the need for an undergraduate library to Mr. Lamont in May, 1941. At that point, Mr. Lamont expressed some interest in the undergraduate library but made no commitment regarding it. When the end of the war seemed to be in sight, Mr. Metcalf wrote Mr. Lamont to inquire if he still was interested in the proposed undergraduate library.[13]

Nothing more transpired until the summer of 1945 when Paul Buck, then Dean of the Faculty of Arts and Sciences, issued this book, *General Education in a Free Society*. After Mr. Lamont read this book, he told Mr. Metcalf that if Harvard was to implement the general education program, it would be necessary to have the undergraduate library that had been under discussion for so many years. Within three months, Mr. Lamont made the money for the building available.[14]

Because additional area would be required to accommodate the classrooms for the general education program, the sum of $1,000,000 that had been originally proposed was no longer sufficient. To be absolutely safe, the architects assigned a new figure of $1,500,000 to cover the additional space needed and to offset the rise in prices.[15]

Equipping the building, buying and processing the books, and doing some renovation at Widener would add an additional $250,000 to the total. A suitable endowment for the library was set at $1,500,000. Operating costs were estimated at $80,000 a year minus about $20,000 that would be saved by closing other unneeded facilities. The total needed reached about $3,000,000. The sum of $848,000 was added to construct the storage area under the Lamont Library for use by both the Widener and Houghton libraries.[16]

In March, 1947, Mr. Metcalf presented a detailed breakdown of the capital costs of the undergraduate library (Table 1). Funds to cover these costs were available from two sources. Mr. Lamont's original gift of $1,500,000 was supplemented by an additional $75,000 which he gave to move and rebuild the Dana-Palmer House. The corporation furnished the remainder of the needed funds: $568,000 for construction costs and $300,000 for other items, plus the $848,000 for the storage areas.

TABLE 1

CAPITAL COSTS OF THE LAMONT LIBRARY

Construction	$1,986,000
Additional labor	115,000
Moving of Dana-Palmer House	42,000
Furniture and movable equipment	150,000
Books	150,000
Total	$2,443,000

Consequently, $1,500,000 was still needed for an endowment fund which would yield an annual income sufficient to provide the necessary operating expenses. The Harvard Fund Council[17] provided this money.[18]

The original budget authorized in 1947 was for $3,291,000 for both the Lamont Library and the storage stacks for Widener and Houghton. The final cost of the building came to $3,040,000.[19]

THE BUILDING

Description

In order to fulfill the objectives of the building, the librarian devised an arrangement whereby there would be long reading rooms on three floors on one side of the building paralleled for their entire length by open stack areas down the center. Specialized reading rooms, such as those for reference, browsing, and the modern poetry collection, were to be on the opposite side of the stack area.[20]

Because the site chosen was in the Harvard Yard, the problem was to design a building, first, that would fit into the available space, and second, that would harmonize in design with its surroundings in the Yard. The building as it was designed is 169 feet 8 inches long, 148 feet 4 inches wide, and eight levels in height. To make the exterior of the building harmonize with the surrounding structures, dark-red brick similar to that of the Chapel and limestone trim like that on the Freshmen Union were used.[21] To reduce the apparent height of the building, three reading rooms were added to the Massachusetts Avenue side, the lowest level was built partly underground, and the General Education Center was located in a low-roof house recessed from the building's perimeter.[22]

The building was planned from the inside out. The "emphasis of interior features in exterior treatment may be seen in the projection of the main entrance motive beyond the face of the north front, increasing the importance of the entrance and giving a valuable accent to the otherwise long unbroken facade." The entrance consists of a wide glass wall in which are set six glass doors "flanked by limestone buttresses carrying a thin roof slab."[23] The large glass entrance helps ease transition from the outside to inside. To further enhance this impression, the lighting in the lobby simulates daylight.

The building itself is a hybrid of modular (modules of 24 feet by 13 feet) and traditional structure. "A combination of different bay sizes was used . . . as a means of taking advantage of the useful features of the modular system and at the same time avoiding the handicaps that it often brings in its train."[24] The reading rooms have high ceilings, where-

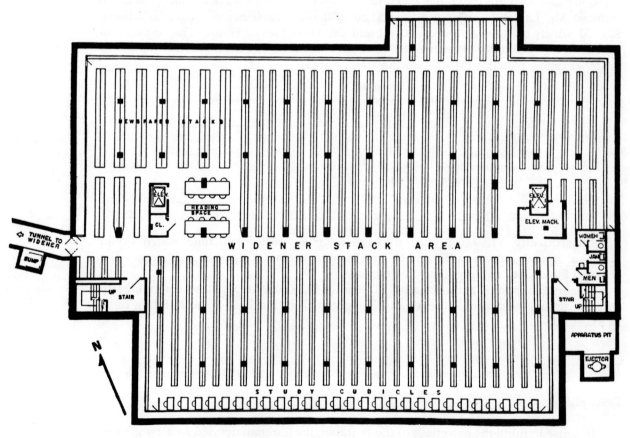

Fig. 1. Widener stack, Lamont Library

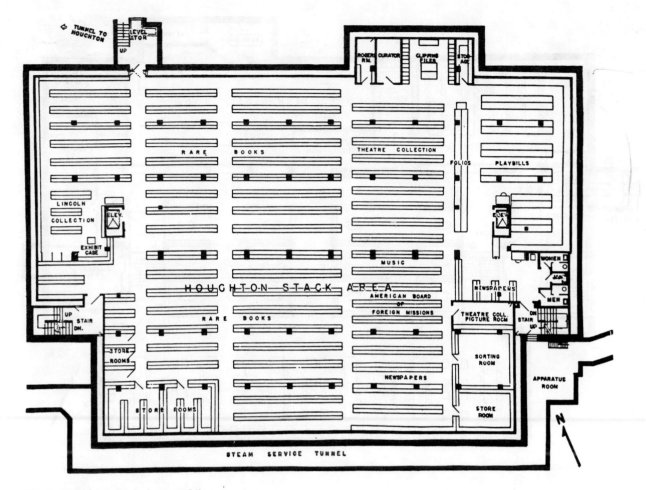

Fig. 2. Houghton stack, Lamont Library

as the stack areas and the mezzanines have relatively low ceilings.[25] The reading areas allow for a certain degree of flexibility within the area, but most areas are well defined by retaining walls.[26]

The structure of the shelving also shows the cross between modular and traditional buildings. Every other floor of the building holds up the floor above it. Therefore, the stacks on the supporting floors are fixed, while those on the other floors are free standing. With such an arrangement, additional stacks can be added anywhere in the building, while on half of the floors the stacks can be rearranged if desired.[27]

In order to break up the large areas in the three main reading rooms, low, open-slatted screens about 7 feet high and 15 feet long projecting from the walls are used to divide the rooms into three parts. Each of the reading rooms is open on one side adjacent to the stacks. Around the perimeter of the three walls are individual carrels.[28]

The building consists of eight levels: basement and mezzanine, first level and mezzanine, third level and mezzanine, fifth level and roof house. The basement and basement mezzanine are known as the Widener stack and the Houghton stack, respectively. These levels provide storage space for both Houghton Library and Widener Library and are the first section of the underground storage unit outlined in the building program proposed in 1940 (Figs. 1 and 2).[29]

Access to the first level is through the west entrance. Most of the space on this level is occupied by a reading area, an alcove area, and a smoking room (Fig. 3). Each alcove houses about 1500 volumes, a table, and chairs. There are twelve alcoves on each of the three main floors. The smoking room provides space for future needs.[30] Adjacent to the

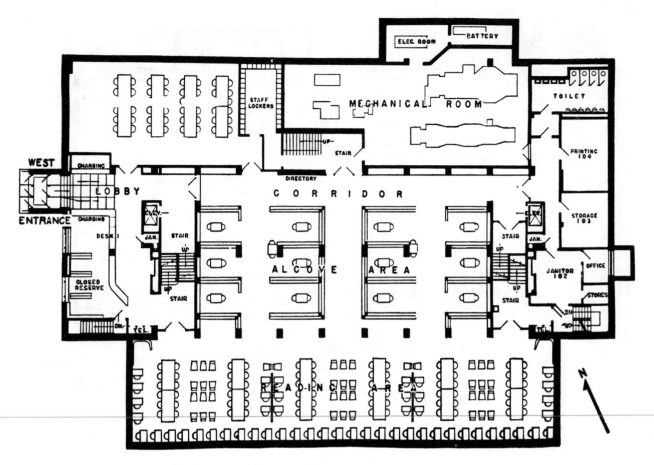

Fig. 3. First level, Lamont Library

reading area are four half alcoves. About 5000 volumes of reserve books for history, government, and economics are housed in the closed-reserve collection at desk 1 at the west entrance. This level also includes a printing room, staff lockers, and the janitors' quarters.[31]

The second level, which is a mezzanine, consists mainly of a stack area housing about 30,000 volumes (Fig. 4). A smoking room with semilounge furniture is on the west end of the floor along with five typing cubicles. On the east end of the floor are two conference rooms. This level has seating for fifty readers in individual carrels and for twenty-eight persons at tables seating four.[32] The stacks contain bound periodicals arranged alphabetically by title.

The main entrance to the building leads to the third level so that there is only one flight of stairs to go either up or down. On either side of the entrance is a charging desk, although only the one on the left (as you enter) is actually used. Provision is made for four exit lanes to be opened at one time, although this has never been necessary (it is possible to open two at the first-level entrance). There are day-and-night book returns outside the main entrance. The reference room is to the right of the main entrance (Fig. 5) and contains the card catalog, the atlas case, the reference collection, and the current periodical section. Seating is provided for sixty-three readers. Beyond the periodical room is a smoking room. The central portion of the floor is arranged in alcoves, and the south side is a large reading area. To the left of the main entrance is the other closed-reserve collection and the circulation desk. Beyond this is the librarian's office and other office space for clerical and professional personnel.[33] The large entrance lobby serves as a distribution point, dispersing the students and their noises before they penetrate far into the building.[34]

The fourth level, a mezzanine level, is similar to the second level, with a smoking room on one end, conference rooms on the other, and a stack area between. The Harvard Collection is on the balcony alcove on this level.[35]

The fifth level is similar in arrangement to the third. A reading area is on the south side; alcoves are in the center of the floor; a smoking room is on the west end; and the General Education Center Offices are on the east end (Fig. 6). Three special-purpose rooms—the Dana L. Farnsworth room, the George Edward Woodberry poetry room, and the Forum room—occupy the north side. The Forum room is a dual-purpose room used by students for library-related meetings. It can seat 108 persons, with the possibility of adding another 40 chairs. The room has a blackboard, motion picture projector and screen, and a public address system. This room can be turned into a reading room for 60 people if the need arises.[36]

The Woodberry poetry room contains a selected collection of poetry, especially contemporary verse, and poetry recordings.[37] The Farnsworth room, previously housed in Widener, contains a collection of general and contemporary reading.[38] Free-standing bookcases are arranged to form alcoves, with additional bookcases recessed into the walls. In order to give the appearance of a private library, floor lamps provide the only lighting.[39]

The General Education Center offices occupied the area along the east wall of the fifth level.[40] Although the Center was not intended to have a library function, it was at Mr. Lamont's request that these rooms were placed in the Lamont Library.[41] However, about a year after the opening of the library, the General Education Division outgrew its quarters and subsequently moved out of the building. The rooms designed as classrooms still serve that purpose.[42]

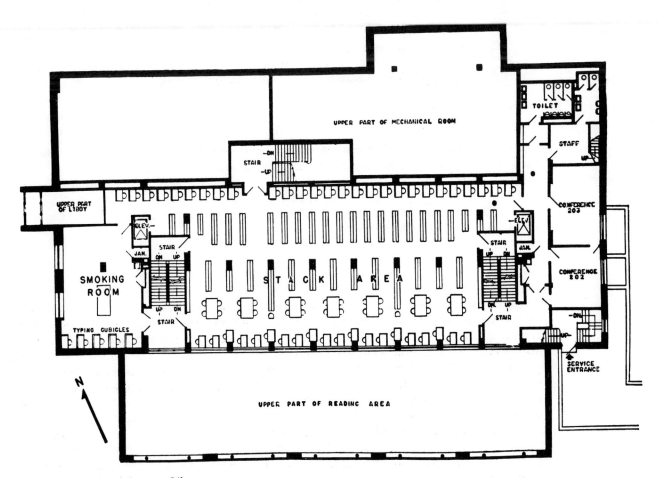

Fig. 4. Second level, Lamont Library

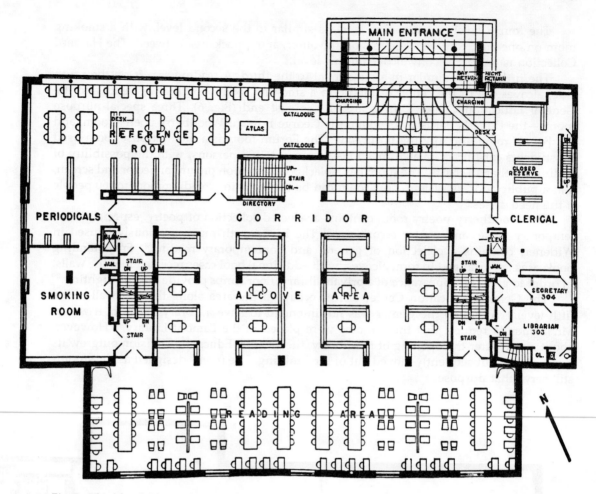

Fig. 5. Third level, Lamont Library

The roof house, or sixth level, contains six conference rooms and the fan room (Fig. 7). Each conference room seats twenty to thirty people and occupies 400 square feet.[43]

The colors used throughout the interior of the building were chosen with the aim of avoiding eye fatigue. The furniture, woodwork, and carrels are all light in color (mostly birch). The lounge furniture is in deep tones of red, brown, and green. The bookcases vary in color with the floor level.

Furnishings

The furniture used in the Lamont Library is almost exclusively of birchwood. The exceptions are the chairs designed by Alvar Aalto and the cherry furnishings in the Farnsworth room. There were two reasons for using light-colored furniture. In 1949, light library furniture was practically the only kind available. The light furniture also makes it possible to cut the cost of lighting by one fourth because of the light intensity. One special feature of the chairs is the inability to tip back.[44] The furniture used in the building varies with the level and rooms, much like the color scheme. In selecting the furniture, five points were taken into consideration: sturdiness, comfort, appearance, cost, and variety.[45]

Of the furniture included, one third provides semiprivate seating (counting the lounge chairs and the individual tables) and about one fifth (15 to 20 percent) consists of lounge chairs. The remainder is at tables seating from four to twelve. Each reader has a work space of 6 square feet providing sufficient space even if all seats are filled, which

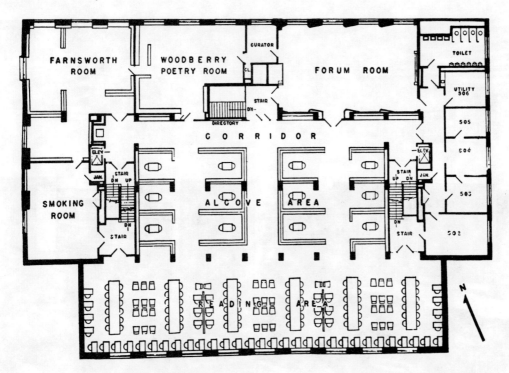

Fig. 6. Fifth level, Lamont Library

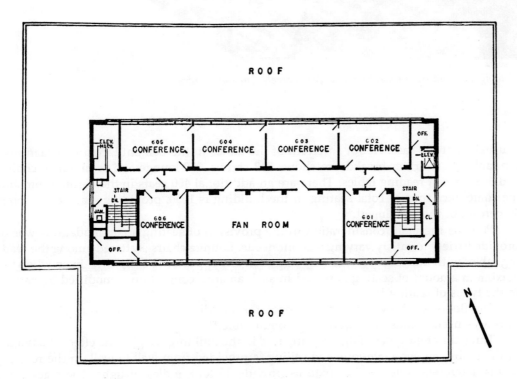

Fig. 7. Sixth level, Lamont Library

Reading area and stack area, first and second levels, Lamont Library

is usually not the case. About 3 percent of the tables in the Lamont Library are slanting-top tables.[46] A further breakdown shows 242 carrels, 250 lounge and semilounge chairs, and 658 seats at reading tables. There are an additional 400 seats in the Forum room and the conference rooms. Total seating in the building is 1550, providing seating for about 30 percent of the enrollment.[47]

Perhaps the main consideration in the provision of seating accommodations was to provide variety to satisfy varying student needs. Lounge chairs scattered among the reading tables with individual carrels help diminish any appearance of rigidity. Even when the maximum amount of seating is placed in such an area, congestion is modified by variety in the types of seating.[48]

The floors are brown cork throughout the building (except for the marble lobby). Cork was used because it is quiet and comfortable.[49]

Three different types of lighting are used in the building. To give the effect of daylight in the lobby, an egg-crate-louvered ceiling is provided from wall to wall. In the reading rooms, louvered-troffer ceiling fixtures provide 25 footcandles of light. The stacks and corridors have louvered fluorescent ceiling fixtures providing 25 footcandles of light. The lighting is "so wired that with comparatively little expense for alterations the intensity can be doubled."[50] However, this has not been necessary.

BOOK COLLECTION

General Collection

In January, 1947, two years before building began, a small group of library staff started selecting books for the Lamont Library under the direction of Mr. Edwin Williams, Assistant to the Librarian.[51] The first step in collecting was to develop criteria for selection. What were they to consist of, what type of books were to be included, what should be the scope of the collection? The collection was based on the premise that students read either for profit, pleasure, or a combination of the two. Selection should include the books that would be most useful to the students.

Part of the problem in selection was that there was no previous guide on which to rely. There were, however, two parts of the collection which were already in existence. The first of these was the reserve books in the Widener reading room, the Freshmen Union, and Boylston Hall,[52] and the other was the reading lists for undergraduate courses which were not on reserve. In addition to providing what the student needed for his courses, the collection was envisaged as something more. Even in relation to courses, students often wanted to go beyond required readings in order to write papers, to prepare reports, and in some cases to satisfy intellectual curiosity. To provide for these instances, there was a need for a general collection. "The general collection may be called Lamont's major bibliographical contribution to the undergraduate."[53]

Faculty recommendations and the House libraries provided the basis of this general collection. Since the faculty helped select the House library collections, these collections acted as a starting point for assembling the Lamont collection.[54]

The selection began with a master card file for all the books found in the seven House libraries.[55] To supplement the list, Charles Shaw's *A List of Books for College Libraries* and the list of titles compiled from the special collections designated for the Lamont Library were used. Since the Shaw list stopped in 1938, 150 scholarly journals were examined to help bring the list up to date.[56] "Cards were made for all books which were favorably reviewed and did not seem obviously unsuitable for the collection."[57]

Another source of books for the Lamont Library was gift books and duplicates available in Widener Library. Some of these had been set aside for inclusion in the Lamont Library before the book-selection project actually began. These titles consisted not only of monographs, but also included some periodical files and current serials.[58]

When cards had been made for all of the above categories of books, the staff checked the required-reading lists against the cards and indicated on the card that these titles would be included in the initial collection because they were required readings. With the addition of the required-reading lists, the file was considered finished. It included a total of 44,500 cards. The next step was to arrange the cards by subjects so they could be sent to the various academic departments for selection. In the process, it was possible to discard more than 4000 cards "because they were out of date, inferior editions, or too specialized."[59] In January, 1948, 40,290 cards sorted into fifty-four subject groups went to twenty-eight departments. The titles in subject areas not sent to departments went to such people as the librarian of the Houghton Library, the curator of the Department of Printing and Graphic Arts, the librarian and dean of the Graduate School of Education, the staff of the Harvard Archives. Members of the Widener staff evaluated the remaining titles.

"Probable use by Harvard undergraduates was the criterion for selection, rather than any theory of what would constitute an ideal book collection."[60] Other factors which influenced selection were such things as the curriculum, the location of other library resources, or availability—some books were hard to obtain.[61]

From the original selection, 7700 titles were rejected and 3809 new titles were added, leaving a total of 36,399 titles for inclusion. The periodical titles and the reference works selected by the library staff were in addition to the above titles. Of the 9832 titles which were required readings or in the reference collection, 6364 were available for transfer from Widener. Only titles duplicated in Widener were transferred. By the time the library opened, there were still about 4000 recommended books that had not been obtained.

Edwin E. Williams said about the Lamont Library collection:

> An undergraduate library can be kept at the same size because no volume in it need re-main there always—one may hope that there will be many copies of Homer in Lamont as long as the building stands but even in ten or twenty years, they will not be the same copies of the same editions that were there in 1949.
>
> The collection is impermanent; so, therefore, are its present deficiencies. All those who use it can help to improve Lamont's book collection, which in a few years, will reflect the original selection less than the later criticism and suggestions made from day to day by students, librarians, and members of the faculty.[62]

The library opened with a collection of 54,755 volumes. The collection itself was stronger in the humanities and social sciences than in the sciences. Sixteen percent, or 5888 titles, treated English and American literature; 15 percent, or 5674 volumes, dealt with history. Government comprised 4993 titles, or 14 percent. On the other end of the scale, Latin and Greek each represented about 1 percent of the total. The sciences were represented by biology (775 titles), mathematics (766 titles), and chemistry (645 titles), each of which made up about 2 percent of the total.[63]

The basic nature of the collection has not changed through the years. English and American literature and history are still the two largest subject areas, while the humanities and social sciences constitute the major part of the collection. In recent years, some effort has been made to add to subjects previously neglected because these areas already had strong branch libraries. Until recently, little science material was bought, but new books "that we think undergraduates would need and appreciate having in their own library" are purchased.[64] Although an effort has been made to broaden the collection, some areas still receive only sparing attention.

Current selection for the Lamont Library follows the original criteria. In selecting books for the Lamont Library, great reliance is placed on the subject journals, while only limited use is made of the more general selection media.[65] One must be aware that all of the titles in the Lamont Library are not essential, useful, or even "good." They were chosen to meet the needs of a particular group of students and, therefore, do not conform to any other set of standards.[66]

An active weeding program has been carried on in the Lamont Library for the past ten years. In 1955, the collection showed a net decrease of 684 volumes.[67] Withdrawals

TABLE 2

WITHDRAWALS FROM THE LAMONT LIBRARY COLLECTION	
1957–58	447
1958–59	1,637
1959–60	474
1960–61	754
1961–62	3,208
1962–63	2,562
1963–64	1,501
1964–65	7,843

Note: Until 1957–58, statistics for the Lamont Library were only given in terms of a net increase or a net decrease, so that there is no way to tell whether any books had been withdrawn. Beginning with 1957–58, both gross increase and net increase were given in the *Annual Report* of the Librarian.

for the succeeding years have varied (Table 2). As the collection ages and grows larger and as the nature of the curriculum changes, old books are withdrawn to make place for new books.

Books withdrawn from the Lamont collection are sent to Widener Library for disposal. In recent years, the weeding has been done not only by members of the Lamont staff but also with the assistance of members of the faculty who have agreed to examine the collection in their subject areas to indicate titles for withdrawal.[68] Even with this weeding program, the collection has continued to grow (Table 3). In 1964–65, the collection contained 142,091 volumes, a net increase of 63 percent in seventeen years.

TABLE 3

GROWTH OF THE BOOK COLLECTION, LAMONT LIBRARY

	GROSS INCREASE	NET INCREASE	TOTAL
1948–49		33,176	87,931
1949–50		6,611	94,542
1950–51		4,850	99,392
1951–52		b	b
1952–53		1,508	103,691
1953–54		3,433	107,124
1954–55		− 684c	106,440
1955–56		2,322	108,762
1956–57		4,665	113,427
1957–58	5,068	3,858	117,285
1958–59	4,937	3,300	120,585
1959–60	6,571	6,097	126,682
1960–61	6,345	5,591	132,273
1961–62	5,733	2,525	134,789
1962–63	5,866a	3,304	138,102
1963–64	7,079	5,578	143,680
1964–65	6,244	−1,589c	142,091

a355 of these were gift books.   bFigures not available.   cNet decrease.

In the original plan, a maximum of 100,000 volumes was set for the collection. Since the Lamont Library was the first undergraduate library built, no experience on the number of volumes appropriate to this type of library was available, so space was provided for at least 175,000 volumes. It was argued that if the collection were to grow much beyond this figure, some advantages of the small select collection would be lost.[69]

The arrangement of books in the Lamont Library emphasizes the same overall pattern of simplicity which pervades the whole plan of the building. Books are arranged consecutively by classification from the first floor to the fifth floor.

Only periodicals indexed in one of the major periodical indexes were included. Although the Lamont Library opened with a small collection of periodical titles, that number grew until in 1962 there were 443 periodical titles currently received. That number has since been reduced to 356.[70] Even though the library receives this large number of titles, not all are retained for permanent inclusion in the collection. Some are kept unbound for about six months and then sent to Widener Library for disposal. The titles that are not bound generally fall into two groups: scholarly publications too specialized for the Lamont Library or titles that might be considered recreational reading.[71]

Reference Collection

The reference collection was selected by compiling a list of recommendations from Constance Winchell's *Guide to Reference Books*. The final inclusion was determined by a committee consisting of the Harvard College librarian, the head of the Processing Division of the College Library, the head of the Lamont Library, and the senior reference assistant.

The guideline for inclusion in the reference collection was "usefulness to undergraduates." Regarding encyclopedias and atlases, this was interpreted as those in English, French, German, Spanish, Italian, and Russian. No such limitation was imposed on the dictionaries. Encyclopedias, dictionaries, handbooks, annuals, and yearbooks in special fields were limited to areas of academic concentration, while bibliographies were included sparingly.[72] In 1962, there were 1652 titles in 3379 volumes.[73]

The Lamont Library provides alcove reference collections on the first, third, and fifth levels. Each of these collections consists of a general encyclopedia, dictionaries, and reference tools in the particular field located in that reading area so that reference books are shelved near the subjects to which they relate.[74]

Reserve Collection

Only required reading was originally considered for the reserve section. Collateral reading was to be a part of the general collection. The general collection and the reserve collection are two separate units in the Lamont Library.[75] A book bought as a reserve book always remains a reserve book. If it is not on a reserve list for a semester, it is removed from the closed-reserve section and put on open reserve. If there are multiple copies of the book, only two or three copies are put on open reserve. The remainder of the copies are stored on the Widener level.

To make books as accessible as possible, those on open reserve are not classified, but are simply grouped by subjects and then arranged alphabetically by author under the subject. If a student is looking for a particular book, it is more accessible in the open-reserve collection than it would be in the general collection. Then too, the student is able "to get almost all the standard works on a particular subject in one area."[76]

The inclusion of a title on a reserve list does not guarantee its purchase. Books are purchased only when they are definitely needed. There is no strict ratio of the number of copies per student, but one copy per ten students is a general, arbitrary guide, with forty or fifty being the upper limit of copies.[77]

Open Access to the Collection

To better serve the needs of the undergraduates, Lamont pioneered in opening the total collection to its clientele. Books and readers were placed in close proximity to encourage further use of books. The books are housed on open shelves (with the exception of those on closed reserve) adjacent to comfortable study facilities in an atmosphere that created a minimum of interference.[78]

SERVICES

Reference

For several reasons, the demand for reference service proved to be less than was expected in the Lamont Library. First, Lamont is largely used as a study hall; second, a major use of the library is for reserve books; third, students can serve themselves in getting books from the open stacks; and fourth, students have learned that to do research in depth, it is necessary to use the larger collection in Widener.[79] Another reason for the lack of demand for reference service may be attributed to the nature of Harvard students. Most of the students are self-reliant and can find what materials they need by themselves. Only when they have exhausted their own resources do they ask for help.[80]

In the Lamont Library, the reference librarian acts as an "interpreter of the collection" and a "guide to its proper and efficient use."[81] If the needs of the student go beyond what is to be found in the Lamont Library, the librarian directs the student to the appropriate library. The policy of the staff in the early years of operation was usually to call ahead the needs of the student so that the librarian at the specified destination would be prepared for the student. The student was ordinarily referred to a specific person for specific materials.[82] This policy is not presently in effect.

When the library first opened, there were three professional librarians giving reference service. Reference service is now provided by library trainees and not by the professional librarians.[83]

Circulation

The circulation system, like the other services of the library, is "centered around the principle of removing barriers between the students and the books."[84] Before the opening of the library, a study was made of the existing systems that were conceivably usable. The result was the decision to use a simple numerical notation.

When each book is acquired, it is given a circulation number (it is not an accession number). On the basis that there would never be more than 100,000 volumes in the collection, the numbers 1 to 29,999 were set aside for reserve books, and those from 30,000 to 99,999 were reserved for general collection books.

When a book is checked out, a predated date due slip on which the circulation number is written is placed in the book pocket. The date due slips are so printed that they can be used four times.[85] Books were originally charged for one week, with all books falling due on Wednesday, thereby limiting the number of files which were necessary.

> The Lamont charging system is simple; it requires no machines; it allows the combining of charging and inspection, with consequent saving in time and money; it gets returned books back into use with as little delay as possible. Its chief value, however, lies in the increased efficiency with which books are made available to the students.[86]

Presently, books are charged out for two weeks and are due two weeks from the date the book is taken out. Because the slips are arranged by circulation number and not by call number, it is not easy to ascertain if a particular book is checked out.

Reserve

When the library first opened, "books for large survey courses, reading period books and a few titles in short supply" were placed on closed reserve. During the 1949 Summer Session, all books were placed on open reserve.[87] Books were taken from open reserve and placed on closed reserve whenever the demand became too great. For titles in heavy demand, two copies were placed on closed reserve and the remainder left on the open-reserve shelves.[88] Although the foregoing policy was envisaged as permanent, it was followed for only a year. Books seemed to disappear from the shelves and were not available when students needed them. As a result, all required readings were put on closed reserve.[89]

The 9000 to 10,000 reserve books are arranged alphabetically by author behind the reserve desk.[90] Reprints of articles, photocopied articles, and books that are rare or valuable provide the only reserve items that do not circulate outside the building. The circulation file for reserve books is arranged by circulation number.[91] To prevent any errors and for possible statistical use, all charge records are kept for one to two years.

Special Services

Two special services of the Lamont Library are the Woodberry poetry room and the Farnsworth room. The collection in the poetry room contained about 3500 to 4000 volumes and 1100 records of poetry readings, folk legends, and Shakespearean plays in 1949.[92]

Since that time, the phonorecord collection has grown to over 2700 records and approximately 600 tapes.[93]

The concept of this room is explained in the term *vocarium,* which implies "that literature be it prose, poetry, or drama, whether spoken or written—belongs in one location, and is readily accessible for study and enjoyment."[94] The collection is aimed at leisure use rather than course-related work.

The vocarium equipment consists of four turntables and four chair stations accommodating a total of thirty-six persons. The chair stations are individual listening posts. With these units, a student may only do "listening browsing," i.e., he may listen to recordings being played on the regular turntables. Records cannot be played at these stations. All controls are at the individual stations.[95]

The collection is particularly strong in modern American and British verse and criticism. The curator of the collection also teaches modern poetry and makes frequent trips to the British Isles to acquire new books. Furthermore, many contemporary poets have taped recordings of their own poetry for this collection. The collection consists almost exclusively of the spoken arts.[96]

The Farnsworth room, on the other hand, is a browsing library "containing a collection of classic and contemporary writings for recreational reading."[97] Like the poetry room, it was transferred from the Widener Library. The collection is made up of two main types of works: standard literary writings and titles of current interest. The collection contains travel books, cartoon books, books on sports and hobbies, science books for the layman, biography, history, and literature (mostly English literature).[98]

There are two other features in the Lamont Library which might be termed special services. On the fifth level, two rooms are provided for the use of blind students.[99] The Harvard Collection "of history, biography, sports, theatricals, class books, and student publications" is on the mezzanine overlooking the reference room. The collection "is designed to reflect the past and present life of the college and its students."[100]

Technical Services

Technical services for the Lamont Library are performed in the Widener Library. The Widener staff does the acquisition and cataloging of Lamont general-collection materials. The staff of the Lamont Library initiates most of its own orders, although members of the Acquisition Department of Widener initiate some orders.[101]

Reserve materials are acquired by the Lamont Library. Orders are generally placed with one of the local bookstores. During the first years the library was open, the secretary or one of the assistant circulation librarians cataloged the reserve books. Notification was sent to the Cataloging Department in Widener so that the title could be added to the union catalog either as an added copy or a new title.[102] However, this process has been changed. All books are now cataloged in Widener. Reserve books are ordinarily handled as rush books, so that they are usually back in Lamont within a few days.[103]

The card catalog in the Lamont Library is a brief finding list, because students are urged to go to the shelves to find their books. To make consultation of the card catalog unnecessary, copies of the index to the Lamont Classification scheme are located in various campus buildings.[104]

The card catalog was originally set up as a divided catalog—author-title and subject—but the subject part of the catalog was not complete. The catalog was divided because "we were afraid if we had a dictionary catalog people would think it is a full subject catalog."[105] Subject cards were provided only for books with two subjects and then only for for the second subject, because the classification number would provide an approach to the first subject. The subject catalog was to be a last resort to finding materials. Because it was incomplete and little used, the subject catalog was discontinued.[106]

A new classification scheme was developed so that the shelf arrangement would be readily apparent and "the numbers should be brief enough for ready memorizing."[107]

The Dewey Decimal system was used as the basis for the Lamont Classification scheme. No more than one decimal place was used and topics were arranged alphabetically when possible for ease in locating them. The classification became more a finding device than an analytical key to subject holdings. Because classification numbers were not to be used for circulation control, classification numbers were put only on the books and cards. Cutter numbers were deemed superfluous.[108]

Three major deviations from the Dewey Decimal Classification were the decisions to put all works on any one topic together no matter how they are treated; to place the works of and by musicians and painters together; and to place language with literature. With the freeing of the 400's, the social sciences (300) were split to relieve overcrowding in that area. Government and economics were left in the 300's, and social relations and education were moved to the 400's.

Simplification and Centralization

The undergraduate library was never planned to provide all library facilities for the undergraduate. It was intended to centralize those facilities that could be concentrated in one place to advantage. Neither was the undergraduate library to deprive the undergraduate student of the research collections housed in Widener or the other collections on the campus. Instead of descending on the research library in masses, undergraduates would go as individuals and could be helped as individuals. "They could be admitted to the stack if they needed to, or they could be given direction by the reference staff in using the catalog and calling books from the stacks."[109]

Shortly after its opening, James Bryant Conant, President of Harvard, spoke of the Lamont Library

> [as] the further elaboration of an already complex library system representing the longest step Harvard has ever taken in the direction of simplification. For the Harvard College Student, the distance and the barriers between the reader and the books have been all but eliminated; the conventional red tape of library bureaucracy has disappeared. The undergraduate in quest of knowledge or inspiration . . . can go directly to the shelves. No longer need he fill out cards, stand in lines at counters and wait while stack messengers or pneumatic tubes perform their functions. Instead he selects the desired volume and proceeds to a nearby table where he can go to work immediately. Or if he wishes, with a few additional steps, he can find a place to read and smoke, or even use a typewriter if he so desires. In brief the new library is both a long stride forward and a good step backward; a step back toward the simple past when the paucity of books and students automatically made a college library easy to access.[110]

Instruction in Library Use

The major aim of the reference staff when the library opened was to teach students to use the library. The concept of reference service at Harvard was "that a large part of a liberal education is learning how to use the library."[111] Over the years this has changed. Presently, there is little instruction in library use. Students are helped as individuals when they ask for aid, but there are few such requests.

STAFF

The first staff consisted of seven professional librarians, sixteen clerical employees, and a curator for the poetry room. Currently, there are two professional librarians with a total staff of twenty-two persons. The librarian and the assistant librarian occupy the two professional positions. The assistant librarian is in charge of both the reserve and circulation operations. In addition, he does some book selection, schedules personnel, hires part-time staff, and assists the librarian in hiring full-time nonprofessional staff. The duties of the librarian, beyond his supervisory and administrative functions, are budget preparation and final decisions for book selection.[112] When there were seven professional librarians, there were three professionals in circulation and three in reference.[113] Such staffing is no longer considered necessary.[114]

The clerical staff, for the most part, has no specific full-time tasks but performs all the various duties involved with the operation of the circulation and the two reserve desks. Since 1955, there has been an assistant in the poetry room who provides general supervision of the poetry room and the Farnsworth room and catalogs the recordings for the poetry room.[115]

As is usually the case, there is a high turnover of clerical help, but this fits into the philosophy at Lamont of not retaining clerical employees more than one or two years. It is felt that persons in these positions get inefficient if they remain too long. There is no means of advancement in the clerical ranks; therefore, if these persons want to advance, they must do it by means of another job.

For several years, the Lamont Library has been using library interns to supplement its staff. The interns attend Simmons Library School part time and work part time. They ordinarily work in circulation or reference and currently fill supervisory positions.[116]

The organization of the Lamont Library during its first few years was based on a functional division. Under the librarian were the head of circulation and the head of reference (Fig. 8). Reporting to each of these two individuals were two professional

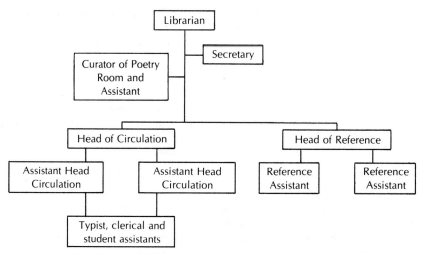

Fig. 8. Former organization chart of the Lamont Library

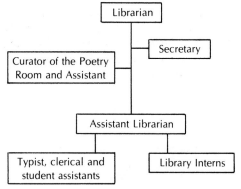

Fig. 9. Organization chart of the Lamont Library, 1965

assistants. The head of circulation was equivalent to an assistant librarian and was the second-ranking official in the library.

The status of the curator of the poetry room has remained the same over the years. He occupies an almost autonomous position in the administrative structure. He is responsible for maintaining both the poetry room and the Farnsworth room, but he does not necessarily keep the librarian informed of his actions.[117]

Because of the present nature of the staff, the organization is simpler (Fig. 9).[118]

LIBRARY USE

All of the emphasis on simplicity for the Lamont Library seemed to have been justified. With the opening of the building on January 3, 1949, many undergraduates came to look at the building, but many more stayed to use it. Soon, students were hard at work with materials they found themselves or with the help of librarians.[119]

Statistics show that there was a marked increase in the use of library facilities at Harvard after the opening of the Lamont Library. There was a negligible decrease in the use of Widener. An increase in circulation of 37,000 volumes was recorded for Widener and Lamont in 1949 over that for Widener in 1948. There was also an increase of 17,000 overnight charges in 1949, although there were 500 fewer students.

General-collection circulation has more than doubled—an increase of 115 percent —since the opening of the Lamont Library (Table 4). Circulation reached its peak in 1960–61 with 74,249 transactions, but since that time has been decreasing and in 1964–65 was down to 66,037. The increase over the years was gradual, as is the decrease, as the percentages point out. The enrollment at Harvard has remained fairly constant over the years so no great increases would be expected, but the decline in loans is an unusual development. The decline could be caused by the smaller number of students who seem to be using the building, or it could be caused by greater pressures exerted on the students in relation to course work.

Reserve loans have varied markedly during the years that the Lamont Library has been in operation (Table 5). Just as with general-collection circulation, reserve loans are in a period of decline. In years in which there were increases, they were never more than 10 percent. The 93 percent increase shown for 1949–50 is not really a true figure, because

TABLE 4

CIRCULATION STATISTICS (TWO-WEEK BOOKS), LAMONT LIBRARY

	LOANS	PERCENT INCREASE
1948–49[a]	30,649	
1949–50	52,714	71
1950–51	55,330	5
1951–52	53,499	− 3
1952–53	47,522	−11
1953–54	47,687	.3
1954–55	46,518	− 2
1955–56	52,651	13
1956–57	57,333	9
1957–58	61,370	6
1958–59	70,081	14
1959–60	72,323	3
1960–61	74,249	2
1961–62	70,178	− 5
1962–63	70,680	.7
1963–64	68,008	− 3
1964–65	66,073	− 2

[a]Jan. through June, 1949.

the total circulation for 1948–49 is only for a six-month period. The 199 percent increase for 1953–54 is also misleading, because "In Building" use figures were not kept until 1953–54. The decrease in reserve loans is puzzling. If one assumes that reserve books are not relied on in teaching as heavily as before, then one would assume that more general, individual reading is being done. But this is not the case, since general circulation is also declining. It seems that students are not using the services of the Lamont Library as much as in the past.

TABLE 5

RESERVE STATISTICS, LAMONT LIBRARY

	IN-BUILDING USE	OVERNIGHT RESERVE	TOTAL	PERCENT INCREASE
1948–49[a]	b	51,117	51,117	
1949–50	b	99,159	99,159	93
1950–51	b	103,756	103,756	4
1951–52	b	99,299	99,299	– 3
1952–53	b	101,386	101,386	2
1953–54	189,996	114,100	304,096	199
1954–55	191,484	121,282	312,766	2
1955–56	177,004	106,997	284,001	8
1956–57	149,366	91,403[c]	240,769	–15
1957–58	165,128	101,772	266,900	10
1958–59	167,982	91,486	259,468	– 2
1959–60	175,276	123,366	277,642	7
1960–61			294,450[d]	6
1961–62			293,121	– .4
1962–63			299,381	2
1963–64			271,162	– 9
1964–65			251,590	– 6

[a]Jan. through June, 1949.
[b]These figures were not kept prior to 1953.
[c]Lower overnight circulation reflects the first full year of extended hours – opened from 10:00 P.M. to midnight.
[d]Since 1960–61, reserve circulation figures have not been broken down into "In Building" and "Overnight Reserve" figures.

Since attendance is not recorded for the Lamont Library, no correlation can be made concerning the number of students actually using the library. Loan figures give an indication of use, but they tell only part of the story. Without the correlation of attendance and circulation, the complete pattern of use is not evident.

One concrete indication of attendance came from a report which the Harvard Student Council prepared in 1955 on libraries serving undergraduates at Harvard. The purpose of the report was to show that use of these libraries — the Lamont Library and the House libraries — warranted extended hours in Lamont. Three reasons were given why students used the library more extensively than had been done previously. Living quarters were becoming crowded, and with more people there was naturally more noise so that the Houses were no longer considered a good place to study. Although the Houses had libraries, they were small and often inadequate in other respects. And lastly, materials needed in connection with courses were to be found only in Lamont. While the extension of hours was primarily at the instigation of the undergraduate students, it was strongly seconded by the graduate students. In fact, it was estimated that 20 percent of the use of the Lamont Library was by graduate students.[120]

Three factors play a role in the graduate-student use of the Lamont Library. First, reserve books for courses open to both graduates and undergraduates are housed in Lamont. Second, many graduate students teach undergraduate courses and hence need to have access to the materials used for these courses. Third, Lamont provides more comfortable surroundings in which to work.[121] Another less obvious reason is that the periodicals are always available in Lamont, because they do not circulate outside the building.[122]

During 1961–62, a record of building attendance was kept to try to determine the amount of usage Lamont was receiving. During a seven-month period, the range of students in the building at one time ran from 884 to 100+ with an average of about 450. According to Henry James, Lamont Librarian,

> There is no feeling of strain on facilities except during peak periods, and even these do not unduly strain Lamont's study capacity of 1001 (omitting classrooms, Farnsworth, Poetry and Forum Rooms which provide another 484 seats).[123]

The Lamont Library receives its heaviest use during the reading periods which are times set aside before mid-year and final exams, but even then the library has never been filled to capacity.[124] When the library first opened, heaviest use was during the day, but after a few years, evening use began to increase while afternoon attendance dropped.[125]

In recent years, overall use of the Lamont Library has been on the decline. A check of Widener's circulation showed 60 percent of its use is by undergraduates. This is attributed in part to the intellectual curiosity of the Harvard student who wants to delve deeper into a subject than the Lamont resources allow and to the stepped-up pattern of education (honors courses, freshman seminars).[126] The decline of both general-collection and reserve circulation also seem to testify to this.[127]

The restriction preventing Radcliffe girls from using Lamont Library surely has an effect on the use of the library. Whatever the reasons for their exclusion (they do use Lamont during the summer and for classes that meet there during the regular terms),[128] this factor obviously cuts down to some extent—and how much or how little cannot be ascertained—on the use of the Lamont Library. Regardless of the locale, the study date is a popular innovation. Granted, most students' motives in going to the library are serious, but there are many who go for social purposes. If these cannot be found in Lamont, the students and their dates are to be found in Widener.

SUMMARY

In 1959, after one decade of operation of the Lamont Library, Paul H. Buck, Librarian of Harvard University,[129] summed up the whole concept of the undergraduate library:

> The idea of a separate undergraduate library was sound. Its physical realization has been triumphantly successful in nearly every detail; Lamont has had a striking influence on academic library policy and architecture throughout the country. For Harvard, the Lamont Library became a vital new tool of educational policy and methods. Quietly, yet effectively and pervasively, it has done much to strengthen the classroom instruction, the concept of teaching and reading, of lecturing, and of study, in all the courses. Just as the Houses are something more than comfortable dormitories, the Lamont Library is more than a group of excellent reading rooms. Like the Houses, it is a vital educational instrument, a source of life-giving blood at the heart of the undergraduate program. Successful as it has been, the full potential of its value to the College has not been realized. The usefulness of the Lamont Library should increase rather than decrease if intelligent administration is constantly alert to opportunities for responding to changing educational needs.[130]

The above statement embodies the whole concept of the Lamont Library. Equating the hopes of yesterday with the realities of today, the Lamont Library has succeeded, at least partially, in providing what was expected of it.

It succeeded in providing a building that was suited to the undergraduates' needs. The book collection began as a basic collection of general literature but has been broadened to meet expanding student needs. However, the division of the collection into so many distinct segments proved to be a detriment to its use. The proliferation of multiple copies for reserve has been extended too far. The reserve system appears to be a contradiction of the original plan of simplicity. Neither the division of the collection into three parts nor the unclassified order provide ease of use if a particular item is sought.

The decrease in reference staff has accompanied a decrease in demand for service. The circulation system in use has satisfied the students' needs. Lamont has been generous in the special services provided for the undergraduates and has succeeded in centralizing undergraduate services, but the efforts at simplification seem to have backfired at Lamont. The decrease in professional staff and the removal of the remaining professional staff from contact with the students does not conform to the standards originally set up for the Lamont Library. Perhaps this has been in part the reason for the decline in use of the library.

NOTES

[1]Keyes D. Metcalf, "The Undergraduate and the Harvard Library, 1937–1947," *Harvard Library Bulletin*, I (Autumn, 1947), 298–99.

[2]Interview with Keyes D. Metcalf, Librarian Emeritus, Harvard University, Oct. 25, 1965.

[3]Keyes D. Metcalf, "To What Extent Must We Segregate?" *College and Research Libraries*, VIII (Oct., 1947), 400.

[4]The Harvard Yard is the original college yard of 1638 which includes most of the principal administration buildings, lecture halls, and the freshmen dormitories.

[5]The Harvard Corporation, which consists of seven members (the president, five fellows, and the treasurer), is the principal governing board of the University. Property is held, appointments are made, and all important business is transacted in its name.

[6]Keyes D. Metcalf, *Planning Academic and Research Library Buildings* (New York: McGraw-Hill, 1965), p.311. Cited hereafter as *Planning Academic . . . Buildings*.

[7]*Ibid.*, p.304.

[8]Keyes D. Metcalf, "Harvard Faces Its Library Problems," in Conference on the Place of the Library in a University, Harvard University, 1949, *The Place of the Library in a University: A Conference Held at Harvard University, 30–31, March, 1949* (Cambridge: Harvard Univ. Library, 1950), p.42.

[9]Interview with Keyes D. Metcalf.

[10]Letter from Chester Hanford, Dean, Harvard College, to Keyes D. Metcalf, Jan. 16, 1946, in the Metcalf Papers (Harvard University Archives, Cambridge, Mass.). Cited hereafter as Metcalf Papers.

[11]Interview with Keyes D. Metcalf.

[12]Keyes D. Metcalf, "The Lamont Library: II. Function," *Harvard Library Bulletin*, III (Winter, 1949), 27–28. The following advertisement appeared in the *Harvard Crimson*, Jan. 12, 1949: "Opportunity— For Radcliffe women. Personable young man with access to Lamont Library." Metcalf Papers.

[13]Letter from Keyes D. Metcalf to Thomas W. Lamont, May 2, 1944, in the Lamont Papers (Harvard University Archives, Cambridge, Mass.). Cited hereafter as Lamont Papers.

[14]Interview with Keyes D. Metcalf. In honor of Mr. Lamont's gift, the undergraduate library was named the Lamont Library.

[15]Letter from Keyes D. Metcalf to Thomas W. Lamont, Aug. 22, 1945, Lamont Papers.

[16]Metcalf, *Harvard Library Bulletin*, I, 300. Because of the interest in costs in relation to building an undergraduate library, an interesting theory evolved. To build an undergraduate library would cost about $2,000,000. This sum would earn $100,000 interest at 5 percent per year. For that sum, it would be possible to "buy enough reserve books so that we could turn over to all the students for the year all the reserve books they needed and let them study in their own rooms." (Interview with Keyes D. Metcalf.)

[17]The Harvard Fund Council is the alumni money-raising group for the University. (Interview with Keyes D. Metcalf.)

[18]Memorandum from Edward Reynolds, Administrative Vice-President, to Mr. James B. Conant, President, Harvard University, March 8, 1947, Metcalf Papers.

[19]Memorandum [by Keyes D. Metcalf], Metcalf Papers.

[20]Henry R. Shepley, "The Lamont Library: I. Design," *Harvard Library Bulletin*, III (Winter, 1949), 5.

[21]Letter from Henry R. Shepley, architect, to Thomas W. Lamont, March 7, 1947, Lamont Papers.

[22]Shepley, *Harvard Library Bulletin*, III, 7.

[23]*Ibid.*, p.8.

[24]Metcalf, *Planning Academic . . . Buildings*, p.50.

[25]Ceiling height varies throughout the building: Level 1, 14'7"; Level 3, 15'1"; Level 5, 9'6". The mezzanines and book stack areas range from 7'9" to 8'. The smoking rooms have ceiling heights of approximately 8'3". The other rooms vary in height. The average clear height is 14'7". (Letter from Keyes D. Metcalf to Miss Myrtle Funkhouser, Librarian, Southern Oregon College of Education, Ashland, Ore., Oct. 21, 1949, Metcalf Papers.)

[26]Shepley, *Harvard Library Bulletin*, III, 10.

[27]Interview with Keyes D. Metcalf.

[28]Shepley, *Harvard Library Bulletin*, III, 10–11; Metcalf, *Planning Academic . . . Buildings*, p.69.

[29]Harvard University. Library, *Annual Report, 1945–56*, p.175.

[30]About two years ago, this room was converted into the map room. The map room is a

Widener function and has no direct relationship to Lamont Library except that it is housed there. (Interview with Keyes D. Metcalf.)

[31]Metcalf, *Harvard Library Bulletin*, III, 22–25.

[32]Morrison C. Haviland, "The Reference Function of the Lamont Library," *Harvard Library Bulletin*, III (Spring, 1949), 297.

[33]Metcalf, *Harvard Library Bulletin*, III, 22.

[34]Interview with Keyes D. Metcalf.

[35]Harvard University. Library. Lamont Library, *Lamont Library Handbook* (Cambridge: Harvard College Library, 1949), p.9.

[36]Metcalf, *Harvard Library Bulletin*, III, 22. The lighting can even be adjusted to make the room a suitable reading area. (Interview with Keyes D. Metcalf.)

[37]*Lamont Library Handbook*, p.11.

[38]*Ibid.*

[39]Shepley, *Harvard Library Bulletin*, III, 10.

[40]Metcalf, *Harvard Library Bulletin*, III, 21.

[41]Shepley, *Harvard Library Bulletin*, III, 5.

[42]Interview with Keyes D. Metcalf.

[43]Shepley, *Harvard Library Bulletin*, III, 9–10.

[44]Interview with Keyes D. Metcalf.

[45]Metcalf, *Harvard Library Bulletin*, III, 28.

[46]Interview with Keyes D. Metcalf; and Metcalf, *Planning Academic . . . Buildings,* p.120.

[47]"Lamont Library Furniture Schedule," Dec. 4, 1947, Metcalf Papers.

[48]Metcalf, *Planning Academic . . . Buildings,* p.323.

[49]Shepley, *Harvard Library Bulletin*, III, 10.

[50]Metcalf, *Planning Academic . . . Buildings,* p.184.

[51]Interview with Mr. Edwin Williams, Counselor to the Director, Harvard University Library, Oct. 27, 1965.

[52]There was a total of 32,700 volumes in the Union Library (22,240) and in Boylston Hall (10,460). Of these, only 5200 titles were selected for inclusion. Most of these books were in the fields of history, government and economics. ("Lamont Project" [by Keyes D. Metcalf], Metcalf Papers.)

[53]Charles A. Carpenter, Jr., "The Lamont Catalog as a Guide to Book Selection," *College and Research Libraries,* XVIII (July, 1957), 387–88.

[54]Edwin E. Williams, "The Selection of Books for Lamont," *Harvard Library Bulletin*, III (Autumn, 1949), 388.

[55]*Ibid.,* p.388–89.

[56]Interview with Edwin Williams.

[57]Williams, *Harvard Library Bulletin*, III, 389.

[58]"Book Selection for the Undergraduate Library," Metcalf Papers.

[59]Williams, *Harvard Library Bulletin*, III, 389–92.

[60]*Ibid.*

[61]*Ibid.*

[62]*Ibid.,* p.394.

[63]"New Library Opened," *Library Journal,* LXXIV (Feb. 1, 1949), 168.

[64]Interview with Theodore Alevizos, Librarian, Lamont Library, Harvard University, Oct. 26, 1965.

[65]*Ibid.*

[66]"Book Collection Account for Lamont," Metcalf Papers.

[67]Harvard University. Library, *Annual Report,* 1954–55, p.10.

[68]Memorandum from Mary Campbell, Library Intern, Reference Department, Lamont Library, May 30, 1963 (in the files of the Lamont Library).

[69]Interview with Keyes D. Metcalf.

[70]Harvard University. Library. Lamont Library, *Statistical Report to the Director,* 1961–62, p.1; 1963–64, p.1.

[71]Interview with Theodore Alevizos.

[72]Haviland, *Harvard Library Bulletin*, III, 297–98.

[73]*Statistical Report to the Director,* 1961–62, p.1.

[74]Haviland, *Harvard Library Bulletin*, III, 298.

[75]"Lamont Reserve System," Metcalf Papers.

[76]Interview with Theodore Alevizos.

[77]*Ibid.*

[78]Harvard University. Library, *Guide to Lamont Library* ("Guides to the Harvard Libraries," No. 7 [Cambridge, Mass.: 1958]), p.1–2.

[79]Interview with Keyes D. Metcalf.

[80]Interview with Theodore Alevizos.

[81]Haviland, *Harvard Library Bulletin*, III, 298–99.

[82]*Ibid.*

[83]Interview with Theodore Alevizos.

[84]Philip J. McNiff, "The Charging System of the Lamont Library," *Harvard Library Bulletin*, III (Autumn, 1949), 438–39.

[85]Haviland, *Harvard Library Bulletin*, III, 297–98.

[86]McNiff, *Harvard Library Bulletin*, III, 440.

[87]Philip J. McNiff and Edwin E. Williams, "Lamont Library: The First Year," *Harvard Library Bulletin*, IV (Spring, 1950), 205–6.

[88]Cynthia A. Saidel, "A Survey of the Lamont Library of Harvard College" (unpublished Master's thesis, School of Library Service, Columbia University, 1952), p.39. Cited hereafter as "A Survey of the Lamont Library."

[89]Interview with Philip J. McNiff, Director, Boston Public Library, Oct. 27, 1965. Mr. McNiff was the first librarian of the Lamont Library.

[90]In the Spring Semester, 1962, there were 10,250 volumes on closed reserve and 10,475 on open reserve. In 1963, there was a total of 22,291 reserve books (open, 9246; closed, 13,045) showing an increase of 1563 volumes. (Harvard University. Library. Lamont Library, *Annual Report,* 1961–62, p.1; 1962–63, p.1–2). In 1964–65, it was estimated that there were between 2500 and 3000 titles on reserve. (Interview with Theodore Alevizos.)

[91]Interview with Gregory Wilson, Assistant Librarian, Lamont Library, Harvard University, Oct. 28, 1965.

[92]McNiff and Williams, *Harvard Library Bulletin*, IV, 209.

[93]Interview with Keyes D. Metcalf.

[94]Frederick C. Packard, Jr., "Harvard's Vocarium Has Attained Full Stature," *Library Journal,* LXXV (Jan. 15, 1950), 69–71.

[95]*Ibid.,* p.72–73.

[96]Interview with Theodore Alevizos.

[97]*Guide to Lamont Library,* p.16.

[98]Interview with Theodore Alevizos.

[99]*Ibid.*

[100]*Guide to Lamont Library*, p.16.

[101]Interview with Theodore Alevizos.

[102]Saidel, "A Survey of the Lamont Library," p.37.

[103]Interview with Theodore Alevizos.

[104]McNiff and Williams, *Harvard Library Bulletin*, IV, 206.

[105]Interview with Keyes D. Metcalf.

[106]*Ibid.*

[107]Richard O. Pautzsch, "The Classification Scheme for the Lamont Library," *Harvard Library Bulletin*, IV (Winter, 1950), 126–27.

[108]*Ibid.*

[109]Interview with Keyes D. Metcalf.

[110]"The Story of Lamont Library," *Harvard Alumni Bulletin*, LI, (Jan. 15, 1949), 301–2.

[111]Interview with Keyes D. Metcalf.

[112]Interview with Theodore Alevizos.

[113]Harvard University. Library, *Directory* (Cambridge, Mass.: 1949), p.19.

[114]Interview with Theodore Alevizos.

[115]Memorandum from W. B. Ernst to D. W. Bryant, Sept. 17, 1959 (in the files of the Uris Library, Cornell University).

[116]Interview with Theodore Alevizos.

[117]*Ibid.*

[118]Saidel, "A Survey of the Lamont Library," p.26.

[119]Harvard University. Library, *Annual Report*, 1948–49, p.2.

[120]"Harvard Student Council Report on the Undergraduate Library," [signed] Steven Reynolds, 1955, Metcalf Papers.

[121]Letter from Peter Calingaert, Secretary, Graduate School Council, Harvard-Radcliffe, to Francis M. Rogers, Dean, Graduate School of Arts and Sciences, Oct. 23, 1954, Metcalf Papers.

[122]Interview with Philip J. McNiff.

[123]Harvard University. Library. Lamont Library, *Annual Report*, 1961–62, p.3.

[124]Interview with Theodore Alevizos.

[125]Harvard University. Library, *Annual Report*, 1956–57, p.7.

[126]Interview with Theodore Alevizos.

[127]Interview with Philip J. McNiff.

[128]Interview with Theodore Alevizos. Beginning with the Spring Term, 1967, the Lamont Library was opened to Radcliffe women. ("The Experimental Desegregation of Lamont," *Harvard Library Bulletin*, XV [April, 1967], 221.)

[129]Mr. Buck retired from this position in 1964 to return to full-time teaching and research.

[130]Harvard University. Library, *Annual Report*, 1958–59, p.12.

The Undergraduate Library, The University of Michigan

The idea of building a separate undergraduate library at Michigan originated in 1945 when William W. Bishop, University Librarian, urged "that universities recognize their undergraduates' needs by a special service, perhaps even a special building."[1] By 1953, the concept of an undergraduate library at Michigan had become more definite and feasible.[2] Previously, the decision had been made to consider the possibility of building an undergraduate library, and an estimate was made of costs. The idea was not proposed by the Librarian, Dr. Warner G. Rice, but by the President of the University, Harlan Hatcher, and the Dean of the College of Literature, Science, and the Arts, Charles Odegaard.[3] In July, 1953, Frederick H. Wagman became director of the university libraries and urged the establishment of the library.

On August 18, 1954, Dr. Wagman issued a "Preliminary Program for the Undergraduate Library." In this statement, he outlined the educational and physical attributes of the proposed library. He cited a two-fold purpose:

> The undergraduate library of the University of Michigan is conceived both as a solution to the problem of the inadequacy of existing library facilities for the students below the graduate level in all colleges of the University and as a general aid to the educational program of the College of Literature, Science and the Arts.[4]

He also stated what the undergraduate library should be to the student:

> The library should be conceived as an intellectual center for undergraduates of all schools, where they may meet for debates and discussions and to listen to music and poetry, recordings, where books are everywhere accessible and visible, where the arrangement of comfortable furniture, the decoration, lighting and other environmental factors are planned to make the atmosphere inviting, beautiful, relaxing, and yet where the student can feel that he has a high degree of privacy and can achieve a sense of intimacy with the books.[5]

One of the major reasons for proposing an undergraduate library at Michigan was that by 1954 the General Library and many of the divisional libraries faced critical space shortages. Thousands of volumes stored in various cellars and attics prevented proper maintenance, slowed service to readers, inhibited the growth of the collections, and created endless administrative problems for the staff. The General Library itself, built to house 800,000 volumes, contained 1,200,000 volumes.

Additional space for readers was also in demand. Space was available for only about 20 percent of the student enrollment. For the undergraduate student alone, the situation was even more discouraging. A total of 899 seats for an enrollment of 6124 provided seating for about 15 percent of the undergraduates in the College of Literature, Science, and the Arts.[6]

Another influencing factor at Michigan was the strongly entrenched system of divisional libraries, and the fact that some of the schools and colleges would eventually be

First floor reading area, Undergraduate Library, University of Michigan

moved to the North Campus.[7] Ideally, these divisional libraries were for graduate students and faculty, but some of the libraries also served undergraduates.

To solve the problem of space shortages for both books and readers, a two-fold plan was suggested. Dr. Wagman recommended that a storage facility for little-used materials be constructed "in a less central location and in a less expensive building." The second point of the proposal was "to [correct] the inadequacy of present library facilities for the undergraduates of the College of Literature, Science and the Arts and the other colleges and to [recognize] the necessity of planning for future undergraduate library needs." Although the trend at Michigan had been toward division by subject, a division was not being made by level of user.

The undergraduate library was to eliminate the high-school study halls "and end the use of the divisional libraries for undergraduate reserve reading."[8] Although the undergraduate would have his own library, he would still retain free access to the collections of the General Library and the divisional libraries.

The second reason for establishing an undergraduate library was the apparent change from the textbook method of instruction to "teaching with books." Teaching in the arts and sciences at the university was a broad range of responsibility, extending from the entering freshman to the advanced doctoral student. As the emphasis recently had swung to research and away from the undergraduate student, the latter was left to shift for himself both in the classroom and in the library. The new student was often confused by the complexity of the large research library. In many respects, the university library was not supporting classroom teaching, especially in the social sciences and the humanities. There were insufficient copies of books, the physical environment was not conducive to study, and necessary books were scattered in varying locations.[9]

Part of this problem could be solved by providing a collection that would not hinder either the student in his search for knowledge or the professor in trying to impart this knowledge to the student. According to Dr. Wagman:

> Such a library will do more than solve the problem of reading space for undergraduates. It will offer the instructor strong support in his teaching and allow him greater freedom in his method of instruction. It should encourage the undergraduate to develop the habit of reading good books. On many, the existence of such a library should have a profound and lasting influence.[10]

Once the decision was made to build an undergraduate library, the next step was to begin planning the project. Dr. Wagman recommended the formation of the Advisory Committee on the Undergraduate Library "to help in formulating objectives and in adapting the building plans to the advantage of the instructional program."[11] This committee undertook to visit some recent library buildings. Lighting, ventilation, furniture, provision of classrooms, smoking, and the reserve system received special attention on these trips.[12] The Advisory Committee on the Undergraduate Library felt that the undergraduates themselves ought to be consulted. James A. Lewis, Vice-President for Student Affairs, designated a student committee for this purpose.[13]

Because some faculty members thought that the general faculty should be consulted in planning the Undergraduate Library, the Advisory Committee on the Undergraduate Library and the director of the university libraries held an open meeting to inform the faculty about the plans for the Undergraduate Library and the advantages it would have for their teaching.[14] The success of the Undergraduate Library would depend on the faculty's use of it.[15]

FINANCING

The Undergraduate Library at the University of Michigan was financed solely by state appropriations. The Michigan legislature appropriated $3,105,000 in 1955 for the building and equipment.[16]

Before Dr. Wagman came to the University of Michigan, the state legislature had approved an estimate for the Undergraduate Library of about $2,000,000. After Dr. Wagman reexamined the plans, it was evident that the sum originally requested was too low. An additional $1,000,000 was requested because two additional floors would be added; these would temporarily house two department libraries, Transportation and Engineering.

TABLE 6

INITIAL BUDGET FOR THE UNDERGRADUATE LIBRARY,
UNIVERSITY OF MICHIGAN[a]

Building	$3,100,000
Equipment	310,000
Books	200,000
Selection and ordering	35,520
Cataloging	107,176
Total	$3,752,696

[a]Taken from memorandum from Stephen Ford, Head, Order Department, University of Michigan, to Frederick H. Wagman, Feb. 10, 1958 (in the files of the University Library).

When these professional schools moved to the North Campus, the libraries would be moved with them, and the released space would be used for expansion of the Undergraduate Library.[17] The initial budget (Table 6) was somewhat above what was finally approved, but it does give an idea of the breakdown of the appropriation.

THE BUILDING

Description

Only one feasible location was available for the building, the site of the automotive laboratory, located on the southeast section of the campus between the Engineering Building and the Clements Library. The shape of the building and its external appearance were governed by the site and surrounding buildings.[18]

What the building would include was decided as the planning progressed. Among additions to the original plan were provisions for the Engineering Library and an audio room.[19] One major change in plans was the elimination of the subbasement that had been included in the first proposal.[20]

A modular building of reinforced concrete was decided upon. The structure of 122 by 233 linear feet was built on modules of 24 by 30 feet in the rear of the building and 18 by 30 feet in the front portion. One of the most important factors in the construction of the building was flexibility, so that the demands of the future would not be hampered by the planning of the past. With this in mind, the lighting, air conditioning, and electric outlets were installed so that partitions could be erected in any desired pattern. There were no interior weight-bearing partitions. Free-standing stacks allowed for rearrangement of bookcases as well as the interchange of bookcases with tables and chairs.[21]

The building consists of five floors, one below ground.[22] The Undergraduate Library occupies two and one-half floors of the building. The third floor is occupied by the Engineering Library, and the fourth by the Transportation Library (these libraries are now one unit) and a Print Study Gallery which is used in conjunction with courses in the fine arts. The Education Library occupies one third of the second floor.[23]

Basically the same arrangement is followed on each floor except for the fourth (Figs. 10–14). Along the west walls, there are group study rooms, a nonsmoking room, a staff office, and a typing room. There are no partitions in the main area of each floor. "Two rows of free standing book stacks in ranges four to six sections each run the length of the floors. They are set at right angles to the room, twenty-seven feet from the outside walls with four foot aisles between sections." The wide floors are broken up with colorful, plastic-covered screens, some of which extend from floor to ceiling. The screens create a sense of privacy for the readers. Individual study tables are attached to both sides of the screens, and individual carrels line the walls on each floor. The rest of the space is occupied by tables for four readers.[24]

Special facilities on each floor are in the front portion of the building. On the basement floor, there are rooms for the blind, the student lounge, and a film-viewing room. There are provisions for three blind students who can be assisted by readers. The student lounge seats fifty persons and is equipped with beverage vending machines.[25] The film-preview room provides a place for students to view educational sound films in viewing booths, each of which has a film projector and headphones. The room can also be used for showing films to small groups.[26]

On the first floor, the front portion of the building has a lobby, the undergraduate librarian's and secretary's offices, a circulation desk, the elevators, inspection exit stations, and an art exhibit area. To the right of the entrance are the secretary's and the librarian's offices. The remainder of the area along the west wall up to the partition, which separates the lobby from the reading area, houses the circulation and reserve desks. The art exhibit area in the lobby has pegboard screens, which extend from floor to ceiling, and lounge furniture.[27] The receiving room, behind the reserve area, has convenient access to the driveway and to the service elevator.

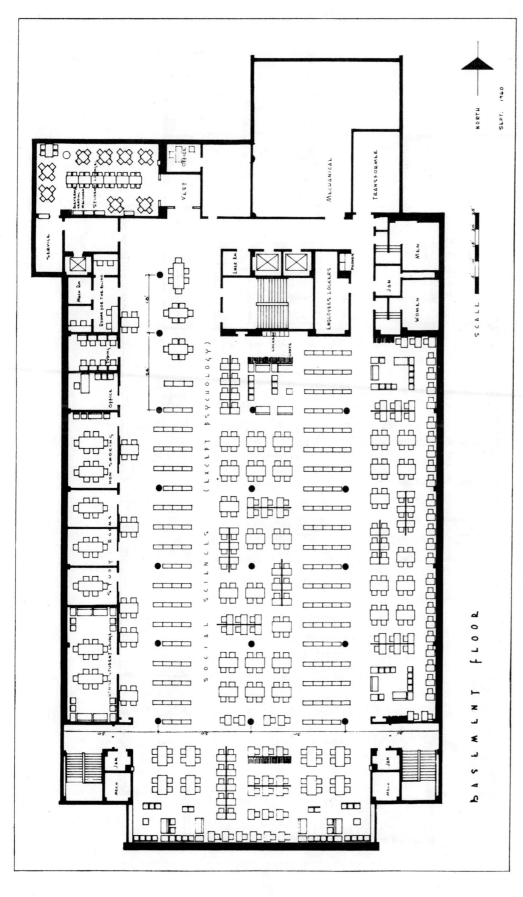

Fig. 10. Basement floor, Undergraduate Library, University of Michigan (original plan)

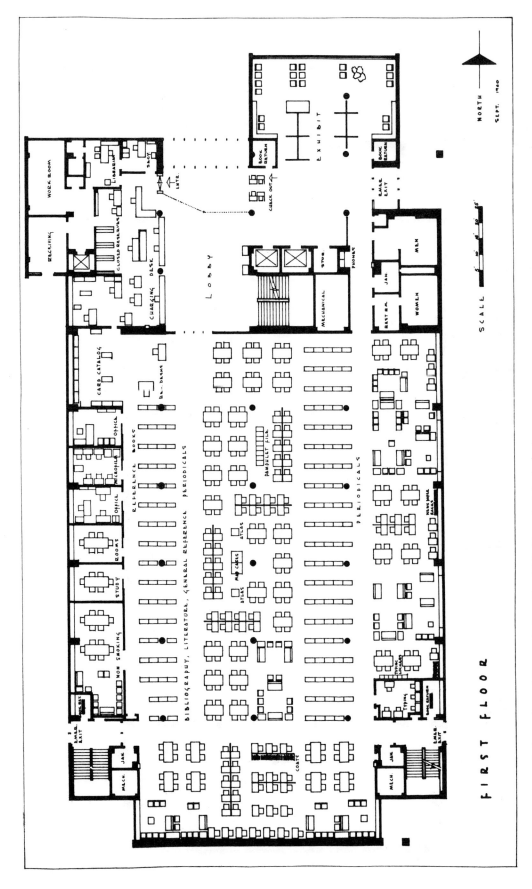

Fig. 11. First floor, Undergraduate Library, University of Michigan (original plan)

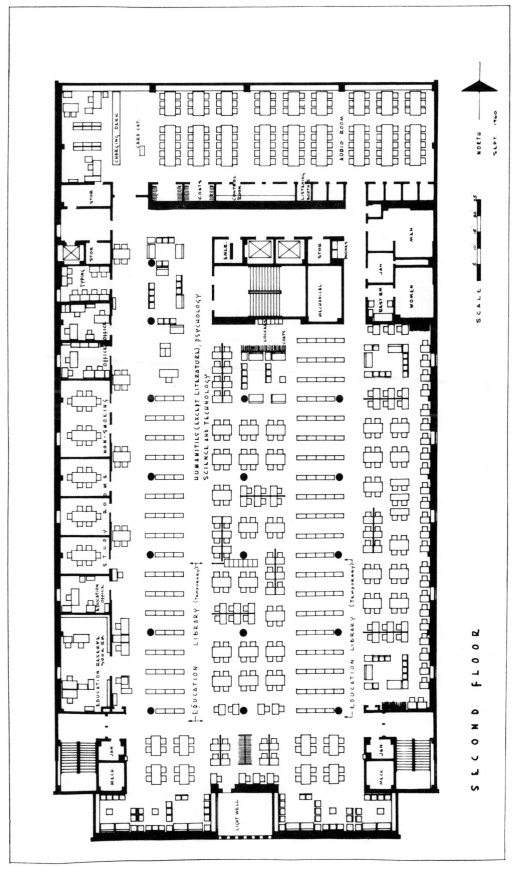

Fig. 12. Second floor, Undergraduate Library, University of Michigan (original plan)

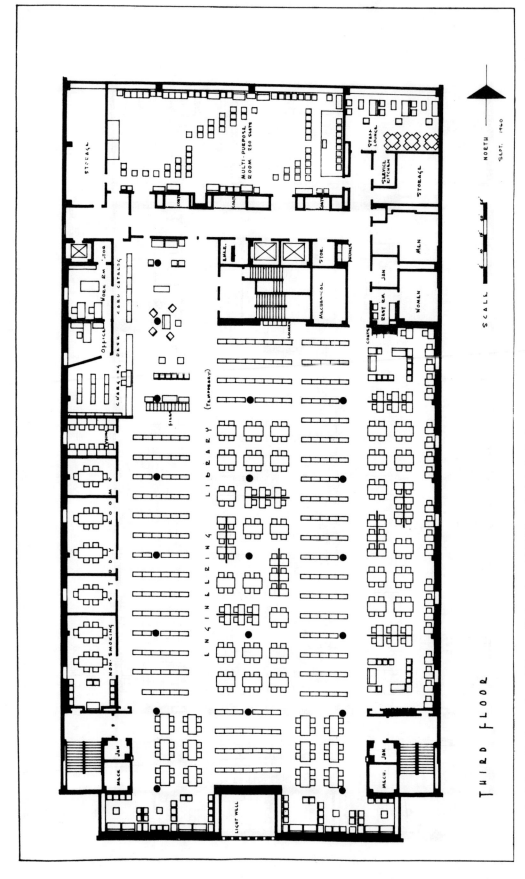

Fig. 13. *Third floor, Undergraduate Library, University of Michigan (original plan)*

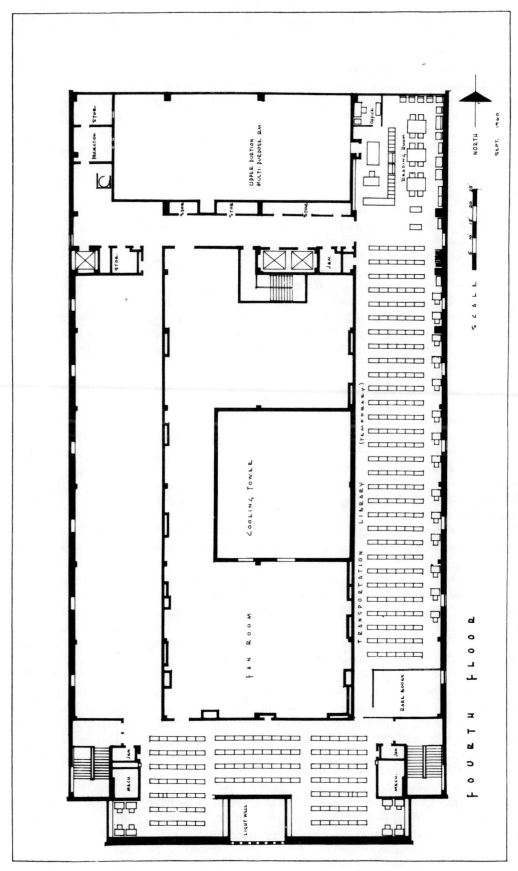

Fig. 14. Fourth floor, Undergraduate Library, University of Michigan (original plan)

The entire front portion of the second floor contains the audio room, which has seventy-two turntables. The room seats 151 people—two at each turntable plus one at each of the seven listening cubicles. A control room allows programs to be played over fourteen channels by either record or tape.[28]

A multipurpose room, providing seating for 230, is located on the north side of the third floor. The room is divisible by an accordion wall, so that it can accommodate two separate activities at one time.

The building actually has four entrance/exits. However, only one—the north or main entrance—is used. The other entrance/exits satisfy the fire regulations and are equipped with panic locks to prevent their use except in case of emergency.[29]

There are four major reading areas:

1. General reference, periodicals, and bibliography
2. Humanities and fine arts
3. Social sciences and education
4. Natural sciences and engineering.[30]

The first, second, and third groups are approximately equal in size. The social sciences, except psychology, are in the basement. The first floor contains bibliography, literature, general reference, and periodicals. On the second floor are the humanities (except literature), psychology, and science and technology. When the library opened, there were 21,000 volumes on the basement floor, 18,375 on the first, and 12,325 on the second.[31]

Furnishings

Special consideration was given to the lighting. Recessed-troffer fluorescent lighting on 6-foot centers provides about 55.5 footcandles. The intensity of the lighting tends to vary with the type of bookbinding, the type of floor covering, and the maintenance of the fixtures. If it became necessary to decrease the size of the aisles to less than 4 feet, bookcases could be placed perpendicular to the light fixtures and still have adequate lighting (this has been done).[32] Lighting is controlled from a pushbutton station on each floor near the main stairway.[33]

An alternate plan of using troffer lights with egg-crate louvers on 3-foot centers was suggested, but the architects pointed out that such an arrangement would occupy a large part of the ceiling and would not be desirable from the standpoint of appearance. It would also interfere with the acoustical character of the building, because some of the acoustical material would have to be omitted to include the extra fixtures. Another considerable factor was the increase in cost—by about 75 percent—that fixtures on 3-foot centers would necessitate.[34] The architects also considered luminous ceilings, but did not recommend them because they would interfere with the acoustics, attract attention, and increase lighting costs and the total height of the building.[35]

The furniture in the building is of three main types: individual carrel seats, seating at tables, and lounge furniture. The arrangement of tables is interrupted by groupings of lounge furniture. No two lounge chairs are placed side by side; an end table is placed between them for the student's convenience.[36] Although there is a disproportionate ratio of seating to bookstacks, "the reader is conscious of the proximity to the books in all parts of the reading areas.[37]

Total seating capacity for the building was 2250, including the student lounge, multipurpose room, etc. Seating for the undergraduate portion of the building (study seats) was about 1100, of which approximately one third was lounge chairs, one third individual seats, and the remaining third divided between tables that seat four and the group study rooms. The emphasis in seating was placed on individual carrels and lounge chairs.[38]

As use of the building increased, the problem of seating became acute, so that at times students would be found sitting on the floors, on the window sills, or on the stairs.

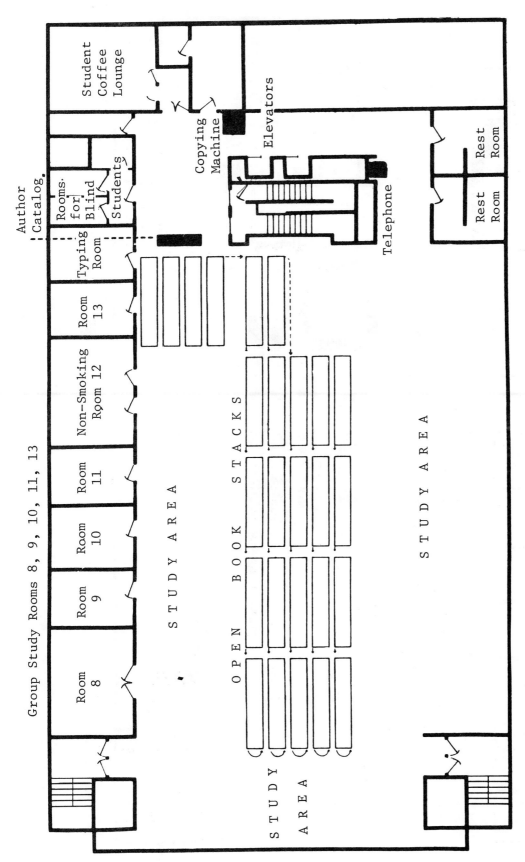

Fig. 15. Basement floor, Undergraduate Library, University of Michigan (drawing of the revised plan, not to scale)

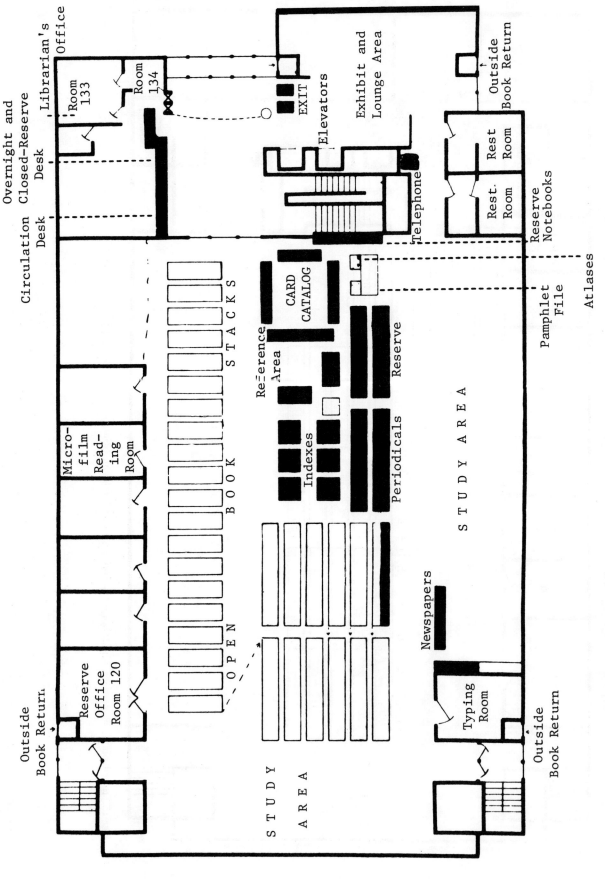

Fig. 16. First floor, Undergraduate Library, University of Michigan (drawing of the revised plan, not to scale)

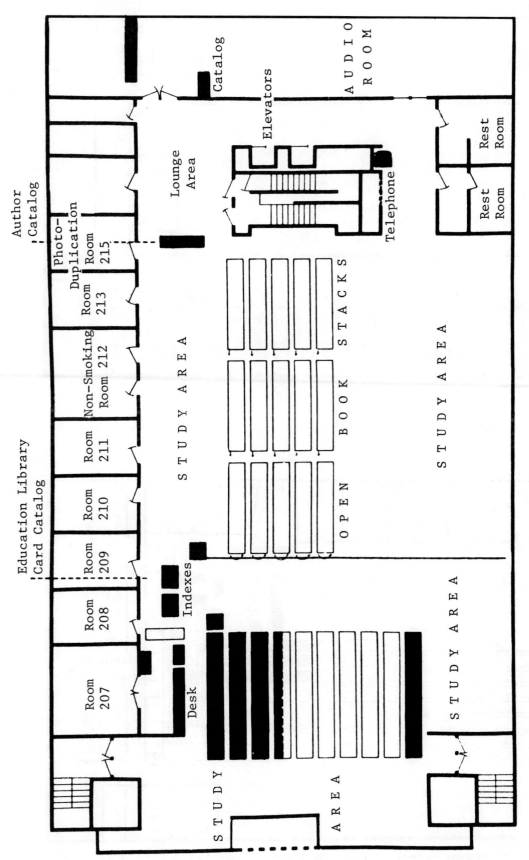

Fig. 17. Second floor, Undergraduate Library, University of Michigan (drawing of the revised plan, not to scale)

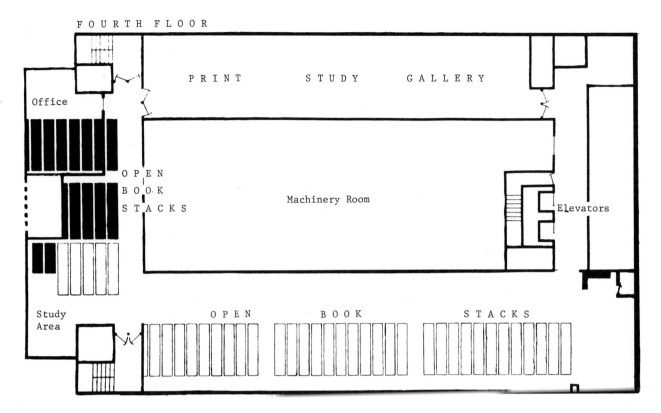

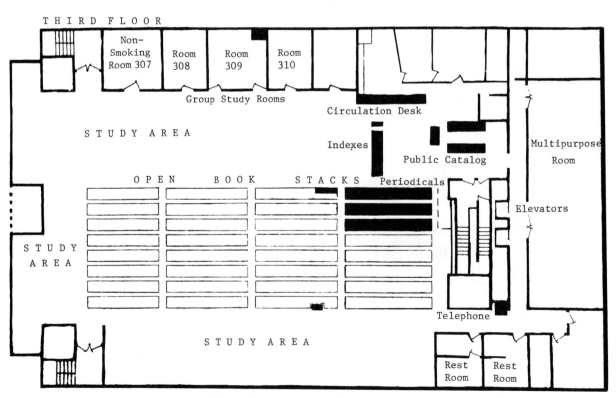

Fig. 18. Third and fourth floors, Undergraduate Library, University of Michigan (drawing of the revised plan, not to scale)

Although it was not desirable to displace the roomy atmosphere of the building, more seating was necessary. During 1964–65, a project was begun to study rearrangements in the building to provide more seating.[39]

During September, 1966, 377 more seats were added to the Undergraduate Library by removing some lounge areas and rearranging existing furniture (Figs. 15–18). The total capacity for the building now stands at 2620; study seats in the entire building number 2315. The Undergraduate Library portion of the building has 1357 study seats.

Lounge furniture was removed, because it was found that many students preferred a table to a lounge chair. Only one lounge area remains on each floor, and seats at divided-top tables have replaced the others.[40] Each table—individual and group—has 6 square feet of work surface per person and has a light-colored surface with low-reflectance value, in addition to being burn and stain resistant. The chairs are designed for comfort and durability, as well as to serve as part of the decorative plan of the library.[41]

Because of the lack of funds, use of color in the furniture provided most of the building's decor. Since upholstered chairs were being used, there was no reason why they should not be colorful. There was also no reason why color could not be added in the screens that were to be used as space breakers. No color was used on the floors or ceilings so they would be unobtrusive. A neutral shade was chosen for the walls to make them appear to recede. However, the back wall on each floor is painted in a bright color.[42]

BOOK COLLECTION

General Collection

Even before beginning the Undergraduate Library building, the process of selecting books for the new library had gotten under way. Mr. Rolland Stewart, Assistant Director of the University Libraries, was in charge of the Undergraduate Library Selection Project. Mr. Stewart's task was to select approximately 40,000 volumes to form the basis of the collection. The desired titles had to be selected, searched, ordered, and processed. If copies of a book were already located in one of the campus libraries, decisions about transfer had to be made.[43]

The criteria for book selection were

> to satisfy the undergraduate's normal library needs—whether for assigned, recommended, or independent reading—through four years of study, and all the way from accounting to zoology.[44]

The object was to provide books to support the curriculum and a good, general, well-balanced collection. The collection was not to reflect the interests and the needs of the lower-division students exclusively but was aimed at the whole range of undergraduates. Although a large part of the holdings of the Undergraduate Library was to be reserve books, it was by no means thought of as a super reserve-book reading room. It was imagined as a liberal arts college library, but one that did not have to be self-contained.[45]

Several categories of books were to constitute the collection. The first was a reference collection. The second category for inclusion was books on assigned-reading lists from the College of Literature, Science, and the Arts. These books were to be on open shelves with other volumes on the same subject to try to interest students in things beyond required reading. The third area of inclusion was books which should be available to undergraduates "for the sake of their general education." Also to be included were the Gold Star periodicals[46] and most of the general interest periodicals. Duplication of a title was not a factor in the choice of any book.[47] Assigned or collateral readings were to be ordered automatically, while it was Mr. Stewart's and the undergraduate librarian's function to select books "to maintain the collection as representative of the best in current and retrospective publications."[48]

The only example of a separate undergraduate library to draw on was the Lamont Library at Harvard. The Lamont Library *Catalogue,* published in 1953, provided a major bibliographic source for the collection at Michigan. It "has the inestimable advantage of offering . . . a large volume of good books in a simple classified arrangement."[49] Mr. Stewart sent one copy of the Lamont *Catalogue* to each department in the College of Literature, Science, and the Arts to check which titles they would like included in the Undergraduate Library.[50]

In the meantime, the staff of the Undergraduate Library Selection Project checked all the titles in the Lamont *Catalogue* against *Books in Print* to determine their availability. As the recommendations came back from the faculty, a card was made for each title and supplied with the basic bibliographic information.[51]

To avoid the weaknesses of the Lamont list, Mr. Stewart resorted to three separate policies:

1. Extensive checking of publishers' catalogues in all fields, routing such catalogues as are divided by subject to members of the teaching staff in the various departments;
2. Large-scale checking of subject bibliographies or bibliographies appended to monographs;
3. Selection from the General Library Shelf List either by myself or by faculty members who will consent to do it for me.[52]

The most valuable "basic preliminary selection medium" was "publishers' catalogs for the English speaking world."[53] Mr. Stewart thought them the best way to get a complete listing of what was available, since neither bibliographies nor reviews in scholarly journals provided as full a listing.[54]

After the Lamont list and publishers' catalogs, the principal selection medium was the University Library. Mr. Stewart first determined the Library of Congress number for the desired subject and then checked the University of Michigan shelf list. He assumed that the University of Michigan Libraries would not have missed many significant publications in any one field. This method was used for about 250 varied narrow subjects.

In addition to seeking the voluntary help of the faculty through the academic departments, Mr. Stewart attempted to hire faculty members to assist in book selection, but there was the problem of finding interested persons. Two persons were hired half time one summer and another for one semester, but the experiment was not satisfactory. Even though these individuals were well versed in their subject matter, they did not know how to go about getting at the books. Of course, one of the major disadvantages to such a project was the great cost involved in hiring these persons.[55]

To supplement all other measures, Mr. Stewart also held personal interviews with representatives of each department. In these conferences, he covered many aspects of the Undergraduate Library, but he stressed the idea of the "sufficiency of the College Library for the undergraduate student body, an emphasis which was and is needed to dispel the notion that the new library is being planned as a glorified lounging facility with lots of good reading matter at hand if other distractions wear thin or begin to cloy."[56]

Time became an important factor in building the collection, because construction of the building was already under way when the selection project began. Since there was to be no special staff in either the Acquisition or Catalog departments to process books, a steady flow of materials was much more desirable than erratic large shipments of material.[57]

Before the actual ordering and buying began, a list of desired titles was compiled on cards. Some categories of books were automatically included, such as the list of titles obtained from the old study halls. However, any title which was not readily available was excluded. There were also cards for faculty recommendations and for the 7000 titles selected by Mr. Stewart from publishers' catalogs.[58]

By November, 1955, cards had been made for 30,437 titles. Another 15,000 titles were marked for inclusion from the Lamont *Catalogue,* and there were approximately 13,000 titles from departmental reading lists, publishers' catalogs, and bibliographies. After editing, the file held approximately 39,447 titles.[59] The total recommendations from all sources numbered about 98,000 titles. Some were duplicates, some were unsuitable for the Undergraduate Library book collection, and others proved to be unobtainable out-of-print titles.

The first stage in actually acquiring the books was a book-buying trip taken by Mr. Stewart in May, 1956. On his first trip, Mr. Stewart went to Baker and Taylor where the books were arranged by publisher, so there was no danger of duplicating titles.[60] For titles of publishers who were not well represented by this wholesaler, Mr. Stewart visited warehouses. From these trips, Mr. Stewart acquired 12,000 to 13,000 titles which could be considered the core of the collection. These were all in-print titles, many of which were from the previously prepared card file, but some were also "impulse" purchases based on Mr. Stewart's knowledge of books.

After these initial forays, the purchasing of the remainder of the collection followed standard library procedures. To determine how much money was available at a given time, an estimate of cost per volume was ascertained at $5.25 and used as an arbitrary measure.[61]

Besides the book-buying trips, several other unorthodox methods were used in obtaining the collection, such as buying a publisher's complete catalog or bookstore stocks.[62] As a result, the initial collection was acquired at a bargain price of about $4.50 per volume. In fact, approximately 44,000 volumes (about 40,000 titles) were acquired with the $200,000 that was available.[63]

The materials acquired by the previous means were mostly in-print materials. The last part of the acquisition procedure was to acquire as many as possible of the out-of-print titles, approximately 1500, included in the list of initial selections. This was done by a search of about ninety secondhand bookstores in Chicago, Boston, Washington, D.C., and New York City and by advertising. In this way, Mr. Stewart acquired all but a few of the desired titles.[64]

The initial collection emerged general and balanced, with predominance in the humanities and social sciences. Since 1958, "the collection has lost some of its early shapeliness,"[65] because purchases in some fields, especially for reserve books, are much higher than in others, giving the collection somewhat of an imbalance. That is not to say that such an imbalance is bad. The collection today reflects a working collection, as opposed to the more theoretical initial collection. The mere fact that a book is on the shelves of the Undergraduate Library "indicates a higher potential demand" than would be the case for any book in a research library.[66]

Since the opening of the library, selection has been broadened to include some subjects which were not considered important in the initial selection. In areas in which there were good divisional libraries, no real attempt was made to build an extensive collection. At the outset, some departmental faculties did not want their students to use the library, but later they changed their minds.[67]

As was previously mentioned, the decision was made to transfer some books from the General Library to the Undergraduate Library. Not only were materials transferred from the stack collection, the graduate reading rooms, and the study halls in the General Library, but it was decided to transfer books from the divisional libraries.[68] Most of the titles that were transferred from the General Library stacks were second copies, and the majority were out-of-print titles.[69]

About 80 percent of the collection was selected from the publishers' catalogs, faculty reading lists, the Lamont Library *Catalogue,* and "lists provided by divisional librarians (to provide materials in specific subject fields)." The titles recommended contained

> the materials out of which can be fashioned a kind of critical anthology of man's intellectual achievement, to the extent that this is possible in a collection of such small compass. It will not be confined to the cold mutton and weak tea laid out in such abundance by books of the type "Introduction to . . . ," "Essentials of . . . ," "Fundamentals of . . . ," etc. It will respond to the unusual student hastening to enlarge his intellectual horizon beyond the curricular needs of the hour. It will invite him to test his powers with scholarly work. Although the collection we are speaking of may be only suggestive of the knowl-

> edge the student may encounter elsewhere in the central research library or the subject divisional libraries that are associated with it, he will because of its representativeness be able to go elsewhere with a larger mind and a surer aim.[70]

The collection is largely a duplication of what is found in the other university libraries (about 98 percent of the initial collection were duplicates of titles already in the system). The same ratio is probably still true.[71]

No great effort was made to draw a sharp line between the graduate book and the undergraduate book. Nor was any attempt made to exclude textbooks.[72] The collection that was assembled was "a small, highly useable, highly flexible general university library which in most respects will satisfy the best of our undergraduate student body."[73]

After the initial book-selection project was over, the function of book selection was divided among the Undergraduate Library professional staff by subject areas. Each person "is also encouraged to do general selection if he sees a title listed which his reference work with students makes him feel would be desirable to have in the collection."[74]

Current general book-selection practice falls into three main areas: important current publications, added copies of titles in heavy demand, and titles lacking in sets or serials and those needed to fill other gaps in the collection.[75] Four factors are taken into consideration:

> the quality and level of the title being considered, the balance of the collection, the book funds available and the tone and emphasis of the basic collection selected by the Assistant Director.[76]

Since the Undergraduate Library is not self-sufficient, it is not expected to provide for all the needs of all undergraduate students. Hence freshmen and sophomores find it adequate, but upper-division students frequently need supplementary materials.

The size of the collection (Table 7) has increased by 122 percent. By 1960, there were about 50,000 titles, while in 1964 there were 57,000 titles included in 107,817 volumes. Considering the policy of duplication for reserve titles, this latter figure seems somewhat remarkable. The collection is now eight years old, but no weeding has been done. Pressed with other duties, the Catalog Department does not have time to withdraw the books. Missing books are withdrawn because the collection is inventoried yearly, and it is desirable to keep the collection updated to that extent (Table 8). However, most of these missing volumes turn up during succeeding searches. The percentage of books missing is not thought high in proportion to other campus libraries.

When the Undergraduate Library opened, it had a collection of about 160 periodicals shelved alphabetically by title on open shelves.[77] They are not classified. To select the titles to be included, a list of 400 periodicals was compiled by the selection project and

TABLE 7

GROWTH OF THE BOOK COLLECTION, UNDERGRADUATE
LIBRARY, UNIVERSITY OF MICHIGAN[a]

	SIZE	PERCENT INCREASE
1957–58[b]	54,000[c]	
1958–59	68,590	27
1959–60	74,222	8
1960–61	81,521	9
1961–62	86,072	5
1962–63	99,486	17
1963–64	107,817	8
1964–65	120,080	11

[a]Figures are for the fiscal year, July 1–June 30.
[b]Includes only Jan. 1–June, 1958. The same will be true for all the following tables.
[c]Approximate size.

TABLE 8

BOOKS FOUND MISSING IN THE ANNUAL INVENTORY, UNDERGRADUATE
LIBRARY, UNIVERSITY OF MICHIGAN[a]

	NUMBER	PERCENT OF COLLECTION
1958–59	1,071	2.00
1959–60	1,219	1.84
1960–61	1,407	1.89
1961–62	1,977	2.42
1962–63	1,914	2.22
1963–64	2,749	2.76
1964–65	2,409	2.23

[a]Figures are for the report year, May 1–April 30. All figures are for the report year in the following tables unless specified otherwise.

circulated to all the academic departments in the College of Literature, Science, and the Arts for their recommendations. Mr. Stewart made the final selection of titles.[78]

Many of the periodicals, namely the Gold Star titles, were transferred from the General Library after the Undergraduate Library opened. The transfers were made mainly because these titles were indexed in *Readers' Guide,* and without sufficient runs, undergraduates would have to use them in the General Library. Since the General Library still had closed stacks when the Undergraduate Library opened, a great strain was placed on the General Library Circulation Department. (The General Library stacks were opened to all students in June, 1958.)[79]

The same policy applies to periodicals as to books: not all titles suggested are added to the collection. Most rejections of periodicals are made on the basis that they are too specialized for the collection. Of the 248 titles in the collection, most are general in nature, but the important scholarly journals in the areas in the College of Literature, Science, and the Arts are included.[80]

Besides the acquisition of books, there was also the problem of acquiring phonograph recordings for the Undergraduate Library audio room. The school of Music made selections from the catalogs of record dealers, and the initial purchase of about 1000 records was made from Sam Goody of New York.[81]

The collection in the audio room consists of all kinds of music — classical, jazz, etc. — on records and tapes. Records that receive heavy use are put on tape to preserve the record. No language records are handled in the audio room. Besides music, the collection contains a number of spoken records — poetry, drama, etc. The collection even contains some foreign language works which are used in conjunction with classes. The collection contains 4158 records and 911 tapes.[82]

Reference Collection

The reference collection began with about 2000 volumes, but it soon became evident that it would have to be enlarged. The collection now numbers about 3100 volumes.[83]

Reserve Collection

The Undergraduate Library has formulated several guidelines in the purchase of reserve books. Reserve books are purchased for all courses (there are some exceptions) numbered below 500 in the departments of the College of Literature, Science, and the Arts. Whenever any title seems to be a questionable inclusion for the Undergraduate Library, the reserve librarian contacts the instructor about its purchase. The Undergraduate Library does not obtain multiple copies of sets containing three or more volumes.[84]

Some of the other internal reserve policies are:

> Some foreign works, expensive sets, volumes of large sets, multiple copies of very expensive titles and very old titles are often borrowed from the General Library. The Reserve librarian decides whether to borrow or order.

> Sometimes a professor asks for multiple copies of a title, when actually what he is concerned with is a short story, play or brief selection which appears in the title. In these instances the Short Story and Play Indexes are for anthologies [*sic*] in the Undergraduate Library which contain the materials.

> Textbooks which students are required to buy are not purchased for that particular course. However, a book used as a text in one course may turn up as Assigned or Suggested reading in another. When this is known, the Undergraduate Library copies are put on Closed Reserve. The book stores will be checked for lists of required *texts* in various courses.[85]

Several other changes were made in certain reserve-book-selection policies. Because one title was occasionally on reserve for several courses, the following change in policy was made:

> List #1 or the course with the larger enrollment will be provided with assigned reading at a ratio of one book per 7 students; List #2 or the course with the smaller enrollment will be provided with a ratio of 1:10; List #3 or after will be provided with a ratio of 1:14 if the Undergraduate Library has 25 or more copies and no additional copies will be provided if the Undergraduate Library has 50 or more copies.[86]

This reserve system often requires an oversupply of materials, making it an expensive operation. During the first years of operation, multiple copies were purchased at the ratio of one copy for each fifteen students for required reading, but only one copy for suggested readings. With large classes, this was ordinarily considered sufficient, while for small classes one copy was not adequate.[87] On July 1, 1960, this was changed to a one to ten ratio.[88]

Even though the ratio of reserve books was increased to provide enough copies, there was still the constant problem of students stealing and hiding reserve titles to be assured of "their" having a copy of the books. A peak of faculty and student resentment during 1961–62 called for immediate attention to the problem. The first cry called for all books to be placed on closed reserve, but the staff of the Undergraduate Library was reluctant to do this because of the educational advantage of the open-reserve system and the increased

TABLE 9

NEW TITLES AND VOLUMES PURCHASED FOR RESERVE, UNDERGRADUATE
LIBRARY, UNIVERSITY OF MICHIGAN

	VOLUMES	TITLES
1957–58	1,268	538
1958–59	2,368	1,157
1959–60	2,585	a
1960–61	3,787	a
1961–62	3,518	1,883
1962–63	11,781	3,612
1963–64	7,988	2,925
1964–65	8,427	2,894

aFigures not available.

costs involved in a closed-reserve system. As an alternate, the ratio was once more reduced, this time to one copy for seven students.[89]

The reserve system is also expensive because many new titles—often in multiple copies—must be ordered each semester (Table 9). It was thought that after two or three years of operation the number of reserve books to be purchased would become smaller as the basic texts were accumulated. This, however, is not the case. The number increases, as does the number of course lists for reserve. Not only do the number of lists in the social sciences and humanities increase as the enrollment grows, but there is a rise in the number of lists for science courses and in the number of titles on each list. This is, however, the objective of the Undergraduate Library: "to offer facilities which would encourage professors to use additional books in their teaching."[90]

Further expense is incurred in buying replacements. If a reserve book is reported missing, no attempt is made to replace it until there is a request for the book. Because of this policy, the replacement cost is not felt to be unbearable or as great as servicing a closed-reserve system. In fact, only about 13 percent of the reserve books purchased in one term are replacements.[91]

Although much money is spent on reserve books, most of it is spent in a few areas. Courses in the social sciences make heavier use of reserve books than the other major disciplines. A further breakdown shows that psychology and sociology require "the greatest number of multiple copies because of the heavy use of library readings in their large elementary courses."[92] Economics and political science also make heavy use of reserve materials.[93]

The number of volumes on closed reserve has varied, although the collection has been maintained at a fairly constant level. In 1958–59, there were 2504 volumes on closed reserve; in 1961–62, this figure rose to 3627; but in 1964–65, it was down to 2815.[94]

Open Access to the Collection

The Undergraduate Library at Michigan provides more open access than any other undergraduate library.

> This library is to have the objective of offering a stimulus to the undergraduate to read good books, to broaden intellectual interests, to develop the lifelong habit of self-education through reading. It should be one of the best educational tools in the College of Literature, Science and the Arts. For this it must do more than provide an adequate number of seats and an adequate number of copies of books which students are required to read for their courses. It must attract the student and hold his interest after it attracts him. All inconveniences, all stumbling blocks that stand between the student and the book must be eliminated. The undergraduate must be given the feeling that this library has been provided for him specifically, for his practical advantage and for his pleasure.[95]

The idea of open access was further defined:

> The book collection of the College Library should be considered as an expendable laboratory collection to which all students of the College should have completely free access. It should be so arranged that the students will feel no bar to its use. The collection should contain an adequate number of copies of all the books that the faculty wish to assign and, in addition, it should contain related works to which we hope interest will extend. Within reasonable limitations of budget, of course, the instructor should feel free to make assignments in outside or collateral reading without the present restrictions that force him to employ textbooks, anthologies, and other canned material.[96]

The provision of such service was seen as exerting constructive and beneficial influence on undergraduate education.[97]

NOTE:

Book Selection in the Undergraduate Library:
The field is divided into ten areas, for each
of which a different librarian has been given
specific responsibility. The areas are (1)
Classical and Romance Languages and Literature;
(2) Journalism, Philosophy and Religion; (3)
English Language and Literature; (4) Germanic,
Far Eastern and Near Eastern Languages and Literature; (5) Education, Psychology and Speech;
(6) American Literature, Reference and Documents; (7) Political Sciences and Natural and
Physical Sciences; (8) Fine Arts, Music and
Slavic Languages and Literature; (9) Anthro-
pology, Geography and Sociology; (10) History
and Economics.

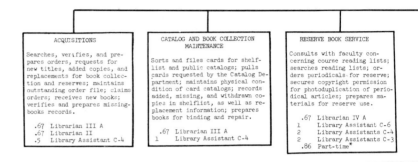

*Full-time Equivalent

Fig. 19. *Organization chart, Undergraduate Library, University of Michigan*

SERVICES

There are eight divisions of function in the Undergraduate Library. They include reference, circulation, catalog and book collection maintenance, periodicals, acquisitions, audio-room service, reserve-book service, and book selection (Fig. 19).

Reference

The original plan for reference service in the Undergraduate Library was to have reference assistants on each floor with a subject reference collection for the areas housed on that floor; however, the advantages of a single reference station and the relatively small staff made it impracticable.[98]

Although reference service has decreased in numbers (Table 10), it has grown in the number of "Under and Over Five Minute" questions and decreased in the number of "Spot" questions. By 1960, it was evident that reference service was acquiring a higher level of quality (more than 40 percent is considered a high figure for this type of question).[99] The decrease in "Spot" questions also indicated that the undergraduate student was a more knowledgeable library user, which could, in part, be attributed to the facilities of the Undergraduate Library.[100]

First plans were for reference service seven days a week, with two reference librarians on duty except for Sunday evening.[101] Because the demand did not warrant such extensive service, it was reduced to one person on reference duty at slack times. No reference service

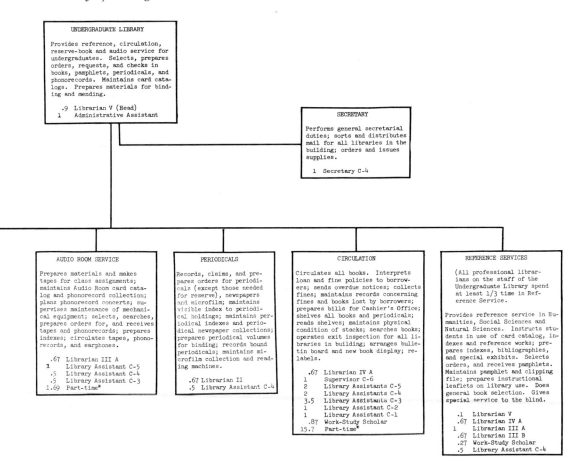

is available from noon to 1:00 P.M., 5:00 P.M. to 6:00 P.M., and 10:00 P.M. to midnight.[102]

Because of space problems, it became necessary to move the card catalog from the lobby alcove into the alcove next to the reference collection, which was considered a great improvement, because it was no longer necessary to help a student to a certain point and then tell him that he must go on to the next librarian for further help.[103]

TABLE 10

REFERENCE STATISTICS, UNDERGRADUATE LIBRARY,
UNIVERSITY OF MICHIGAN

	UNDER AND OVER FIVE MINUTES	SPOT QUESTIONS	TOTAL	PERCENT OF TOTAL WHICH WERE NOT SPOT QUESTIONS
1957–58			14,635	
1958–59	14,288	32,537	46,825	31
1959–60	16,899	24,958	41,857	40
1960–61	18,404	20,162	38,566	48
1961–62	23,327	15,103	38,430	61
1962–63	26,950	12,164	39,114	69
1963–64	31,844	11,610	43,454	73
1964–65	25,550	14,726	40,276	63

Circulation

The librarian gave much consideration to the selection of a circulation system for the Undergraduate Library. She wanted a system whereby books could be returned to the shelves without delay in waiting for them to be discharged. The system finally decided upon was a transaction number system "which involved stamping a transaction number in duplicate on the charge slip submitted by the student and on the date due slip fastened inside the book, together with preprinted sheets of these transaction numbers which would serve as a check list."[104] This system got the books back to the shelf as quickly as possible, but it resulted in many errors in the overdue routines, so a new system was adopted which uses a duplicate carbon-interleaved charge slip instead of the single slip. The library retains both slips; one is filed by transaction number under the date due and the other by call number. When the book is returned, the slip in the transaction number file is removed. Using the first slip, the second slip is then pulled from the circulation file. This system allows the book to be returned to the shelf immediately, segregates overdue books with no effort, and eliminates congestion at the file.

When the library first opened, books were charged on all three floors of the Undergraduate Library. Because of staff shortages, this practice was given up in August, 1958. Charging of all books was moved to the circulation desk on the main floor.[105]

Reserve

The reserve system in the Undergraduate Library at the University of Michigan is unique among undergraduate libraries. There is no separate reserve collection except for a small section of about 2000 volumes behind the reserve desk. All other reserve books are placed on the open shelves in their normal position with distinctive markings to indicate that they are reserve books. This system was chosen because it was felt that a student should be exposed to the total holdings on a particular subject rather than to one book. The educational advantages of such a system far outweigh other disadvantages.[106] Besides the educational advantages, this system also relieved the staff of having to charge and discharge the same books all day.[107]

When the system was first set up, there was only one type of reserve book.[108] Since then, two other types of reserve have been adopted.[109] The first of these was for a one-week circulation period. The first semester this was used 42 percent of reserve titles were on one-week reserve.[110] The second type of reserve was the closed-reserve book. After one semester of operation with all books on overnight open reserve, there were faculty requests asking that a few titles in heavy demand be placed on closed reserve.[111]

In the fall of 1958, a small closed-reserve collection was set up. Three categories of books were placed on closed reserve: (1) out-of-print books in the Undergraduate Library for which there were not sufficient copies; (2) "books borrowed from other campus libraries (all out-of-print)"; (3) "personal copies of books and other materials provided by the professors."[112] Books are also placed on closed reserve when there is pressure on the use of the book or when the instructors request it. These books remain on closed reserve only for the period of heavy use.[113]

The successful functioning of the open-shelf reserve system depends on a constant program of reshelving. Ideally, reserve books should be given top priority by shelving them every hour during the day, but because of heavy book use and insufficient staff, this goal has not been reached.[114]

There are two serious disadvantages to the open-shelf reserve system. First, a small group of students sometimes monopolizes books for a long time. Second, it is easier for students to steal books from open shelves. They are usually returned when the need has passed, but it is too late for the other students involved. Pressure is increasing to change the reserve system so that the reserve books will be more available. It may be necessary to change to a closed-reserve policy.[115]

Since the library opened, there has been the recurring problem of reserve lists not arriving in time to be processed before the semester begins. Such tardiness inhibits the library's service. To alleviate the situation, each semester a reading-list form is sent to all faculty members teaching courses below 500. Faculty submit their reading lists in triplicate: one copy is supplied with call numbers and the number of copies and serves as a master list; the second copy is provided with the same information and placed in a loose-leaf notebook by subject areas for student consultation; the third list with the same information is returned to the professor.

The increase in the number of periodical articles placed on reserve provides a new problem, because these may not be reproduced in quantity without permission. Copies of the journals containing the needed articles have to be ordered from publishers or permission obtained to duplicate them. Such a service takes a great deal of time and money.

After one year's experience, the philosophy of the reserve system seemed to be sound. Students' comments led the staff to believe that when the students "seek out their required readings in the midst of the total collection in a given subject," they are stimulated to do further reading.[116]

Special Services

Unlike most libraries, the Undergraduate Library at Michigan was to include uncommon special services, because the Undergraduate Library was conceived "as something more than a library in a very strict sense"; it was to be a "cultural center" for the students.[117]

Special facilities provided in the Undergraduate Library are the multipurpose room, group study rooms, student lounge, rooms for the blind, typing rooms, and exhibit area (all are described above). "All programs scheduled for the Multipurpose Room must in some way provide service to part of the undergraduate population." Only recognized student organizations may use it. "Programs must be 'educational' rather than 'social' and no admission may be charged of persons attending the scheduled programs" nor are students allowed to use library equipment without obtaining a professional person to operate it.[118] The multipurpose room is considered "a place where the students' cultural activities would center"—more than in any other building on the campus.[119] It is a place where they hold meetings, listen to lectures, watch films, or have discussions or debates.

When the library first opened, groups of students could reserve the group study rooms, but after it was determined that only 50 percent of the reservations were kept, the use of the rooms was placed on a first-come, first-served basis.[120]

Perhaps the most popular and most appreciated facility in the building is the student lounge. In fact, the use of the room is so heavy during the evening hours that an attendant maintains order and prevents drinks from being taken throughout the building.[121] A student lounge per se is not a feature often found in a library. It was included because students seemed to be spending more time in the library and "there was no reason . . . why a student should not be able to get up and stretch and go have a cup of coffee to break up his work."[122] The room, which seats only fifty persons, is much too small. At one point, a university room-use survey indicated ninety-eight persons in the room at one time.[123] The student lounge provides a "great safety valve." If the lounge were not there, the students would do their visiting in the study area and the library would not be as effective a study center.[124] So from that point of view, it is a good feature.

The film-preview room, located in the basement, had intermittent use. For the most part, faculty members who wanted to show films other than during class periods used the room.[125] Because of the relatively small use of the film-preview room, used to show about fifteen or twenty films a year, it was converted into a sorting room in March, 1965. Previously a small passageway on the second floor was used for this purpose.[126]

The library also has two typing rooms available for student use. Each room seats ten people and is provided with type-a-line electric coin-operated typewriters.

There is a small exhibit area on the first floor near the entrance to the building which provides the Fine Arts Museum with a place for exhibits where they are readily accessible to the students.[127]

The largest of the special services is the audio room, which provides two types of service: phonorecords are loaned to the student for playing on the turntables and programs are transmitted from the control room. Use of fourteen channels is "made up of class assignments, three simultaneous concert programs of selections from the record collection, and broadcasts from WUOM, the University of Michigan FM radio station."[128] In addition, a program of three concerts a day is scheduled, but because of class assignments, it is not always played. As the audio room catches on, the demand for its service increases, and the concert and WUOM programs have had to be dropped.[129]

Another special service is the pamphlet and clipping file. It contains inexpensive items which are left uncataloged.[130] Emphasis is placed on "quality, coverage and timeliness of the material."[131] The pamphlet collection was to be maintained at a relatively constant figure, but this policy has not been adhered to, since the collection has grown from 3675 items in 1957–58 to 16,863 items in 1964–65. In 1960–61, a weeding program was begun, but the collection has grown to over five times its original size.[132]

Technical Services

The only technical services provided in the Undergraduate Library are card catalog maintenance and ordering of books. When the library opened, it had five catalogs: the complete dictionary catalog; the audio room catalog; and author catalogs (to be used as finding lists) on the lower and second floors and at the rear of the main floor. The author catalogs contain cards for those books found on that floor.

One problem arose in regard to the audio room card catalog. Cards were so soiled that almost the whole catalog had to be retyped. Because of some dissatisfaction with the plastic covers used in the main catalog, the cards in this catalog were laminated. No changes are made on these cards so lamination was not a problem.[133] But after only one year of use, the lamination began to break loose from the cards most heavily used.[134]

Simplification and Centralization

The preliminary plans for the Undergraduate Library centered on simplification and centralization. The layout of the building, the interspersing of books and readers, and the ready accessibility of books were devices to make the library easy to use. The building was located centrally in the classroom area near the other campus library facilities for ease of access by the students.

Instruction in Library Use

It is the function of the reference staff to help the student use the book collection and to teach him how to use the card catalog and the other basic bibliographic tools.[135] Once the student has exhausted these sources in the Undergraduate Library, he is sent to the General Library or to one of the specialized collections. Thus, undergraduates continue to use other collections despite the heavy use of the Undergraduate Library.[136]

The staff tried to get the student to approach the collection through the card catalog, because it was felt that the undergraduate would miss so much by simply browsing.[137] For instance, the student might miss books treating his subject but filed elsewhere, or some volumes might not be on the shelf when he browsed. But most important, the Undergraduate Library was considered a "training library," where the student learns the basis of how to use a library to enable him to move on to a more complex situation.[138]

The philosophy of service in the Undergraduate Library holds that

> a reference librarian who works with undergraduates is a teacher who makes use of every contact with students to instruct them in the use of the library and to stimulate them to go beyond the minimum requirements in the use of books.[139]

In helping the student, the librarian works jointly with the student, guiding and explaining the methods used in finding particular information.

The role of a librarian in the Undergraduate Library is

> as adjunct teacher for all departments, acting as interpreter and intermediary between professor and student. He has a unique opportunity to help students expand their intellectual horizons, see relationships between the various areas of their studies, appreciate books as a means of intellectual stimulus and growth, clarify their assignments, learn expert use of a library's resources and become aware of the utility of individual reference works.
>
> The purpose of this method is to teach students to use library resources to the maximum and to develop in them a conviction that books are a necessary part of their lives. Since the alertness of the reference staff is essential to the success of such a program, it is important that the reference librarians continue to grow in their work.[140]

STAFF

In planning the Undergraduate Library, staffing was not considered a major problem. The first staff member appointed was the librarian, Mrs. Roberta Keniston, who assumed her duties on July 1, 1957. Six professional positions were originally allocated, but this was later changed to eight after an analysis was made of the work to be done. When the Undergraduate Library opened in January, 1958, the staff consisted of nine professionals, seven clericals, and 1098 part-time hours for an operation of 100 hours per week.[141] The size of the staff has grown slowly. On July 1, 1964, there were ten professional positions, two work-study scholars,[142] twenty-two clericals, and 33,000 part-time hours.[143]

The staff was originally organized on a flexible basis which provides for full staff cooperation in an area of stress. Such organization promotes good group morale, but because of the increasing work load and the high proportion of professional staff, it also abuses the professional staff in that often they are performing clerical tasks. The high ratio of professional staff was considered necessary to get to the point "where our supervision could be taken care of in the various areas of the library."[144]

Although there has been the usual high turnover of clerical staff, the professional staff has been stable partly because of good staff morale. Roberta Keniston felt "it was a sense of pride of being part of a new and different kind of library" which gave the professional staff a sense of pioneering and the feeling of making a real professional contribution.[145]

Until December, 1965, the undergraduate librarian reported directly to the director of the university libraries. But since the reorganization in December, 1965, the undergraduate librarian reports to the assistant director in charge of readers services.

LIBRARY USE

The success of the Undergraduate Library from the first day it opened can be determined in part by the number of people who use the building. On January 16, the first day the library opened, 7678 persons entered the building. Not all of these, of course, were students and not all came to study. But the majority who came remained to study or to read.[146] As Mrs. Keniston described it:

> The undergraduates swarmed into the building and settled down to study as if they had been using the library for years. It was a fascinating study in group behavior to watch a vast building being taken over and put to use by thousands of students, to observe them transform themselves from a chaotic mass into a group with patterns of behavior and even "tradition" in a few days.[147]

It was thought that building use would drop sharply after the first day and then begin to increase slowly. This was not the case. During the first semester of operation, the librarian reported:

> So soon after opening, on one evening at the height of the semester every seat was oc-
> cupied, students were sitting on the floors and stairways and even standing up reading
> books. Many times people have speculated as to where these students had been study-
> ing before . . . .[148]

In just a few years' time, on "an average day (6000 entries) the seats in the building were filled 40% of the time, while on a peak day (exceeding 9000 entries) this was raised to 60%." Peaks of use came at 10:00 A.M., 3:00 P.M., and 8:00 P.M.[149]

In an analysis of how students use their time while they are in the library, it was found that 65 to 70 percent of the student's time is spent studying, 10 to 13 percent is spent sleeping or daydreaming, 10 percent in getting settled, and the remainder in socializing and various other activities.[150]

Just as the presence of the Undergraduate Library did not remove all undergraduates from the General Library, neither did it have a perceptible effect on circulation in the General Library. It did drop some, but circulation in the Undergraduate Library equalled or surpassed that of the General Library during each month of the Spring Semester, 1958. Therefore, between the two libraries, circulation almost doubled over that of the previous semester, showing that the Undergraduate Library filled a need. Here use can definitely be attributed to need and not to an increase in enrollment.[151]

A comparison was made of Undergraduate Library and General Library circulation for the first semester that the Undergraduate Library was open (Table 11). The figures show that about 70 percent of the Undergraduate Library's use was by undergraduates and about 70 percent of the General Library's use was by graduate students.

TABLE 11

COMPARISON OF UNDERGRADUATE AND GENERAL LIBRARY CIRCULATION,
UNIVERSITY OF MICHIGAN[a]

STUDENT USE	UNDERGRADUATE LIBRARY PERCENT	GENERAL LIBRARY PERCENT
Freshman	13.65	5.3
Sophomore	15.88	4.7
Junior	21.96	10.8
Senior	24.58	16.6
Graduate	23.92	62.4

[a]Taken from the Undergraduate Library *Annual Report*, 1958–59, p.45.

In order to gather information about book use, a notation was put on the call slip asking what course the book was being used for or an indication of "none" if the book was not for course-related work. From a sample taken after one semester's use of the collection, the results showed that 24.5 percent of the books circulated were for voluntary reading or noncourse-related reading.[152] One year later 37.5 percent of the circulation was for voluntary reading. Undergraduates accounted for 45.9 percent of this circulation. For three years, the Undergraduate Library kept statistics on voluntary-reading circulation, excluding overnight circulation (Table 12). These figures seem to be "a striking testimonial of the intellectual stimulus which the Undergraduate Library book collection is providing for the student body."[153] Graduate students made up the largest single class of students doing voluntary reading.

There seems to be no question that students make more use of the library. Since the Undergraduate Library opened, enrollment has increased 29 percent, while total book use has increased 112 percent and attendance has risen 35 percent in a seven-year period. The people who use the library seem to use it heavily, since the average increase in attendance is 4.8 percent while the average increase in book use is 13 percent.

TABLE 12

PERCENTAGE OF CIRCULATION FOR VOLUNTARY READING, UNDERGRADUATE
LIBRARY, UNIVERSITY OF MICHIGAN

	FALL 1958–59	SPRING 1958–59	FALL 1959–60	SPRING 1959–60	FALL 1960–61	SPRING 1960–61
Freshman	39.4	39.1	35.1	39.5	40.3	37.2
Sophomore	38.0	40.5	34.4	37.2	34.8	38.4
Junior	33.2	38.3	35.8	37.4	34.2	34.7
Senior	32.2	38.4	46.2	48.8	35.3	43.5
Graduate	45.9	48.3	65.1	62.7	51.3	62.7
Average all classes	37.5	41.8	45.1	44.2	38.9	42.7

But circulation and attendance figures do not provide a complete picture. Based on a collection of 64,000 volumes in 1958–59, circulation showed that each volume in the collection had been used an average of seven times. In 1964–65, it was 8.89 times. While attendance for the same year had increased only 12.7 percent, book use had increased 58.2 percent.[154]

Book use is known to be higher than circulation figures show. According to a study conducted by Dr. Richard Meier, two persons use each book removed from the shelves before it is reshelved. Reserve books are used by about three persons each time the book is charged out, according to Meier's findings. During periods of heavy library use,

> the standard student ploy upon entering a crowded library was to seek out someone in the class rather than to look for the required reading on the appropriate shelf, because in that manner it was more probable that information as to the actual location of the volume could be obtained.[155]

Building use has continued to increase but in no way comparable to the increase in home circulation and building use of books, which seems to indicate that the Undergraduate Library is being used more for its resources than for its chairs.[156]

Circulation statistics (Table 13) for home use and building use of books show that home use has increased by 81.7 percent (since the first full year of operation), building use of books has increased 108.1 percent, and the total increase in book use is 100.3 percent.

TABLE 13

HOME CIRCULATION STATISTICS, UNDERGRADUATE LIBRARY, UNIVERSITY OF MICHIGAN

	HOME CIRCULATION	PERCENT INCREASE	BUILDING USE OF BOOKS	PERCENT INCREASE	TOTAL	PERCENT INCREASE
1957–58	35,971		78,569		114,540	
1958–59	141,624		339,888		481,512	
1959–60	164,998	16.9	479,958	41.2	644,956	33.9
1960–61	167,008	1.5	498,938	3.9	665,946	3.2
1961–62	196,391	17.6	482,610	-3.2	679,001	1.9
1962–63	213,429	8.6	593,448	22.9	806,877	18.8
1963–64	249,272	16.7	680,475	14.6	929,747	15.2
1964–65	257,425	3.2	707,475	.3	969,900	4.2

Use of reserve books is definitely increasing (Table 14) as the number of lists placed on reserve and the closed-reserve circulation indicate. No accurate picture of reserve circu-

TABLE 14

RESERVE STATISTICS, UNDERGRADUATE LIBRARY,
UNIVERSITY OF MICHIGAN

	NUMBER OF LISTS[a]	TITLES ON RESERVE[b]	VOLUMES ON RESERVE	COPIES BORROWED	CLOSED RESERVE CIRCULATION
1957–58	188	3,521	5,501	717	16,220
1958–59	539	7,629	14,470	676	16,598
1959–60	594	8,213	16,534	487	32,070
1960–61	619	9,973	20,211	373	24,120
1961–62	609	9,602	18,608	217	34,033
1962–63	634	10,072	29,638	128	35,693
1963–64	675	11,329	30,986	179	43,553
1964–65	747	12,952	34,079	320	58,184

[a]Excludes periodical reading lists.
[b]Figures for the fiscal year.

lation can be ascertained because of the nature of the reserve system. About 90 percent of the reserve books are on the open shelves, and no count is made of their use in the building. Those reserve books which are used in the building are included in the "Building Use of Books" figure, but not separately.

There seems no doubt that the predominant use of the Undergraduate Library has

TABLE 15

			PERCENTAGE OF CIRCULATION BY LEVEL OF USER,		
	FALL 1958–59	SPRING 1958–59	FALL 1959–60	SPRING 1959–60	FALL 1960–61	SPRING 1960–61
Freshman	13.65	13.09	22.86	19.82	17.73	19.80
Sophomore	15.88	10.24	14.81	15.58	15.91	17.48
Junior	21.96	19.58	21.69	22.47	20.93	23.42
Senior	24.58	25.43	30.60	30.13	25.91	21.52
Graduate	23.92	31.60	10.06	11.91	19.52	17.71

been by undergraduates. During the first full year of operation, 73 percent of the borrowers of two-week books were undergraduates (Table 15). The average has been about 83 percent undergraduate use.

While the Undergraduate Library is not used primarily as a study hall, this is one valid segment of use since crowded conditions in dormitories and apartments leave no adequate place for study besides the library.[157] On March 11, 1965, a count was taken in the university libraries to determine to what extent the library is used as a study hall. In the case of the Undergraduate Library, there was a total of 1292 "readers"; 760, or 59 percent, were using library materials. The overall average for the university libraries showed that 34.5 percent of the "readers" were using library materials, while the remaining 65.5 percent were studying their own books or notes. The high percentage of book use in the Undergraduate Library could be due to the presence of reserve books or to the general accessibility of the books. It may indicate that the Undergraduate Library is not as much a place to study as the General Library is (77.5 percent of use of the Main Reading Room and 75 percent of the use of carrels was for study hall purposes).[158]

The figures given above do not imply any definite trends. Study hall use of the library is difficult to ascertain, because a student may come to the library to read a reserve book and then remain to study from his own books or notes. Study hall aspects of use also vary with the time of term.[159]

SUMMARY

The Undergraduate Library at Michigan is a well-planned building which was too small the day it opened. Some of the planning faults have been corrected. The book collection has been developed to meet the undergraduate's curricular needs, and it is a well-rounded working collection. The reserve collection has grown quickly, especially in a few areas. Placing it on open shelves has provided greater freedom of access than in other undergraduate libraries. Unfortunately, students have abused the privilege.

Reference service has not been in great demand, and most of the needs are readers advisory rather than bibliographic. The present circulation system becomes more cumbersome as circulation grows. The audio room has proven to be one of the popular features of the library. Services have been centralized, for the most part, in the Undergraduate Library for the lower-division student. For the upper-division student, this is not true because his needs carry him beyond the resources found in the Undergraduate Library. The Undergraduate Library is certainly a simpler tool than the research library. The arrangement of books, the card catalog, etc., are areas where simplification is most evident. Instruction in library use is achieved through orientation lectures and by individual instruction by the reference librarians. Instruction is in the form of how to do it—the work is not done for the student.

The staff, which is helpful and informative, has proven satisfactory in serving the needs of the undergraduates. The use of the Undergraduate Library has been greater than anticipated, testifying to its adequacy.

TABLE 15–Continued

UNDERGRADUATE LIBRARY, UNIVERSITY OF MICHIGAN

FALL 1961–62	SPRING 1961–62	FALL 1962–63	SPRING 1962–63	FALL 1963–64	SPRING 1963–64	FALL 1964	WINTER 1965
19.90	16.61	16.59	15.45	24.78	15.40	16.89	19.20
17.87	19.63	17.38	18.07	20.01	17.26	15.37	16.04
21.58	23.78	22.45	23.37	24.24	21.69	20.86	21.05
22.92	22.11	25.74	24.49	12.76	25.56	27.94	24.64
17.74	17.88	17.83	18.62	18.21	20.09	18.94	19.07

NOTES

[1]Letter from William W. Bishop, Director of the University Libraries, the University of Michigan, to Keyes D. Metcalf, Nov. 23, 1945, Metcalf Papers (Harvard University Archives, Cambridge, Mass.).

[2]Letter from Samuel W. McAllister, Associate Director, University of Michigan Libraries, to Mrs. Edna H. Byers, Librarian, Agnes Scott College, Decatur, Ga., Dec. 29, 1953 (in the files of the University Library).

[3]Interview with Dr. Frederick H. Wagman, Director of the University Libraries, the University of Michigan, March 10, 1966.

[4]Frederick H. Wagman, "Preliminary Program for the Undergraduate Library," Aug. 1, 1954, p. 1 (in the files of the University Library).

[5]*Ibid.*

[6]Frederick H. Wagman, "The Library Situation and the Program of Plant Extension." Statement presented to the Library Committee of the College of Literature, Science, and the Arts, Nov. 3, 1954 (in the files of the University Library). Cited hereafter as "The Library Situation."

[7]The North Campus development was begun about 1951 to provide space for additional growth of the University. It is a 700-acre tract of land located about five miles northeast of the central campus.

[8]Wagman, "The Library Situation."

[9]Letter from Charles E. Odegaard, Dean of the College of Literature, Science and the Arts, the University of Michigan, to Marvin L. Niehuss, Vice-President for Student Affairs and Dean of Faculties, the University of Michigan, March 20, 1956 (in the files of the University Library).

[10]Wagman, "The Library Situation."

[11]Letter from Frederick H. Wagman to Marvin L. Niehuss, Nov. 27, 1953 (in the files of the University Library).

[12]Minutes of the Meeting of the Advisory Committee on the Undergraduate Library, March 29, 1954.

[13]Letter from Frederick H. Wagman to James A. Lewis, Vice-President for Student Affairs, Dec.

21, 1954 (in the files of the University Library).

[14]Memorandum from Frederick H. Wagman to Department Chairmen, College of Literature, Science, and the Arts, Dec. 16, 1954 (in the files of the University Library).

[15]Memorandum from Frederick H. Wagman to Department Chairmen, College of Literature, Science, and the Arts, Dec. 27, 1954 (in the files of the University Library).

[16]Roberta Keniston, "Circulation Gains at Michigan," *Library Journal,* LXXXIII (Dec. 1, 1958), 3357.

[17]Interview with Frederick H. Wagman.

[18]Frederick H. Wagman, "The Undergraduate Library of the University of Michigan," *College and Research Libraries,* XX (May, 1959), 184.

[19]Memorandum from W. K. Pierpont, Vice-President in Charge of Business and Finance, the University of Michigan, Nov. 11, 1954 (in the files of the University Library).

[20]Conference Notes, Jan. 25, 1955 (in the files of the University Library).

[21]Michigan. University. Advisory Committee on the Undergraduate Library, "Program for an Undergraduate Library," by Frederick H. Wagman (Ann Arbor: 1955), p.3.

[22]The early plans for the building included an underground book-storage area connecting the Undergraduate and General libraries. This plan had to be abandoned because of the difficulties "in moving the steam tunnels that lace this campus." (Interview with Frederick H. Wagman.)

[23]The provision for these libraries was not included in the initial plans but was added later. When the idea of the building was first formulated, the audio room was not included but was added at the same time that the decision was made to house the additional libraries in the building. (Memorandum from W. K. Pierpont, Nov. 11, 1954.)

[24]Keniston, *Library Journal,* LXXXIII, 3358.

[25]Rose-Grace Faucher, "The Undergraduate Library." Talk given at the Library Science Convocation, Ann Arbor, Mich., Sept. 30, 1965.

[26]Keniston, *Library Journal,* LXXXIII, 3358.

[27]*Ibid.*

[28]Wagman, *College and Research Libraries,* XX, 185.

[29]"Program for an Undergraduate Library," p.4–7.

[30]*Ibid.,* p.5.

[31]Michigan. University. Library. Undergraduate Library, *The Undergraduate Library Building of the University of Michigan* (Ann Arbor: University of Michigan Library, 1960), p.4–6; memorandum prepared by Samuel M. McAllister [no date] (in the files of the University Library).

[32]Report of a meeting on the Undergraduate Library, Aug. 26, 1955 (in the files of the University Library).

[33]Report of a meeting on the Undergraduate Library, Nov. 1, 1955 (in the files of the University Library).

[34]The lighting of the Undergraduate Library received an award as the outstanding lighting project completed in Michigan in 1957. (Letter from Albert Kahn, Associated Architects and Engineers, to W. K. Pierpont, May 15, 1958 [in the files of the University Library].)

[35]Conference notes on the Undergraduate Library, Aug. 26, 1955 (in the files of the University Library).

[36]Letter from Frederick H. Wagman to Mr. Sol King, Albert Kahn Associated Architects, Oct. 4, 1954 (in the files of the University Library).

[37]Wagman, *College and Research Libraries,* XX, 184.

[38]"Program for an Undergraduate Library," p.4–7.

[39]Michigan. University. Library. Undergraduate Library, *Annual Report,* 1964–65, p.21.

[40]Interview with Miss Rose-Grace Faucher, Librarian, Undergraduate Library, University of Michigan, Oct. 8, 1965.

[41]Wagman, *College and Research Libraries,* XX, 185.

[42]Interview with Frederick H. Wagman.

[43]Memorandum from Frederick H. Wagman to Robert H. Muller, April 16, 1956 (in the files of the University Library).

[44][James Packard] "The Undergraduate Library," *Research News,* XV (May, 1965), 4.

[45]*Ibid.*

[46]The Gold Star Periodicals were a collection of frequently used periodical titles which were housed immediately behind the circulation desk in the General Library for the sake of convenience. Each volume had a gold star on its spine as an identification mark.

[47]Letter from Frederick H. Wagman to Professor Warner G. Rice, Chairman, Department of English, April 5, 1955 (in the files of the University Library).

[48]Memorandum from Robert H. Muller to Frederick H. Wagman, June 18, 1957 (in the files of the University Library).

[49]Rolland C. Stewart, "Building Undergraduate Library Collections: Questions, Realities, and Prospects." Speech given before the Illinois Library Association, College and Research Section, Chicago, Ill., Oct. 29, 1965. Cited hereafter as "Building Undergraduate Library Collections."

[50]*Ibid.;* interview with Mr. Rolland C. Stewart, Assistant Director for Public Services, University of Michigan Library, Dec. 16, 1966.

[51][Packard] *Research News,* XV, 5.

[52]Memorandum from Rolland C. Stewart to Frederick H. Wagman, Sept. 28, 1955 (in the files of the University Library).

[53]Stewart, "Building Undergraduate Library Collections"; interview with Rolland C. Stewart.

[54]*Ibid.*

[55]Interview with Rolland C. Stewart.

[56]Memorandum from Rolland C. Stewart to Frederick H. Wagman, Sept. 28, 1955.

[57][Packard] *Research News,* XV, 5.

[58]Letter from R. W. Pidd, Harrison M. Randall Laboratory of Physics, the University of Michigan, to Frederick H. Wagman, July 22, 1955; letter from

Frederick H. Wagman to R. W. Pidd, Aug. 8, 1955, (in the files of the University Library).

[59]Memorandum from Rolland C. Stewart to Frederick H. Wagman, Dec. 7, 1955 (in the files of the University Library).

[60]Interview with Rolland C. Stewart.

[61][Packard] *Research News*, XV, 8.

[62]One such instance was the purchase of about 1500 books for $1 apiece from Wahr's Bookstore in Ann Arbor. Many standard works were obtained in this way. (Interview with Rolland C. Stewart.)

[63][Packard] *Research News*, XV, 9.

[64]Interview with Rolland C. Stewart. Mr. Stewart expressed doubt that he would repeat such a venture because the results do not warrant the effort.

[65][Packard] *Research News*, XV, 8–11.

[66]*Ibid.*

[67]Interview with Roberta Keniston.

[68]Letter from Rolland C. Stewart to Frederick H. Wagman, Sept. 24, 1956 (in the files of the University Library).

[69]Letter from Roberta Keniston to Billy R. Wilkinson, Librarian, Uris Library, Cornell University, Dec. 20, 1961 (in the files of the University Library).

[70]Stewart, "Building Undergraduate Library Collections."

[71]Interview with Frederick H. Wagman.

[72]Textbooks are not now knowingly purchased for the reserve collection.

[73]Memorandum from Rolland C. Stewart to Frederick H. Wagman, Sept. 28, 1955.

[74]Michigan. University. Library. Undergraduate Library, *Annual Report*, 1957–58, p.25.

[75]*Ibid.*, 1959–60, p.11.

[76]*Ibid.*, 1961–62, p.13.

[77]Michigan. University. Library. Undergraduate Library, *Annual Report*, 1957–58, p.19.

[78]Memorandum from Rolland C. Stewart to Frederick H. Wagman, Dec. 7, 1955.

[79]Interview with Roberta Keniston.

[80]"Book Selection Policy for the Undergraduate Library" (in the files of the Undergraduate Library).

[81]Interview with Rolland C. Stewart.

[82]Interview with Rose-Grace Faucher.

[83]Michigan. University. Library. Undergraduate Library, *Annual Report*, 1957–58, p.18.

[84]Letter from Roberta Keniston to Rolland C. Stewart, Nov. 28, 1960 (in the files of the University Library).

[85]Memorandum from Rolland C. Stewart to Frederick H. Wagman, March 25, 1964 (in the files of the University Library).

[86]Michigan. University. Library. Undergraduate Library, *Annual Report*, 1962–63, p.7–8.

[87]Michigan. University. Library. Undergraduate Library, *Annual Report*, 1957–58, p.21–22.

[88]*Ibid.*, 1959–60, p.8.

[89]*Ibid.*, 1962–63, p.7–8.

[90]*Ibid.*, 1959–60, p.8.

[91]Interview with Rose-Grace Faucher.

[92]Michigan. University. Library. Undergraduate Library, *Annual Report*, 1962–63, p.8.

[93]Interview with Rose-Grace Faucher.

[94]Michigan. University. Library. Undergraduate Library, *Annual Report*, 1958–59, p.25; 1961–62, p.25; 1964–65, p.30.

[95]Letter from Frederick H. Wagman to Lynn W. Fry, Oct. 16, 1953 (in the files of the University Library).

[96]Letter from Charles E. Odegaard to M. L. Niehuss, March 20, 1956.

[97]*Ibid.*

[98]Memorandum from Frederick H. Wagman to Lynn W. Fry, Oct. 14, 1955 (in the files of the University Library).

[99]Michigan. University. Library. Undergraduate Library, *Annual Report*, 1961–62, p.3.

[100]*Ibid.*, 1962–63, p.5.

[101]*Ibid.*, 1957–58, p.9.

[102]*Ibid.*, 1959–60, p.3.

[103]Interview with Roberta Keniston.

[104]Michigan. University. Library. Undergraduate Library, *Annual Report*, 1957–58, p.6.

[105]Interview with Roberta Keniston.

[106]Letter from Roberta Keniston to the members of the faculty of the College of Literature, Science, and the Arts, Dec. 16, 1957 (in the files of the University Library).

[107]Interview with Frederick H. Wagman.

[108]Letter from Roberta Keniston to the members of the faculty of the College of Literature, Science, and the Arts, Dec. 16, 1957.

[109]Michigan. University. Library. Undergraduate Library, *Annual Report*, 1957–58, p.19.

[110]*Ibid.*, 1958–59, p.13.

[111]*Ibid.*, 1957–58, p.22.

[112]*Ibid.*, 1958–59, p.14.

[113]*Ibid.*

[114]*Ibid.*, 1959–60, p.6.

[115]Interview with Frederick H. Wagman. During the Fall Term, 1967, the Undergraduate Library changed to a closed-reserve system. All reserve books are now located in one area on the first floor.

[116]Michigan. University. Library. Undergraduate Library, *Annual Report*, 1957–58, p.19–22.

[117]Interview with Frederick H. Wagman.

[118]Letter from Rose-Grace Faucher to Mr. Lucien W. White, Director, Public Service Departments, University of Illinois Library, Nov. 22, 1963 (in the files of the University Library).

[119]Interview with Frederick H. Wagman.

[120]Michigan. University. Library. Undergraduate Library, *Annual Report*, 1958–59, p.30.

[121]*Ibid.*, 1959–60, p.19.

[122]Interview with Frederick H. Wagman.

[123]Interview with Rose-Grace Faucher.

[124]Interview with Mrs. Roberta Keniston, Assistant Librarian, Eastern Michigan University, Feb. 22, 1966. Mrs. Keniston was the first librarian of the University of Michigan Undergraduate Library.

[125]Michigan. University. Library. Undergraduate Library, *Annual Report*, 1957–58, p.28.

[126]*Ibid.*, 1964–65, p.16.

[127]Interview with Frederick H. Wagman.

[128]Michigan. University. Library. Undergrad-

uate Library, *Annual Report*, 1958–59, p.26.

[129]*Ibid.*, 1959–60, p.15.

[130]*Ibid.*, p.14.

[131]*Ibid.*, 1962–63, p.13.

[132]*Ibid.*, 1958–59, p.26.

[133]*Ibid.*, 1959–60, p.13.

[134]*Ibid.*, 1961–62, p.11.

[135]Letter from Frederick H. Wagman to Mr. Robert H. Blackburn, Chief Librarian, University of Toronto, Oct. 1, 1957 (in the files of the University Library).

[136]Michigan. University. Library. Undergraduate Library, *Annual Report*, 1957–58, p.18.

[137]Interview with Roberta Keniston.

[138]*Ibid.*

[139]Michigan. University. Library. Undergraduate Library, *Annual Report*, 1957–58, p.17.

[140]"Reference Service to Undergraduates" (in the files of the Undergraduate Library).

[141]Memorandum from Roberta Keniston to Mr. Warren Owens, Personnel Officer, the University of Michigan Libraries, April 25, 1958 (in the files of the University Library).

[142]The University of Michigan Library sponsors several work-study scholarships each year for students who are enrolled in the Department of Library Science. These grants give the student a chance to work in one of the university libraries gaining library experience. In addition to an annual stipend, the university pays the course fees for these students. Each scholar works thirty hours a week and carries an average course load of six hours.

[143]Michigan. University. Library. Undergraduate Library, *Annual Report*, 1964–65, p.1.

[144]Interview with Roberta Keniston.

[145]*Ibid.*

[146]Letter from Frederick H. Wagman to Dr. Harlan Hatcher, President, the University of Michigan, Jan. 17, 1958 (in the files of the University Library).

[147]Michigan. University. Library. Undergraduate Library, *Annual Report*, 1957–58, p.11.

[148]*Ibid.*, p.29.

[149]Richard L. Meier, *Social Change in Communications-Oriented Institutions* (Mental Health Research Institute, University of Michigan, Report No. 10 [Ann Arbor: University of Michigan, 1961]), p.26–27. Cited hereafter as *Social Change*.

[150]*Ibid.*, p.28.

[151]Interview with Roberta Keniston.

[152]Michigan. University. Library. Undergraduate Library, *Annual Report*, 1957–58, p.24.

[153]Memorandum from Roberta Keniston to Frederick H. Wagman and Rolland C. Stewart, Nov. 24, 1958 (in the files of the University Library).

[154]Michigan. University. Library. Undergraduate Library, *Annual Report*, 1958–59, p.17.

[155]Meier, *Social Change*, p.30.

[156]Michigan. University. Library. Undergraduate Library, *Annual Report*, 1959–60, p.9.

[157]Interview with Roberta Keniston.

[158]Letter from Frederick H. Wagman to Dr. Roger W. Heyns, Vice-President for Academic Affairs, the University of Michigan, March 29, 1965 (in the files of the University Library).

[159]Interview with Frederick H. Wagman.

The Undergraduate Library, The University of South Carolina

In the mid-1950's, an acute shortage of space developed in the McKissick Memorial Library, involving both readers and books. There was also a feeling that there was need to provide more satisfactory library facilities for undergraduate students.

After a proposed addition to McKissick Memorial Library was rejected as inadequate,[1] Keyes D. Metcalf, Librarian of Harvard University, was selected as a consultant to study the building problem. His recommendation was that the $1,000,000 necessary for remodeling be spent for a separate undergraduate library, which would include storage space for little-used materials. He believed that this would achieve the same goals in a much more satisfactory manner.

Metcalf's plan was approved by Donald S. Russell, President of the University, and Mr. Metcalf was retained as consultant for the building. The firm of Lyles, Bisset, Carisle and Wolff, of Columbia, South Carolina, was retained as architects. They submitted the initial plans to Mr. Metcalf and to Mr. Alfred Rawlinson, Director of the University Libraries at South Carolina, whose recommendations for changes were incorporated into the plans. After the basic design and floor plan had been settled upon, Edward D. Stone, of New York City, was called in as consulting architect. His contributions were the "dramatic" touches that gave the building its character: the white marble, the red rug, the dark furniture, and the gold-anodized aluminum.

FINANCING

The Undergraduate Library was financed by a bond issue. At that time, the state of South Carolina had a program for permitting state institutions of higher education to issue bonds for construction. The amount of the bonds could not exceed a certain percentage of anticipated annual revenue, a limitation imposed for assurance of easy refunding.[2]

THE BUILDING

Description

Mr. Metcalf's original specifications called for a seating capacity of 400 and storage capacity for 60,000 books on open shelves. After some consideration, the seating capacity was raised to 600, providing seating for about 14 percent of the university enrollment in September, 1959, and 9 percent of the 1965 undergraduate enrollment. With the addition of new shelving in 1964–65, the book capacity now stands between 75,000 and 80,000 volumes on open shelves, with an additional 150,000 volumes in the storage area beneath the library.[3]

The cost of the building, including furnishings, was $900,000, or approximately $18 per square foot. The bid for the building itself came to $735,860.[4] In other areas of the country, it was costing $23 or $24 per square foot for buildings which had none of the

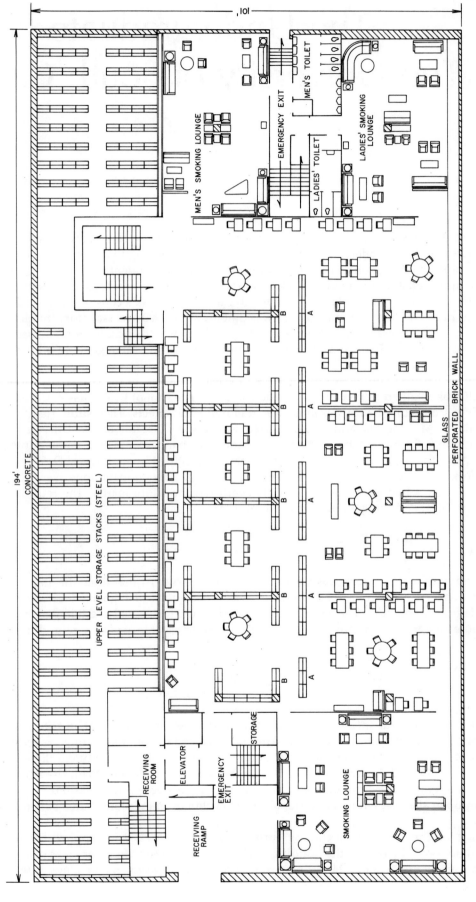

Fig. 20. Ground floor, Undergraduate Library, University of South Carolina

extra touches found in the South Carolina library: marble exterior, solid mahogany paneling, high ceilings. Low labor costs, simple design, and the deliberate policy not to buy expensive furniture all contributed to the low cost.[5]

The site chosen was on Davis Field on the "new campus" south of Green Street. The Undergraduate Library at South Carolina was not located adjacent to the central library or in the center of the campus. Instead, it was built at a distance from both the main library and from classroom facilities, because the site was considered the new geographical center of the campus,[6] and because it would be located in the center of the undergraduate residence facilities, in recognition of the fact that the library would serve largely as a study hall.[7] In addition, this particular site offered enough available space for future expansion and the reunion of library facilities, and it afforded a slope which would allow entrance to the building on the center floor.[8]

Because the campus buildings are both traditional and contemporary in design, a merger of the old and new of the two campuses was a major objective in the design of the new library. The white marble, the columns in front, and the dark furniture characterize the old. The openness of the building, its simplicity, and the extensive use of glass are concessions to the new.[9]

The exterior of the building is constructed of white Georgia marble on the east and west sides; the north and south walls are entirely of glass. A gold-anodized aluminum screen in a honeycomb pattern on the south side of the building deflects the sunlight from the glass wall. On the north side, panels of metallic curtains made of gold-anodized aluminum discs, mounted on strips of flexible brass, are alternated at intervals with equal areas of unobstructed glass, complementing the exterior screen treatment on the south side. The extended overhang of the roof further protects the north glass wall from the sun.

The building, contemporary in style, is constructed as an open-stack, self-service library with a single entrance and exit for control purposes and operational economy. The building consists of three floors: ground, first, and mezzanine. The total area comprises 40,000 square feet (there is an additional 10,000 square feet in the storage area), with the ground floor being 100 by 200 feet, the first floor 75 by 150 feet, and the mezzanine 52 by 150 feet.

The basic design is similar to that of the Lamont Library, with the books in the center and reading areas on either side. The ground floor (see Fig. 20) is different only in that on the east and west ends there are smoking lounges: on the east end, one for men and one for women and on the west end, a general lounge. On the east end of the first floor (Fig. 21) are the circulation desk, the library offices, and the card catalog. The mezzanine has no special areas (Fig. 22).

Metal and bamboo screens break up large reading areas on the mezzanine and ground floors. The interior design is striking, with solid-mahogany paneled walls and African mahogany shelving.

Furnishings

The furniture in the building—card catalog, tables, circulation desk, and chairs—is walnut and was specially designed for the building.[10] The chairs were chosen because they had proven satisfactory in Russell House, the student union. Relatively inexpensive covered lounge furniture was purchased along with inexpensive reading tables.[11]

There are three different kinds of seating: 79 individual carrels, 245 lounge chairs and sofas, and seating for 276 at tables, giving a total capacity of 600. Although there are 600 seats by actual count, it would be difficult to seat that many people at one time, because the settees rarely accommodate more than one person.[12]

The furniture is arranged in groupings. On the first floor at the front of the building, there is a spacious grouping of lounge furniture. Tables are scattered between the stacks, and the area along the back of the building is furnished exclusively with reading tables.

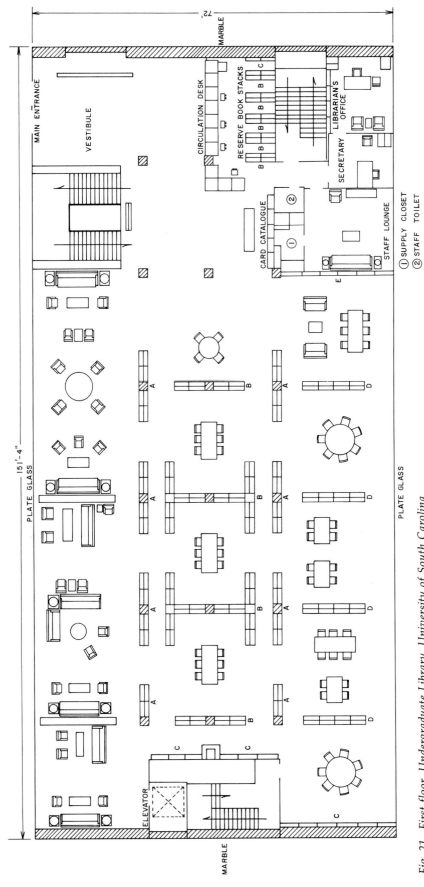

Fig. 21. First floor, Undergraduate Library, University of South Carolina

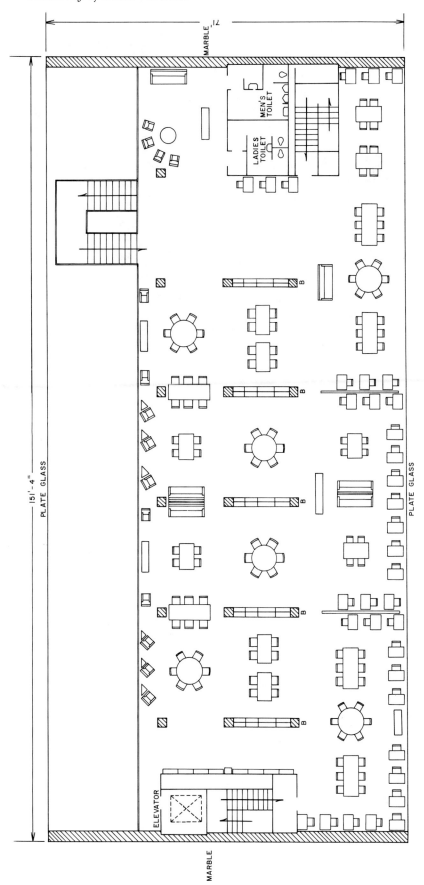

Fig. 22. Mezzanine floor, Undergraduate Library, University of South Carolina

First floor reading area, Undergraduate Library, University of South Carolina

On the mezzanine, the same basic pattern is followed, but individual carrels line the east, west, and south walls. On the ground floor, the lounges are furnished almost exclusively with lounge furniture, although there are a few tables and carrels in the general lounge. Carrels line all the walls on this floor, and the remainder of the seating (at tables) is placed among the stacks and on the south side of the floor. The stacks themselves form semi-alcoves similar to those found in the Lamont Library.

Because the furniture is relatively inexpensive, it was not expected to last indefinitely, especially with the anticipated heavy use. As a result of an accumulation of dirt and some fraying of the material, the lounge furniture had to be recovered in 1964–65, and the original fabric upholstery was replaced with similarly colored plastic material.[13]

Even though all fixtures were to be movable, the bookcases, which might fall because they stood on carpeting, were bolted in place to prevent their turning over.

Carpeting is one feature not found in the other undergraduate libraries. Scarlet carpeting was used with dark furniture and white marble "to create an atmosphere of elegance in the building."[14] The entire public area, with the exception of approximately 20 square feet inside the front entrance, is carpeted, including the stairway which carries almost all traffic.[15] The offices and the area behind the charging desk have rubber-tile flooring. Glazed brick is used for the floors in the smoking lounges.[16]

A wool needlepoint-weave carpet was laid on a carpet cushion on concrete floors, which were first covered with a coat of regular floor sealer to reduce the problem of dust created by lime in the cement.[17] Maintenance of the carpet is provided by daily vacuuming and annual or semiannual shampoos. After the initial purchase of the cleaning and shampooing equipment, the daily cost of maintenance is found to be lower than that for rubber tile or other types of floor covering. The carpeted flooring has three main advantages: "ease of maintenance, its tremendous contribution to noise reduction in the building, and its general aesthetic appeal in creating an atmosphere of beauty and dignity within the library."[18]

Recessed fluorescent fixtures of 50 footcandles provide lighting for the building.[19] One special feature about the lighting is that it can be set at three different levels of intensity. Although the lighting could probably be cut to minimum intensity on many days or at many times during the day, this has not been done because of the trouble involved in changing it with constant weather changes.[20] To get full capacity from the lighting, it was recommended that all light tubes be replaced annually or at least biannually. When only the burned-out tubes are replaced, full lighting capacity is never reached, but the intensity is not so low as to hamper reading.[21]

BOOK COLLECTION

General Collection

When the library opened, it had a collection of 12,000 volumes, "chosen to supplement the work of the classroom and laboratory, and to provide material for recreational reading and the pursuit of special interests."[22] Initially, the collection was planned for 40,000 volumes, but this figure was later greatly reduced. The major factor in the choice of books was the need of the undergraduates. No effort was made to avoid duplication of titles located in other libraries on campus. However, materials the undergraduate might need for research were not provided in the Undergraduate Library; they were to be found only in the Main Library.[23] The collection for the Undergraduate Library was envisaged as one which would change constantly. As new titles were added, old ones would be withdrawn and returned to the Main Library.

Factors taken into consideration in selecting the book collection were "readability, format, scope of interest appeal."[24] Not until last year was a definite acquisition policy adopted for the Undergraduate Library. It read as follows:

> The Undergraduate Library seeks to make available to Undergraduate students reading material to supplement their work in the classroom and laboratory; to provide reading material to be placed on closed reserve by faculty members for special assignments; and to provide material for recreational reading and for the pursuit of special interests and hobbies. . . . In summary the basic purpose is to provide a live, relevant, working collection containing the book material to which any undergraduate should have ready access during the course of his undergraduate education. . . .
>
> Recommendations of titles to be purchased should be further limited generally to materials in the faculty member's own specific field of competence. Likewise a title should not be recommended unless a faculty member has reasonable grounds for believing that it will be used by an undergraduate in the normal course of his undergraduate pursuits. One very practical basis for making this determination is whether or not the title will be discussed in the classroom, listed on assignment sheets, or otherwise noted in reading lists and bibliographies distributed to the student. . . . In no instance should a title be recommended for the Undergraduate Library simply because it is a title deemed "desirable in any university library collection."[25]

In setting up the policies and techniques in building the collection of the Undergraduate Library, the experiences of similar libraries were considered, but the librarian realized that no single plan could be wholly adapted since each institution has its own peculiar needs. Three methods were proposed for selecting titles for the collection. First, recommendations were to be solicited from the faculty; second, pertinent bibliographies were to be consulted; and third, titles available locally were to be examined to determine their suitability for the collection.[26] Although these were the proposed procedures, they were not used. In the first place, even though actively sought, faculty response was limited. Therefore, Alfred Rawlinson, the University Librarian, necessarily chose the collection almost *in toto*. Furthermore, the amount of funds that would be available for the collection was not known until March, 1958, when $50,000 was made available.[27]

Having been hampered up to this point by lack of funds and lack of faculty participation, Mr. Rawlinson selected six basic book-selection guides and marked two copies of each of them, indicating his preferences for inclusion in the Undergraduate Library. These six aids were:

1. McNiff, Philip J. Catalogue of the Lamont Library, Harvard College. Harvard University Press, 1953.
2. Larrabee, Eric, ed. American Panorama. New York University Press, 1957.
3. Hoffman, Hester R. Bookman's Manual. 8th ed., rev. and enl. Bowker, 1958.
4. Costello, Harry Todd. Books for a College Student's Reading. (The Trinity College Booklist, 5th ed., largely rewritten). Hartford, Conn., Trinity College, 1958.
5. Deason, Hilary J. Books of the Traveling High School Science Library. Published by the American Association for the Advancement of Science and the National Science Foundation, Washington, D.C., 1957.
6. Bertalan, Frank J., comp. Books for Junior Colleges. American Library Association, 1954.[28]

Since time was short — the building was already under construction — normal acquisition routines were not considered practical. Too much time would be needed to order each title individually. Mr. Rawlinson checked copies of the selection tools and sent one to A. C. McClurg and Company and the other to Colonial Book Company. He instructed McClurg to send $25,000 worth of the items on any of the checked lists which they had available. This procedure was for current in-print materials. For the out-of-print materials, there was a similar agreement with the Colonial Book Company for materials in certain categories, mainly from the Lamont list, at the initial list price up to the sum of $10,000. The library submitted no orders; the books were simply crated, invoiced, and sent.[29]

This collection was acquired at an average cost of $5 per volume, including the in-print, out-of-print, and reference works.[30] About 25 percent of the collection is unique to the Undergraduate Library. It is assumed that this ratio fluctuates but probably continues in the same pattern as the collection grows.[31]

Not all of the collection was acquired by purchase. Three collections then housed in McKissick Memorial Library were transferred to the new library. These included the reserve-book collection of about 3000 titles, the English reading collection of about 1000 titles, and the Blue Star collection of about 300 titles.[32]

One year before the library opened, about 10,000 titles had been chosen. Of these, 1607 titles came from faculty reading lists and recommendations, 5434 were selected from the titles listed above, 360 were reference titles, 2500 were out-of-print items obtained from the Colonial Book Company, and 650 titles were 1958 current publications selected by Mr. Rawlinson from periodical reviews.[33]

Although there was little faculty participation in building the original collection, the picture has greatly changed. At the present time, the faculty selects 70 to 80 percent of the additions to the collection.[34]

The strengths and weaknesses of the general collection reflect to a large extent the curriculum at the university. The main emphasis is in the humanities, especially in literature and philosophy. History, sociology, and psychology are the strongest areas in the social sciences.[35] The weaknesses of the collection are mainly in the fine arts, business administration, and nursing.[36]

This undergraduate library is different in that it does not provide permanent files of periodicals or any of the periodical indexes. Fifty current titles comprise the periodical collection.[37] All titles are of a general nature, the policy being not to subscribe "to any periodical that is limited to one specific subject field."[38] Besides the general titles, most are news and recreation titles.

Exclusion of back files of periodicals was a matter of economy and a deliberate policy to prevent the Undergraduate Library at South Carolina from becoming a complete library in itself. Obviously, if back runs of journals had been purchased out of the initial book appropriation of $50,000, there would have been money for little else.[39]

A small collection of current local newspapers is available in the library. They are duplicates of those in the Main Library and are kept only for a brief time.

Reference Collection

The reference collection contains about 1000 titles, containing generally basic reference tools. On the mezzanine and ground floors, there are small duplicate collections consisting of two or three general encyclopedias, standard bibliographical tools, dictionaries, and sources relating to the subject matter on that floor.[40]

Reserve Collection

When the library first began operation, about 90 percent of the books placed on reserve were borrowed from the Main Library. That figure has now been reduced to about a third of those on reserve. Most of the borrowed books fall into two categories: titles that are out-of-print and therefore unavailable, and books that the Undergraduate Library does not own when they first appear on a reserve list. The books in the latter category are purchased if they are available, and the Main Library copies are then returned. The Undergraduate Library does not purchase books for graduate reserves, so these titles have to be borrowed.[41]

To supplement and replace closed-reserve books, the Undergraduate Library has a liberal policy of providing multiple copies for the open-stack collection. Most of the additions to the original collection have been secured from faculty reading lists. A general rule of one copy to eight students is followed—with many variations—for the first forty students. After this, the ratio drops drastically. Another rule that is generally followed is the automatic purchase of two copies of any book that is on an active reserve list as a long-range economy. With the rapid rise in campus population, "the danger of having too many copies just does not exist any more."[42] Except under unusual circumstances, no more than twenty copies of a title are purchased. Up to fifty copies are presently provided, for a few large courses required for all freshmen.

Book losses have not been much of a problem. Two inventories have been taken, and in both instances, the loss factor has been less than 1 percent. In five years, only 1047 books have been lost.

Open Access to the Collection

The main service to be provided was access to a well-developed book collection. All books except some reserve titles were placed on the open shelves. In order to reduce the number of books on closed reserve, multiple copies were purchased when possible in the hope that their presence would make it unnecessary to put those titles on closed reserve. An effort was made to provide the student with books which would take him beyond his regular class work and help him develop a lifetime reading habit.[43]

In some cases, Mr. Reames, the Undergraduate Librarian, works closely with the faculty member to build up a collection in a particular field so that the student has a wide range of books to choose from on the open shelves, rather than a select number of titles on closed reserve. This has proven to be a successful policy, and it has been helpful in convincing other faculty members to abandon the closed reserve system. A system of open-shelf reserves without the reserve restrictions has resulted.[44]

SERVICES

Reference

Reference service is administered from the circulation desk, the only service point in the building.[45] The reference collection is shelved adjacent to the circulation desk, so the problem of service has not been difficult. The reference collection is uncomplicated so most students are able to use it without assistance.[46]

Circulation

Because the McBee Keysort circulation system was used in the Main Library, it was also adapted for use in the Undergraduate Library. In case the McBee system did not prove satisfactory, a book pocket was placed in each book to facilitate the change to a book card system. The author, title, and call number were placed on the pocket to help the student get the correct information on the call slip. Often, students cannot discern the correct information from the title page of the book, or they have by-passed the card catalog to find the book they want, so they do not find the information there.[47] The book pocket also holds the date due card, which is used instead of the date due stamp in each book.[48]

When the library opened, the McBee card had a carbon copy for overdues. However, only about 25 percent of the carbon slips were actually used, therefore the double card was discontinued. Overdue notices are now prepared by making a thermofax copy of the original charge card.[49]

Reserve

The Undergraduate Library at South Carolina maintains six different kinds of closed reserve: one week, three day, two day, overnight, and building use only. To keep the collection small, the reserve area has space for only 3000 volumes.[50]

With the opening of the Undergraduate Library, all reserve-book functions were transferred to the Undergraduate Library, including those for graduate courses.[51] One reason for doing this was the problem of staffing two separate service points. Then, there was the problem of making the decision how to split books in courses open to both graduate students and undergraduates. But perhaps the most important consideration was the validity of the closed-reserve system on the graduate level. Rightly or wrongly, "the closed reserve system, whatever its justification on the undergraduate level, was completely unjustified on the graduate level."[52] Therefore, there was no feeling of obligation to a system which was not favored in the first place.

To keep the number of books on closed reserve at a minimum, a report is sent at least once a year to faculty members showing them how many books they placed on reserve, the number of times the books were used, and the number of books never used at all. If books are not being used or are used very little, the faculty member is urged to take these titles off closed reserve and put them on the open shelves to make them more accessible.[53] This method of keeping in close touch with the faculty has led some faculty members to abandon the use of closed reserves or to place only a few titles on closed reserve, thereby enhancing access to the collection and thus producing the reduction in reserves advocated in the policy adopted toward open access.[54]

Although in actuality there are only closed reserves, most of the general collection could be considered open-reserve materials. The original reserve policy was that a book would be put on closed reserve "if it is going to have extensive use in a short period of time and a large number of students are going to have to see it. But if it is just something that is on a reading list, we have used every power of persuasion at our disposal to keep it off reserve."[55] By adhering to this policy, it has been possible to reduce the number of books placed on reserve.

Technical Services

The Main Library handles technical services for the Undergraduate Library, including ordering and physical preparation of books. The staff of the Undergraduate Library prepares orders and does preliminary filing in the card catalog. When there were three professional librarians, the Undergraduate Library staff did all of the filing in the card catalog. When the professional staff was reduced to two, a clerk took over preliminary filing, and the cataloger from the Main Library, who does the cataloging and classification of Undergraduate books, revises the filing on a weekly basis.

Books in the Undergraduate Library are classified according to the Lamont Classification scheme, because "the Lamont scheme had been specially worked out for an open stack collection and does bring with it certain advantages of pulling things together that the other system [Dewey] spreads out."[56] On the whole, the Lamont scheme has proven satisfactory.

Special Facilities

No provision was made in the Undergraduate Library at South Carolina for any special facilities such as are found in the other undergraduate libraries. The only space set off from the reading area are three smoking lounges on the ground floor (the only places smoking is allowed).[57]

Extensive audio facilities already were available on the campus, and there was no reason to duplicate them. Typing facilities were not provided because a previous experience with such facilities in the library had not proven successful. The matter of the increased cost of such extra facilities also had to be considered. It was thought preferable to provide well-serviced, basic library functions instead of a larger scope of functions improperly serviced because of inadequate staff and funds.

Simplification and Centralization

A separate building for the Undergraduate Library delineated the services between undergraduates and the graduate students and faculty. In this way, the undergraduate could be given more attention and he could be given the type of service relative to his needs. The separate building also centralized undergraduate services, making the students' use of the library easier and more meaningful.

Even though simplification is one of the major goals outlined for the undergraduate library, South Carolina accepted this principle only in part. The administration did not want a library which from the students' point of view was too easy to use, because it felt that such a library would discourage students' learning how to use a more complex library system. One means of reaching this objective was to exclude journals. In this way, it was hoped that the student would go beyond the resources of the Undergraduate Library.[58]

Instruction in Library Use

The librarian feels that the weakest point in the library's service to students is in terms of teaching the student to use the library. The whole philosophy of reference service is envisaged as "interpreting the collection to the student. It is at this point that some of the most intimate teaching goes on on the campus if you are able to do it."[59] There is a need to establish an initial contact with the student who comes to the library but does not know what to do or where to begin. The reference librarian has to know when the student needs this help, and he has to know how to offer it to him in such a way that he is willing to accept it.[60]

STAFF

A staff was selected and began work in July, 1958, by processing books already received. There were two reasons for having the new staff process these books. First, there was not sufficient staff available in the Main Library to undertake a task of this magnitude; second, it provided a means for the staff to "become" acquainted with the holdings.

The staff consisted of three professional positions[61] – director of the Undergraduate Library, circulation-reference librarian, assistant circulation librarian – and three clerical. The professional staff remained constant until 1962 when the assistant circulation librarian retired. Since then, there have been two professional and four clerical positions.[62]

Previous to 1965, the circulation-reference librarian was in charge of the circulation desk and reference service. However, the position has been redefined primarily as a reference position but with a responsibility for understanding the circulation system and working at the desk when necessary. The primary responsibilities in this position are:

(a) to assist students in learning the techniques of using a library;
(b) to interpret the collection to students;
(c) to render simple, ready reference service to students;
(d) to render complete reference service within the limitations set by the collection;
(e) to refer students to other campus library resources for assistance in extensive research problems.[63]

In addition, the circulation-reference librarian also participates in book selection, with primary responsibility for preparing desiderata both for immediate needs and long-range purchases, and he is responsible for supervising student assistants. He is expected "to maintain cordial, friendly relationships with students and faculty members by giving the best library service possible."[64]

The director of the Undergraduate Library, besides being responsible for the overall operation of the library, does book selection and reference work. He makes the final decision in book selection and provides reference service when needed.

Staffing has been one of the weak points in the operation of the Undergraduate Library at South Carolina. Only in the first two years of operation was professional service available during the whole time the library was open. Now, professional service is available only during the day and two evenings a week. The remainder of the time, clericals, who have gained some skill in helping patrons but cannot provide professional service, staff the library.[65]

To date, the staff has been sufficient as far as full-time clerical employees are concerned. The number of student-assistant hours has been increased to take care of additional shelving and various duties. No additional professional staff will probably be added until the building is enlarged.

Administratively, the head of the Undergraduate Library reports directly to the director of the university libraries. Because of previous decentralization in the university library system, it was decided to integrate the Undergraduate Library as much as possible with the Main Library.[66]

LIBRARY USE

In planning the Undergraduate Library at South Carolina, the librarian assumed that about 50 percent of its use would be as a study hall, and current figures seem to bear this out. Much of the use is by the student who brings his own books and notes and is simply looking for a quiet, comfortable place to study. The location of the library in the residential area of the campus seems to have been a good decision.[67]

It was anticipated that about 90 percent of the undergraduate's needs would be satisfied by the Undergraduate Library. However, because of the size of the collection and the lack of journals, students must go to McKissick Memorial Library for serious research, ranging from a freshman theme to a senior thesis. It is difficult to believe that such a large portion of the undergraduate's needs have been met. However, neither the McKissick Memorial Library nor the Undergraduate Library keeps a breakdown of circulation, so this cannot be determined with certainty.

Use of books and of the building has grown progressively. Circulation of two-week books and reserve books has more than doubled in the six years the library has been open (Table 16). Book use has not risen dramatically, but there has been a steady increase in the total number of books circulated, indicated by a 118 percent increase in book use since the library opened. The increase in two-week circulation is 130 percent, in reserve books for building use 122 percent, and in reserve books for home use 103 percent. The increases have been erratic, especially in reserve books.

TABLE 16

CIRCULATION STATISTICS, UNDERGRADUATE LIBRARY, UNIVERSITY OF SOUTH CAROLINA

	TWO-WEEK CIRCULATION	PERCENT INCREASE	RESERVE BUILDING USE	PERCENT INCREASE	RESERVE HOME USE	PERCENT INCREASE	TOTAL	PERCENT INCREASE
1959–60	16,693		9,281		4,935		30,909	
1960–61	21,985	24	9,247	– .3	3,693	–33	37,799	22
1961–62	26,053	13	12,463	32	5,990	62	44,506	20
1962–63	29,981	14	18,096	45	5,292	–13	53,380	19
1963–64	34,689	15	18,122	1	5,620	6	57,431	7
1964–65	38,522	11	20,632	13	8,297	47	67,451	17

Two factors must be considered when looking at the circulation figures: the size of the book collection and the size of the student body. The book collection was initially small (Table 17), but in six years, it has increased by 153 percent. The librarian has made an effort to restrict the rate of growth.

TABLE 17

GROWTH OF THE BOOK COLLECTION, UNDERGRADUATE LIBRARY, UNIVERSITY OF SOUTH CAROLINA

1958–59	14,348
1959–60	18,230
1960–61	21,627
1961–62	25,544
1962–63	28,309
1963–64	32,409
1964–65	36,336

While the collection has grown slowly, the student body has increased from 4273 when the Undergraduate Library opened in the Fall Semester, 1959, to 6244 in the Fall Semester, 1964, making an increase of about 68 percent in six years. The growth of the collection has, therefore, outstripped the growth of the student body.

Use of the building has grown increasingly (Table 18). The increases began slowly, but in the past two years, the rise in attendance has been more dramatic. Considering the size of the enrollment, the use of the library is even more stunning.[68]

TABLE 18

ATTENDANCE STATISTICS, UNDERGRADUATE LIBRARY,
UNIVERSITY OF SOUTH CAROLINA

1959–60	113,012
1960–61	130,901
1961–62	147,276
1962–63	132,432[a]
1963–64	188,363
1964–65	220,659

[a]Because of a clerical error, attendance was not recorded for a period of time. This figure is, therefore, an incomplete one.

Heaviest use during the year comes in October and March.[69] During the first year of operation, on peak days, as much as 20 percent of the student enrollment used the library, while on a normal day, this figure was about 10 percent.[70]

When the library opened, it was agreed that "we would only make rules that we considered essential to be able to operate and that we would be as consistent as we possibly could in enforcing the few rules that we made."[71] Perhaps this has been part of the reason why there have been no real discipline or noise problems. The Undergraduate Library does not play the role of a social center or a cultural center for the students. In one or two instances when there was an indication that the Undergraduate Library was serving as a gathering or meeting place, the matter was dealt with forcibly to discourage any future recurrence. Many of the problems that are arising are only because there are so many students.[72]

SUMMARY

The goals of the Undergraduate Library at South Carolina were to make access to books easier for the undergraduate, to separate undergraduates and graduate students and faculty so that the undergraduate could receive the type of service he needed, and to make the learning process easier and more satisfactory for him. Open access to the book collection was provided with the exception of some titles on closed reserve. The building and the organization of services are arranged so that the undergraduate receives the personalized service he needs and can use the facilities easily. Ease of use was facilitated by the location of undergraduate facilities in one building.

The book collection at South Carolina, including reserve books, is carefully selected to support the curriculum. The collection does not include general interest reading unrelated to the curriculum, but it does include general books on subjects in the curriculum.

The Undergraduate Library at South Carolina does not provide any special facilities. Instruction in use of the library is provided through reference service. Students receive instruction in library use only as individuals so that the instruction they receive is tailored to their individual needs.

NOTES

[1]Letter from J. Mitchell Reames, Librarian, Undergraduate Library, University of South Carolina, to Dr. Edward B. Stanford, Librarian, University of Minnesota Library, Oct. 16, 1959 (in the files of the Undergraduate Library).

[2]Interview with Alfred H. Rawlinson, Director of Libraries, University of South Carolina, Nov. 4, 1965.

[3]_Ibid._; letter from J. Mitchell Reames to the author, April 14, 1966.

[4]_Columbia Record_, March 6, 1958.

[5]Interview with Alfred H. Rawlinson.

[6]The campus at the University of South Carolina is divided into "new campus" and "old campus." The original campus or "old campus" is that which is located around the central horseshoe and contains the classroom buildings and some dormitories. The "new campus" which is south of Green Street is the area outside of the "walls" which surround the "old campus." The dormitories comprise the pre-

dominant type of structure in this area.

[7]Interview with J. Mitchell Reames, Librarian, Undergraduate Library, University of South Carolina, Nov. 2, 1965.

[8]Interview with Alfred H. Rawlinson.

[9]Interview with J. Mitchell Reames.

[10]J. Mitchell Reames, "The Undergraduate Library, University of South Carolina," *Southeastern Librarian*, X (Fall, 1960), 132–33.

[11]Interview with Alfred H. Rawlinson.

[12]Interview with J. Mitchell Reames.

[13]*Ibid.*

[14]Reames, *Southeastern Librarian*, X, 133.

[15]American Library Association, Library Technology Project, *The Use of Carpeting in Libraries* (Chicago: A.L.A., 1962), p. 3. The elevator is located at the west end of the building and therefore is little used. The steps are usually quicker.

[16]Letter from J. Mitchell Reames to Mr. Charles E. Butler, Librarian, Longwood College, Oct. 24, 1960 (in the files of the Undergraduate Library).

[17]Letter from J. Mitchell Reames to Frazer G. Poole, Director, Library Technology Project, Aug. 31, 1960 (in the files of the Undergraduate Library).

[18]Letter from J. Mitchell Reames to Frazer G. Poole, March 8, 1962 (in the files of the Undergraduate Library).

[19]Reames, *Southeastern Librarian*, X, 133.

[20]Interview with Alfred H. Rawlinson.

[21]Interview with J. Mitchell Reames.

[22]Reames, *Southeastern Librarian*, X, 134.

[23]Letter from J. Mitchell Reames to Mr. N. Stockdale, Acting Librarian, the Australian National University, April 4, 1960 (in the files of the Undergraduate Library).

[24]"Suggested Policies and Techniques for the Selection of Books for the Undergraduate Library at the University of South Carolina," May 5, 1957 (in the files of the Undergraduate Library). Cited hereafter as "Suggested Policies and Techniques."

[25]"Acquisition Policy—Undergraduate Library," July 23, 1965 (in the files of the Undergraduate Library).

[26]"Suggested Policies and Techniques."

[27]Interview with Alfred H. Rawlinson.

[28]"Aids Used in Selecting Books for the Undergraduate Library" (in the files of the Undergraduate Library).

[29]Interview with Alfred H. Rawlinson.

[30]*Ibid.*

[31]South Carolina. University. Library. Undergraduate Library, *Annual Report*, 1961–62, p.1.

[32]"Suggested Policies and Techniques."

[33]J. Mitchell Reames, "The Undergraduate Library, The University of South Carolina." Speech given at the meeting of the Columbia Library Club, Columbia, S.C., Sept. 24, 1958.

[34]Interview with J. Mitchell Reames.

[35]Reames, *Southeastern Librarian*, X, 134.

[36]Because of the local situation at the University of South Carolina and because nursing is an undergraduate curriculum, the nursing collection was transferred from the Main Library to the Undergraduate Library.

[37]Interview with J. Mitchell Reames.

[38]*Ibid.*

[39]Interview with Alfred H. Rawlinson; letter from J. Mitchell Reames to the author, April 14, 1966.

[40]*Ibid.*

[41]Interview with J. Mitchell Reames.

[42]*Ibid.*

[43]Reames, *Southeastern Librarian*, X, 134.

[44]Interview with J. Mitchell Reames.

[45]Library hours are: Monday through Friday, 9:00 A.M. to 11:00 P.M.; Saturday, 9:00 A.M. to 5:00 P.M.; Sunday, 2:00 P.M. to 10:00 P.M.

[46]Interview with Alfred H. Rawlinson.

[47]Letter from J. Mitchell Reames to Mr. William A. Pease, Undergraduate Librarian, the University of North Carolina Library, Feb. 25, 1963 (in the files of the Undergraduate Library).

[48]Interview with J. Mitchell Reames.

[49]*Ibid.*

[50]Letter from J. Mitchell Reames to Mr. William A. Pease, Sept. 9, l963 (in the files of the Undergraduate Library).

[51]*Ibid.* The enrollment at the University of South Carolina is primarily undergraduate as there are only 300 or 400 graduate students which comprise less than 10 percent of the total enrollment.

[52]Interview with Alfred H. Rawlinson.

[53]Memorandum from J. Mitchell Reames (in the files of the Undergraduate Library).

[54]Interview with J. Mitchell Reames.

[55]*Ibid.*

[56]*Ibid.*

[57]Letter from J. Mitchell Reames to Mr. Lucien W. White, Director, Public Service Departments, University of Illinois Library, Nov. 22, 1963 (in the files of the Undergraduate Library).

[58]Interview with Alfred H. Rawlinson.

[59]Interview with J. Mitchell Reames.

[60]*Ibid.*

[61]One of the professional positions was actually only two-thirds time. One person worked a schedule of nights and Saturdays. (Interview with J. Mitchell Reames.)

[62]Interview with J. Mitchell Reames.

[63]"Job Description—Circulation-Reference Librarian—The Undergraduate Library" (in the files of the Undergraduate Library).

[64]*Ibid.*

[65]Interview with J. Mitchell Reames.

[66]Interview with Alfred H. Rawlinson.

[67]Interview with J. Mitchell Reames.

[68]Library attendance at the University of South Carolina is counted manually by means of two small tickers so that the figures arrived at are not necessarily exact, but they do give a relatively close indication.

[69]Interview with J. Mitchell Reames.

[70]South Carolina. University. Library. Undergraduate Library, *Annual Report*, 1959–60, p. 2.

[71]Interview with J. Mitchell Reames.

[72]*Ibid.*

The Undergraduate Library, Indiana University

The idea for an undergraduate library at Indiana took shape about 1950, when Dr. Robert A. Miller, Director of Libraries, suggested a "new and separate library building for undergraduates."[1] Dr. Miller considered an undergraduate library

> a big step toward equalizing library privileges. It affords the underclassman with a curious mind the opportunity to lengthen his intellectual tether and it provides the less curious student a convenient place to read what he must.[2]

Consideration was first given to remodeling the Central Library building to include adequate facilities for the undergraduates, but it soon became evident that such a plan was impractical. "The presence of a multi-tier stack wall, the impossibility of expanding the present building except for additional stacks, its location, and the impossibility of opening large areas for the seating required make it impossible to secure the improvement desired for the undergraduate program."[3]

Dr. Miller felt that the concept of an undergraduate library was important because undergraduates often received poor library service. The proposal for a separate undergraduate library was presented to the Faculty Council and, in principle, received its approval.[4]

An analysis of the existing library facilities for undergraduates was made. These were four in number: (1) general and humanities reading room; (2) social sciences reading room; (3) documents and periodical reading room; and (4) stack collection. These facilities provided seating for 460 readers and open access to about 18,000 volumes, including the general and humanities and the social sciences collections, the reference collection, and unbound periodicals. All other materials—reserve books, documents, and stack collection—were housed in closed stacks, with the card catalog being the only means of access.[5]

The library administration carefully delineated the purposes the library was to serve by indicating how and why undergraduates use the library. First, undergraduate students used the library to read and study their own books. The study hall concept of use was "legitimate and undergraduates should be encouraged in this activity by having adequate space and pleasant surroundings."[6] Second, about 30 percent of undergraduate use of the library was for reading assignments in reserve books. No great change in the method of instruction was anticipated to change this situation. Third, undergraduates used the library for doing collateral reading, and "evidence is available to prove that the policy of providing such books is educationally sound."[7] Fourth, only a few students used the library for independent reading, but their reading could be encouraged if they had ready access to books and "surroundings conducive to study." Fifth, undergraduates used library materials for their term papers and reports. Sixth, in freshman English courses and some undergraduate library science courses, students had to prepare special projects that teach library use. Seventh, the library was a traditional meeting place for friends and small study groups.[8]

To meet these needs, six space requirements were established: (1) seating for 1500 students with a minimum of 25 square feet per reader, equaling a total of 37,500 square feet; (2) shelving for 75,000 volumes with a total of 8300 square feet for stack space; (3) meeting and smoking area of 1800 square feet; (4) rooms to accommodate conversation, group study, and blind students, consisting of 2300 square feet; (5) office space comprising 400 square feet; and (6) typing rooms consisting of 400 square feet. Total assignable space requirement was 52,200 square feet.[9]

However, the proposal for the undergraduate library had to be put aside because of more pressing needs for a new classroom building. The Library Committee went "on record as supporting a plan for a new stack addition, future use of the Student Building,[10] and the construction of a central library building as soon as possible after the classroom structure is completed."[11] With this statement, the idea of a separate undergraduate library building was rejected in favor of combining all library facilities in one structure. Division of the collection was opposed by many faculty members.[12]

Shortly after completion of the addition to the Central Library in 1955, the university received a gift from the Eli Lilly Company for a rare-book library. Although this was a most welcome gift, another postponement of a central library building was necessary.[13]

In the meantime, to improve service to readers and to accommodate the ever growing numbers of undergraduate students, the Student Building was to be renovated as an undergraduate library, if it could be done economically. The new undergraduate library to be housed in the Student Building was to provide adequate facilities for the next twenty years and make the Central Library building better suited to the needs of graduate students and faculty.[14]

THE BUILDING

Although the use of the Student Building as a library adjunct had been considered as early as 1954, a definite decision was made about five years later. At that time, a new Physical Education Building was being built to accommodate the Women's Physical Education Department, then housed in the Student Building. Since the building was adjacent to the Central Library building, Vice-President Briscow suggested that the library occupy the building even though it was inadequate in many ways.[15]

The Undergraduate Library does not occupy the whole building. The Women's Physical Education Department still maintains the swimming pool in the basement, and Central Library offices, which have no connection with the Undergraduate Library, occupy the second and third floors of the east wing. Even before the renovation of the building was begun, it was recognized that the results were not going to be completely satisfactory, nor would the building be a permanent solution. The work, begun in 1961, took almost a year for completion.[16]

Description:

The building consisted mainly of three gymnasiums—one in the basement and two on the first floor—and some smaller areas on the second and third floors which were adapted for use. Each of the gymnasiums was converted into a large reading area, one housing the basement reading room and the other two housing the general collection.[17]

The basement includes the basement reading room, open-reserve shelves, and closed-reserve desk (Fig. 23). The lobby contains a lounge and smoking area equipped with comfortable furniture. The basement reading room houses the open-reserve books and provides space for students to work on assigned readings. It is the only air-conditioned area in the library.

The first floor contains a lobby, the new-book shelf, card catalog, unbound and bound periodicals, and two reading rooms (Fig. 24). The card catalog is the center of the lobby, the new-book shelf along the west wall, the exit control to the right of the southwest entrance, the reference desk adjacent to the exit control, and the small alcove behind the

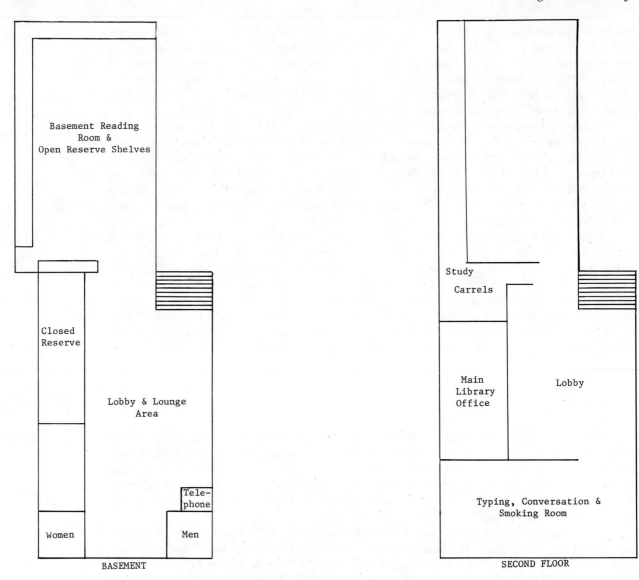

Fig. 23. Basement and second floors, Undergraduate Library, Indiana University

reference desk houses the collection of college catalogs. The librarian and one reference librarian have their desks in the office area to the left of the entrance. The circulation area is beyond the offices.

The reading room in the west wing houses Library of Congress classes A through N and the reference collection. Shelving lines the walls on the north and east sides of the room but stands perpendicular to the west wall. Seating is at tables arranged in rows for the length of the room. The center reading room, which houses Library of Congress classes P through Z, has a similar arrangement. Bookstacks line the west, north, and east walls. Free-standing shelves are arranged in U-shaped alcoves on the south side of the reading room. The back part of the alcove is closed off with a partition, and the area behind this partition provides a corridor for students going to the periodical reading room. In this way, students do not have to walk through the reading area disturbing those who are studying.

The east wing of the first floor consists of the *New York Times* alcove, which contains a five-year back file of bound volumes of the *Times,* and the periodical reading room. Unbound periodicals are shelved in the north periodical reading room along the west wall, while the remainder of the shelving contains the bound periodicals. The periodical indexes are in the south periodical reading room.

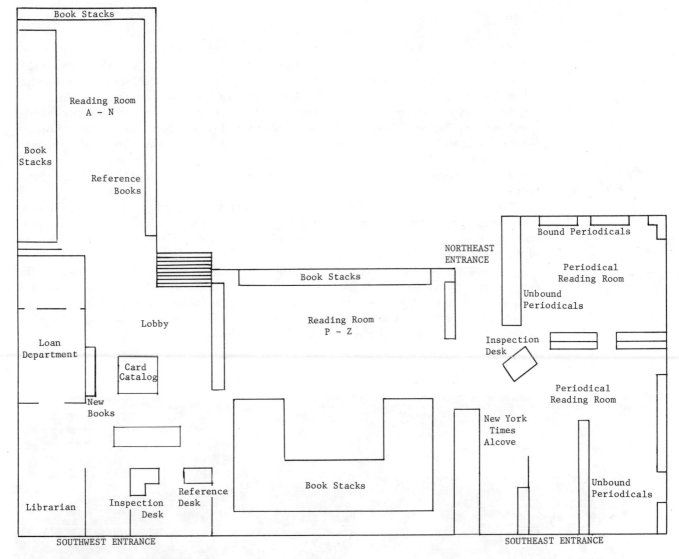

Fig. 24. Main floor, Undergraduate Library, Indiana University

The west wing of the second floor has a lobby, balcony study carrels, and a typing, conversation, and smoking room (Fig. 23). The balcony, which overlooks the first floor reading room, is just wide enough for one row of carrels and an aisle. The one office on this floor was previously occupied by the typing and conversation room, but the Central Library took over the space. The typing and conversation room is now combined with the smoking room. The lobby is furnished with lounge furniture.

The arrangement of functions was largely determined by the layout of the building. Reserves were placed in the basement, because it is the only room in the library which can be shut off from the rest of the building and so could remain open as a study hall after regular hours. It was necessary to remove the reserve books from the Central Library as soon as possible, so they were placed in the basement, the first area to be completed.[18] The loan desk is near the entrance for easy access, and the card catalog is near both the circulation desk and the reference desk so that the student can obtain either information for locating a book or help in using the catalog. The periodical reading room is in the east wing of the first floor, because that seemed to be the most logical place, even though the reference librarian is at some distance from the periodical indexes. The arrangement of books is simple and was dictated by the layout of the building and by the absence of an elevator. Hence, all the books are on the first floor or in the basement.[19]

Furnishings

The furniture in the Undergraduate Library is birch. Purchased new for the Undergraduate Library, it has worn well with heavy use. Three kinds of seating are provided:
tables, individual carrels, and lounge furniture. Out of the total of 620 seats (in the Central
Library, a total of 865 seats was available for 7124 undergraduate students, providing seating for about 12 percent of the enrollment, or half the capacity usually recommended),
there are only 20 individual carrels and probably not many more lounge seats. Lounge
furniture is mainly in the three lobbies, but a few lounge chairs are in the reading rooms.
All carrels are on the second floor balcony. The majority of the tables are 4 feet by 6 feet,
but there are some round tables. The reading table chairs are straight-back birch chairs
without arms.

New lighting was installed when the building was renovated for library use. Fluorescent lights hang from the high ceiling by steel rods. Although the fixtures are covered
with egg-crate louvers to defract the light, illumination directly over the glossy surfaces
of the reading tables produces some glare.

Because the flooring throughout the building (except for the vinyl tile used in the
east wing) is hardwood, the noise created by walking is somewhat of a problem. Rubber
mats did not muffle the footsteps, so in June, 1964, carpeting was laid in the main and
lower lobbies of the west wing and on the stairs. Runners of carpeting were also installed
near the edges of the reading rooms to provide walkways.[20]

First floor reading room, west wing, Undergraduate Library, Indiana University

BOOK COLLECTION

General Collection

The book collection for the Undergraduate Library was originally thought of as containing "75,000 duplicate copies of books, journals, and reference volumes."[21] Selection of the collection at Indiana did not begin until 1961. Mrs. Barbara Fischler, who was in the Reference Department at the Central Library, was appointed assistant undergraduate librarian beginning with the Spring Semester, 1961, with responsibility for selecting the book collection.[22] A special appropriation was made for this purpose. In addition, Ford Foundation funds were available to purchase the initial collection.[23]

The shelf list of the University of Michigan Undergraduate Library served as the basic selection tool. Undergraduate reserve books housed in the Central Library were moved to the new library, but the collections housed in the social sciences reading room and the general and humanities reading room really provided the core of the collection. The total collection in these two rooms consisted of approximately 15,000 volumes. Mr. Neil Boardman, Undergraduate Librarian (now Administrative Assistant), purchased another segment of the collection.

Using the Michigan list, Mrs. Fischler made selections for the Undergraduate Library collection. She also personally talked with members of the faculty in all departments except those with department library services. The books suggested in this way were ordered through regular channels.

As the time for opening the library approached, it became evident that the stock of books on hand for the general collection was too small. To facilitate matters, Mr. Boardman made a trip to New York City and purchased many secondhand books. Except for a small list of titles which could not be purchased through regular channels, the purchases were based on Mr. Boardman's experience and knowledge. Most of the titles were standard works in the social sciences and humanities. Little purchasing was done in the area of the sciences except for the more outstanding layman titles. Because of the short time available to assemble the collection, the size of the collection when the library opened was only about 19,000 volumes.[24]

The procedures used for book selection after opening the Undergraduate Library are somewhat different than those found in other undergraduate libraries. To assure the maintenance of a good collection, the undergraduate librarian is assisted in her purchasing by several subject specialists in the Central Library. If one of these specialists sees a title which he feels would be appropriate for the undergraduate collection, he orders it. In a like manner, the undergraduate librarian orders books for the Central Library collection.[25] Whenever the Undergraduate Library initiates an order for a title which the Central Library does not have, the undergraduate librarian also orders a copy for the Central Library. Therefore, the undergraduate collection is nearly a 100 percent duplicate of books in the Central Library with one exception, paperbacks. The Central Library does not necessarily purchase paperbacks which the Undergraduate Library does. In purchasing the initial collection, no effort was made to make it a wholly duplicate collection.[26] The matter is further complicated because the Undergraduate Library pays for the books which it orders for the Central Library. These purchases account for about 20 percent of all Undergraduate Library book funds.[27]

An effort has been made to develop a general collection around the needs of (but in no way strictly limited to) the curriculum. Consideration is given to books that undergraduates use not only for specific class assignments (reserve reading) but also for papers and reports. It is necessary, then, to have sufficient materials in the areas more prevalent for report topics.[28]

Faculty members give little assistance in book selection for the general collection outside of their reading lists. As a result, the undergraduate librarian does almost all of the book selection for the general collection. Required readings fall within the province of the reserve desk, but are a means of adding new titles to the collection. The librarian makes an effort to purchase all supplementary titles that are in print, but out-of-print books are acquired only in unusual cases. Needs are also determined by "holds" placed on books. All hold slips are retained and examined. When the transaction involves undergraduate students and a fairly basic book, another copy is ordered. When the hold involves a graduate student or faculty member, it is referred to the Central Library. Not all hold books are ordered automatically. Missing books can be included with this group. After a book has been missing for a month, the librarian orders another copy if there is not already one in the library.[29] These categories probably constitute no more than a third of the books ordered each year, with replacements constituting 8 percent of the total and added copies 5 percent of the total.[30]

Most books are acquired by reviewing the selection media. The library should have "the latest scholarship on [relevant] subjects," so the librarian tries to acquire the good new books. On the whole, only highly recommended books are purchased, except in cases where there is really nothing else on a subject. If the topic is timely and is apt to interest the undergraduate, it is represented in the library. Heaviest dependency in selection is placed on *Choice,* from which the majority of the new purchases are selected.[31] New books constitute about 56 percent of all purchases for the Undergraduate Library.[32]

As a rule, only one copy of a title is ordered for the general collection, because it is hard to predict potential use. Exceptions are made for titles for which demand can be predicted, but no more than five copies of any title are purchased. Two copies of paperbacks are always purchased, because it is felt that they do not last long. Some copies of paperbacks (especially those for reserve) are not cataloged, on the assumption that they wear out quickly. However, few of those copies have actually worn out from use.

No conscious effort is made to maintain a balanced collection except "by size of department involved and their use of outside reading."[33] The patron's immediate needs play a more important part in the development of the collection than does any aesthetic ideal of a balanced collection. As a result, the collection is stronger in the social sciences than the humanities, while the pure sciences and the fine arts, heavily represented in several department libraries, are represented by minimum collections. Growth of the book collection in the social sciences, and especially in history, has been greater because many instructors send their reading lists to the Undergraduate Library to use as buying guides, and because the history specialist in the Central Library works with the undergraduate librarian in developing the collection in this area. Current events and works on the American Negro represent smaller areas of strength in the collection. The emphasis on the social sciences is attributed to the publication of more books in that area.[34]

A breakdown by subject was set up as a guide for purchasing new books for the Undergraduate Library. There are five subject areas: language and literature; history and other social sciences; reference, general, and other; and science and mathematics. Language and literature, comprising 33 percent of the new-book purchases, includes fiction, language, literature, poetry, and drama. History constitutes 30 percent of the new-book purchases. Other social sciences, education, philosophy, psychology, religion, sociology, economics, sports, recreation, and travel account for 30 percent of the purchases. Only 6 percent of the new books is for reference, art, general works, music, and biography. One percent of the new books treats mathematics, science, medicine, technology, and home economics.[35] In science, mathematics, medicine, technology, and home economics, department libraries satisfy undergraduate needs. Recently, however, the Undergraduate Library has been buying books to supplement department library holdings for the sake of weaker students who want further aid.[36]

The collection is intended to satisfy about 80 percent of the needs of the average undergraduate. The collection, numbering about 40,000 volumes, is still not large enough (the collection was supposed to have reached 100,000 volumes by the time the new building was completed in the summer of 1969) nor are there enough multiple copies of many books.[37]

The book collection has not grown rapidly at Indiana (Table 19). The totals listed in Table 19 are for cataloged items only. When uncataloged items are added, the collection

TABLE 19

GROWTH OF THE BOOK COLLECTION, UNDERGRADUATE LIBRARY, INDIANA UNIVERSITY

	VOLUMES IN COLLECTION	PERCENT OF INCREASE
1961–62	19,150	
1962–63	32,079	67
1963–64	36,673	14
1964–65	39,916	8

totals 42,453. Uncataloged items include pamphlets, college catalogs, borrowed reserve books, and photocopied articles for reserve.

Although the collection continues to grow, the rate of growth is declining (Table 19). One factor limiting growth of the collection is an insufficient book budget (Table 20). Although the initial book budget was $150,000 (spread over a two-year period), subsequent budgets have been inadequate to meet purchasing needs and have forced the library to purchase only one copy of a title even if multiple copies are needed. The fact that serials and standing orders are not paid from Undergraduate Library book funds stretches the budget. These books are paid for by the Serial Department with Central Library book funds. That 700 to 800 books are lost annually also helps explain the apparent slow growth of the collection (Table 20 shows net, not gross, growth).[38]

TABLE 20

BOOK BUDGET, UNDERGRADUATE LIBRARY,
INDIANA UNIVERSITY

1961–62	$75,000
1962–63	75,000
1963–64	26,000
1964–65	28,000

The periodical collection consists of fifty-seven titles with holdings of about 1600 volumes.[39] "The periodicals cover a wide range of subjects, and were selected after a special study had been made of titles most frequently requested by undergraduate students."[40] The present policy is to have ten-year back runs of the periodicals, which extends most titles back to 1951. The indexes cover the same period. Because ten-year back runs do not provide sufficient coverage, runs of some selected titles are being extended to 1948.[41]

Most of the titles included in the periodical collection are of a general nature, and their small number constitutes a weakness in the collection. The biggest gaps are in the general social science periodicals and in education journals. Titles that are added tend to be more specialized.[42]

Beginning the Spring Semester, 1964, an effort was made to initiate a weeding program. The staff began a list consisting mainly of superseded editions. Books to be weeded were also found by checking the date due slips to determine the extent of use of the book. The project had to be discontinued, because the Catalog Department did not have time to withdraw the books.[43]

In order to keep the collection updated, the staff takes an annual inventory. At first, only half of the collection was to be inventoried, but in practice, the whole collection is checked. After a book has been missing for a year, catalog records are pulled and stored in the Undergraduate Library if the book is unavailable (i.e., it is out of print). If the book is not found in three years and is still unavailable, it is officially withdrawn from the collection.[44]

Reference Collection

The reference collection contains 1478 volumes. It consists primarily of general reference tools. Money and space limitations have kept the collection smaller than was anticipated, especially when considering the depth of searching which the staff does.

Reserve Collection

The reserve collection contains required readings. After a few years, it was anticipated that the basic collection of reserve books would have been purchased and the number of books needed to be added would decrease. But the opposite has been true. The number of books purchased for reserve has been slowly increasing, even though there is a limit of five copies of all titles purchased. Yet many of the reserve books (about a fourth) are never checked out.[45]

By sending book cards which show the amount of use for each book to the instructors each semester, the staff tries to retain the collection as a working collection. However, the response is not significant considering the amount of work involved in carrying out such a project. As a result, books which were requested for both the Fall and Spring semesters are placed on permanent reserve. New lists are not mandatory each semester.[46]

The number of books placed on reserve is growing continually. From the Fall Semester, 1964, to the Fall Semester, 1965, there was an increase from 280 lists to 400 lists of books placed on reserve. In the Fall Semester, 1965, there were approximately 2000 volumes on closed reserve (about 1500 volumes are on permanent reserve) and about 1000 volumes on open reserve. More professors are now placing their reserve books on open reserve. However, space considerations limit the number of books on open reserve.

Books which are not available in the Undergraduate Library and cannot be purchased are borrowed from the Central Library for reserve use in the Undergraduate Library. Each semester this amounts to about 800 volumes. There are 268 Central Library books permanently on reserve in the Undergraduate Library.[47] Reserve books are borrowed only from the Central Library. If a book is available only in a department library, it is put on reserve there rather than in the Undergraduate Library.[48]

Open Access to the Collection

The library administration at Indiana wanted to create the atmosphere and the "selectivity of a small college library in the midst of a large educational enterprise."[49] The inadequacy of library facilities for undergraduates was clearly recognized. Except for the collections housed in the three reading rooms mentioned above, the undergraduate did not have direct access to books. "Admittedly the undergraduate is not likely to have interest in or need for the great bulk of the library collection, but his intellectual appetite can be sharpened and his course work benefited by access to a larger collection of books."[50]

It was also felt that the card catalog was often an insurmountable barrier "with its 1,500,000 cards . . . and stands as a complex, irritating septum to book procurement."[51] A simplified catalog and reference service would increase the undergraduate's understanding and use of the library. When the undergraduate competed with graduate students and faculty for the same service, he often lost out, because the other two groups were more vocal and demanding.

The location of the Central Library building on the western edge of the campus was another detriment to library service for the undergraduate student. The building was some distance from classroom facilities and even a greater distance from the dormitories. The Central Library building did not provide any area where students could smoke or where groups could study together or talk while taking a study break.

The Undergraduate Library is seen as an experiment in undergraduate education; one which supports "the increasing emphasis on quality education for underclassmen."[52] To do this, the library features "an open shelf collection of the most useful books, reserve book space and study facilities" which are designed to encourage "frequent and continuous use."[53]

SERVICES

Reference

In most cases, the services administered by the staff are relatively simple. This is the case with reference service. Usually the questions are easily answered: location questions (about a fifth of the total), help with the card catalog, or short-answer questions. Much of the reference service is in terms of readers advisory functions.[54] Because many of the reference questions are biographical and because the reference collection is somewhat removed from the reference desk, all biography reference books were removed from their regular place in the collection and shelved near the reference desk.[55]

The bulk of reference work falls to the professional in charge of reference and to the librarian in charge of circulation. The undergraduate librarian and the librarian in charge of reserve are not regularly scheduled for reference duty, although they help out when needed.[56]

Circulation

The Undergraduate Library at Indiana maintains circulation control on McBee Key-sort cards. The McBee system was chosen because it was used in the Central Library, and it was desired to maintain uniformity in the system.

A double-slip charge card is used. The carbon or second slip is placed in the book. On return of the book, it is stamped with the date and time of receipt to prevent any problems arising from assertions of students about the date or return of specific books. The two-week loan period applies to all users of the library regardless of status.

Besides the regular student and faculty charges, cards are kept for books on reserve, missing books, and reference books. Charges for reference books are kept in the file, because previous to 1964 reference location was not indicated in the card catalog.[57]

Reserve

The Undergraduate Library uses open and closed reserves. Books on open reserve are in the basement reading room, and the books on closed reserve are behind the reserve desk in the lobby. Previous to the Spring Semester, 1966, requests for closed-reserve books were made orally, but this was considered inefficient and now a reserve slip is used.[58]

Open-reserve books are for room use, but they circulate overnight, as do the closed-reserve books. Open-reserve books are largely suggested, rather than required, reading. Placing the books on the open shelves gives the student a chance to make the choice from the books which are available.[59]

Special Services

Four special services are provided in the Undergraduate Library. About 350 college catalogs are provided for the student's convenience. The collection has not been expanded, because college catalogs are also available in the Registrar's Office.[60] Holdings are kept on IBM (International Business Machines) cards, and current print-outs are made available each semester.[61]

A pamphlet and clippings file is also serviced and maintained by the reference staff. Because of a lack of staff time, the pamphlet file has not received much attention. At present, it contains about 326 pamphlets, exclusive of other items.

The Undergraduate Library maintains a collection of tests for undergraduate courses in the College of Arts and Sciences. Faculty members send sample tests to keep the file up to date. When the Undergraduate Library opened, the tests were part of the reserve collection, because they are limited to building use. But because pressures on reserve materials and tests usually coincide, in October, 1964, the tests were transferred to the Circulation Department to help alleviate the pressure on the reserve staff. At the same time, the file was reorganized and weeded, and each test was indexed on an IBM card for handling ease. To keep the collection up to date, each semester print-outs are sent to the departments for them to indicate items for removal. Even with this innovation, the file continues to grow. Presently, it comprises approximately 1000 items.[62]

In the Fall Semester, 1965, a listening room was installed on the third floor of the west wing. The room, which accommodates twenty persons, features nonmusical tape recordings for course-related and recreational listening. There are no records or musical recordings.[63]

Technical Services

The Undergraduate Library performs no technical services. The Central Library does the acquisition and cataloging of books, but the Undergraduate Library initiates and prepares its own orders. The Undergraduate Library does part of the physical preparation of the books. The book has the call number on the spine, but the Undergraduate Library staff puts in the date due slips and the book pockets.[64]

Simplification and Centralization

The provision of a separate facility augmented the centralization of undergraduate services at Indiana. The undergraduate no longer had to use four different library locations to get his materials. Almost all of the books and services were centralized in one building. The great bulk of the Central Library collection had been a deterrent to use. The Undergraduate Library helps alleviate this problem by providing a selective but complete collection covering most subjects in the Central Library.[65]

Areas within the library are arranged as simply as possible. Shelving books adjacent to the reading areas makes use easier. The provision of open reserve simplifies use by giving the student a chance to make his own choice of titles.

Instruction in Library Use

The staff helps the student in learning how to use the card catalog and some specific reference tools, in understanding the arrangement of the library (physical location), and in finding materials. The student is given personal assistance when possible.[66] Not as much of this is done as is needed because the staff is not large enough, but when the Undergraduate Library is "staffed by energetic librarians, who work closely and exclusively with both students and faculty, it is possible to relate such a library more closely to the work that goes on in the classroom."[67]

The only formal instruction is tours given by the staff at the beginning of the term. The students have a chance to see the building and to learn briefly about the services and facilities afforded.[68]

STAFF

A staff of two professional librarians was appointed to administer the Undergraduate Library when the reserve desk began operation in September, 1961. A third professional librarian, a reference librarian, was added in January, 1962, when the remainder of the building opened.[69] In July, 1963, another reference librarian was added, making a total of four professional librarians. One librarian works two evenings a week to supplement the regular staff. There is a total of five nonprofessional positions and a varying number of student assistants.[70]

Until July, 1965, all authority for decisions in the Undergraduate Library rested with the undergraduate librarian. Although staff members had specific assignments, they had no executive authority. As the operation of the library grew, it became more evident that such an administrative structure was impracticable. Such an organization also made it necessary to forego decisions on problems in the absence of the librarian. As a result, responsibility in several areas of operation was delegated to the three other professional librarians, "with only major decisions of policy to come to the Librarian."[71] The three areas of responsibility are: reserve; circulation and hiring and scheduling of students; and shelving, card catalog, reference inventory, and new books.

One prerequisite for the staff is that they be "the most helpful, the most gracious, the most personable people that you can possibly find."[72] It is the one place in the university library system where people with general backgrounds are useful. Personality is almost as important as background. The staff at Indiana has been a young one. "And the turnover is of no importance because what is important is that they are willing to help people and to go to some lengths to help them."[73]

The administrative structure of the Undergraduate Library is a very simple one. The undergraduate librarian reports to the assistant director for operations and services. In turn, each professional librarian reports to the undergraduate librarian (Fig. 25). The clerical employees report to the three other professional librarians, with the exception of the one library assistant who is responsible for book orders.

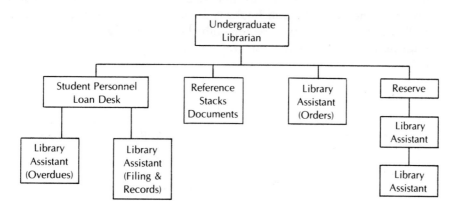

Fig. 25. Organization chart, Undergraduate Library, Indiana University

LIBRARY USE

Use of the collection has increased markedly since the opening of the Undergraduate Library (Table 21). Building use of books alone has increased 61 percent since the first full year of operation, while circulation of two-week books has increased 82 percent. The yearly rate of increase is dropping, but this is not unusual. In the areas of reserve and

TABLE 21

CIRCULATION STATISTICS, UNDERGRADUATE LIBRARY, INDIANA UNIVERSITY[a]

	BUILDING USE	PERCENT INCREASE	TWO-WEEK CIRCULATION	PERCENT INCREASE	TOTAL TOTAL	PERCENT INCREASE
1961–62[b]	8,571		12,330		20,901	
1962–63	40,899	399	48,224	291	89,113	331
1963–64	55,303	35	71,765	48	127,068	42
1964–65	66,074	19	87,921	22	152,995	21

[a]Taken from the Central Library Annual Reports.   [b]Jan. to June, 1962.

circulation, use has increased 400 percent while enrollment has only risen 21 percent in the same period. In 1961–62, use per volume was 2.9 times; in 1964–65, it was 6.0 times.

No attendance count is kept, but periodic head counts indicate that at peak hours (midevening, for example) about 400 persons are in the building. Although all 620 seats have never been full, this figure indicates that the building is beginning to reach capacity.[74] For practical purposes, the librarian considers the building full when there are over 500 people in it, because it is actually too noisy and too crowded for serious study.

Heaviest use of the building is in the afternoons and the evenings. Lunch hours and dinner hours have not, until recently, been busy times. Slack periods are, however, becoming more infrequent, although morning use is still light.[75]

In a study of two-week loans, undergraduates accounted for about 67 percent of the circulation. The remaining 33 percent was to faculty, graduate students, staff, and others.[76] A closer breakdown shows that in the Spring Semester, 1964, 59 percent of the users were undergraduates; 31 percent were graduate students; and 10 percent were faculty, staff, and other borrowers. In 1965, the number of undergraduate users rose to 62 percent, while graduate-student use decreased to 29 percent and use of all other borrowers dropped to 9 percent.[77]

Even though many reserve books are not used, use of the reserve collection is increasing (Table 22). The percentage of books charged out shows a large increase in the second year of operation, but it must be remembered that the figure for 1961–62 is only for a six-month period. In 1963–64, there was a slight decrease in the number of books charged out.

TABLE 22

CIRCULATION OF RESERVE BOOKS, UNDERGRADUATE LIBRARY, INDIANA UNIVERSITY

	BUILDING USE	CHARGED OUT[c]	PERCENT INCREASE	TOTAL	PERCENT INCREASE
1961–62	[a]	26,460[d]		26,460	
1962–63	[a]	54,988	92	54,988	107
1963–64	6,613[b]	54,249	–1	60,862	10
1964–65	24,216	63,159	16	87,375	43

[a]Figures not available.   [c]Includes overnight and two-hour books.
[b]Jan. through June, 1964.   [d]Jan. through June, 1962.

After the opening of the Undergraduate Library, there was an overall increase in the use of reserve books: more titles were put on reserve, more lists were serviced, and more books were checked out. This was surprising, because it reversed the trend of reserve use that was apparent while the reserve collection was still housed in the Central Library.[78]

A factor which helps keep reserve use at a manageable level is duplication of some heavily used reserve books in the Halls of Residence libraries. These titles are duplicated for eight basic departments which make heavy use of reserve material. Instructors indicate on their reserve lists which titles are used heavily enough for duplication in the Halls of Residence libraries.[79]

In a survey conducted in November, 1965, a sampling showed that almost 50 percent of the students who came to the Undergraduate Library came to study from their own materials, while only about 5 percent actually withdrew a book. Many come to use library materials in the building, such as reserve materials or books used in conjunction with writing a paper or preparing a speech. Likewise, 90 percent of the persons using the Undergraduate Library were undergraduates, the remaining 10 percent being largely graduate students. Furthermore, only about 5 percent of the students go to the shelf to find their books. The usual approach is through the card catalog.[80]

If circulation follows the pattern set by book selection—i.e., if circulation is proportionate to purchases in the various fields—then the circulation pattern has remained nearly the same as it was for undergraduate use in the Central Library. During the two years preceding the opening of the Undergraduate Library, a study was made of the circulation of books to undergraduates. According to the findings, the order of heaviest to highest use by fields was: language and literature; education; United States history; philosophy, psychology, and religion; and social sciences.[81] Purchasing now follows this sequence: language and literature; history and other social sciences; reference, general, and other; and science and mathematics. The only real change is the omission of education books from the current purchasing sequence. This is understandable in the Undergraduate Library, because education is covered by a department library; therefore, the Undergraduate Library makes no real attempt at building a collection in this area.[82]

SUMMARY

The Undergraduate Library at Indiana began and still functions in a building below the standards for a model undergraduate library, but it is expected that the problem will be solved by completion of the new library building. Even with its physical handicaps, the building has satisfied some of the needs of the undergraduate by giving open access to the book collection. The book collection is limited in size and scope due to space and budget limitations and to the method of selection. Reserve books have been satisfactorily handled by using both open and closed reserve, although the advantages of open-shelf reserves are evident. The operation of reserve, circulation, and reference has been satisfactory. Indiana does more bibliographic searching than the other undergraduate libraries.

Staff organization, until the reorganization in 1965, was not practical or functional. Further division of book-selection duties would aid the development of the collection. The staff at Indiana has been a young one for a young clientele, and in this situation, the combination has worked well.

NOTES

[1]Indiana. University. Library, *Library News-letter*, Nov., 1950, p.[1].

[2]*Ibid.*

[3]Indiana. University. Library, *Statement of a Program for an Undergraduate Library at Indiana University* (Bloomington: 1952), p.16–17. Cited hereafter as *Statement of a Program for an Undergraduate Library*.

[4]Indiana. University. Library, *Report on the Libraries of Indiana University*, 1950–51, p.3.

[5]*Statement of a Program for an Undergraduate Library*, p.13–14.

[6]*Ibid.*, p.17.

[7]*Ibid.*, p.19.

[8]*Ibid.*

[9]*Ibid.*, p.20–23.

[10]The Student Building was located adjacent to the Central Library. It was known that the department which then occupied the building would be moving out in a few years and the building would be available for other use.

[11]*Library News-letter*, May, 1954, p.[1].

[12]*Ibid.*

[13]*Report on the Libraries of Indiana University*, 1955–56, p.[1].

[14]*Library News-letter*, Jan., 1959, p.[1].

[15]Interview with Dr. Robert A. Miller, Director of Libraries, Indiana University, Jan. 12, 1966.

[16]Interview with Mr. Neil S. Boardman, Administrative Assistant, Indiana University Libraries, Jan. 13, 1966.

[17]Interview with Robert A. Miller.

[18]Interview with Neil Boardman.

[19]Interview with Mrs. Janet S. Horton, Librarian, Undergraduate Library, Indiana University, Jan. 12, 1966.

[20]Memorandum from Mrs. Janet S. Horton to Robert A. Miller, April 3, 1964 (in the files of the Undergraduate Library).

[21]*Statement of a Program for an Undergraduate Library,* p.17–18.

[22]Interview with Neil Boardman.

[23]*Report on the Libraries of Indiana University,* 1961–62, p.[1].

[24]Interview with Neil Boardman.

[25]Interview with Robert A. Miller.

[26]Interview with Janet Horton.

[27]Memorandum from Janet Horton to Robert A. Miller, Aug. 6, 1965 (in the files of the Undergraduate Library).

[28]Interview with Neil Boardman.

[29]Interview with Janet Horton.

[30]Memorandum from Janet Horton to Robert A. Miller, Aug. 6, 1965.

[31]Interview with Janet Horton.

[32]Memorandum from Janet Horton to Robert A. Miller, Aug. 6, 1965.

[33]Interview with Janet Horton.

[34]*Ibid.*

[35]Memorandum from Janet Horton to Robert A. Miller, Aug. 6, 1965.

[36]Interview with Janet Horton.

[37]Interview with Robert A. Miller.

[38]Interview with Janet Horton.

[39]*Ibid.*

[40]*The Undergraduate and the Library* (Bloomington: Indiana University Libraries, 1965), p.[3].

[41]Indiana. University. Library. Undergraduate Library, *Summary of Library Operations, 1964–65,* p.7–8.

[42]Interview with Janet Horton.

[43]*Summary of Library Operations,* 1963–64, p.5; interview with Janet Horton.

[44]*Summary of Library Operations,* 1963–64, p.5–6.

[45]Interview with Janet Horton.

[46]*Summary of Library Operations,* 1963–64, p.4.

[47]Letter from Janet Horton to the author, April 8, 1966.

[48]Interview with Janet Horton.

[49]*Library News-letter,* Oct., 1959, p.[l].

[50]*Statement of a Program for an Undergraduate Library,* p.15.

[51]*Ibid.,* p.16.

[52]*Library News-letter,* Sept., 1963, p.[1].

[53]*Ibid.*

[54]Interview with Aguanita Kuo, Reference Librarian, Undergraduate Library, Indiana University, Jan. 13, 1966. Reference librarians are on duty all hours the library is open (Monday through Saturday 8:15 A.M. to 10:30 P.M.; Sunday 11:00 A.M. to 10:30 P.M.) except dinner hours on Friday and Sunday and on Saturday after five o'clock.

[55]*Summary of Library Operations,* 1963–64, p.2.

[56]Interview with Janet Horton.

[57]*Ibid.*

[58]*Library News-letter,* Feb., 1966, p.[3].

[59]*The Undergraduate and the Library,* p.[4].

[60]Memorandum from Robert A. Miller to Janet Horton, Nov. 21, 1963 (in the files of the Undergraduate Library).

[61]*Summary of Library Operations,* 1964–65, p.9.

[62]Interview with Janet Horton.

[63]*The Undergraduate and the Library,* p.[4]; letter from Janet Horton to the author, April 8, 1966.

[64]Interview with Janet Horton.

[65]*The Undergraduate and the Library,* p.[3].

[66]*Ibid.,* p.[4].

[67]*Library News-letter,* Jan., 1959, p.[1].

[68]Interview with Janet Horton.

[69]Interview with Neil Boardman.

[70]*Summary of Library Operations,* 1963–64, p.[1].

[71]*Ibid.,* p.[3].

[72]Interview with Robert A. Miller.

[73]*Ibid.*

[74]Memorandum from Janet Horton to Robert A. Miller, Nov. 26, 1963 (in the files of the Undergraduate Library).

[75]Interview with Janet Horton.

[76]*Summary of Library Operations,* 1963–64, p.[3].

[77]"Undergraduate Library Statistics" (in the files of the Undergraduate Library).

[78]Interview with Janet Horton.

[79]*Ibid*

[80]Interview with Robert A. Miller.

[81]Esther R. Whitely, "Undergraduate Use of the Stack Collection of the Indiana University Library as Indicated by Circulation, April 1959–March 1961" (unpublished Master's thesis, Library School, Indiana University, 1962), p.26.

[82]Memorandum from Janet Horton to Robert A. Miller, Aug. 6, 1965.

Uris Library, Cornell University

The undergraduate library at Cornell University, Uris Library, was the fifth library to be housed in a separate building. Many of the circumstances that promoted undergraduate libraries elsewhere—the need for space, more adequate service, open access to books, a selective collection, etc.—contributed to the establishment of this one.

Pleas for additional space were voiced at Cornell as early as 1947. Through the years, as the holdings of the University Library increased, additional space was provided to store the overflow from the main library in various buildings over the campus. The creation of department libraries alleviated some of the space problem. Plans were finally made to enlarge the existing library and were presented to the Planning and Development Committee of the Board of Trustees in September, 1949. The plans were unacceptable to the committee. As an alternative plan, the committee suggested an off-campus storage building, an undergraduate library, and "the possibility of adapting existing academic buildings to library use."[1]

After further study of these proposals and others by the members of the Library Board,[2] the Ad Hoc Committee recommended three proposals, any of which were satisfactory to the Library Board. They were:

1. The expansion of the present library building to the north and west by approximately 1,000,000 cu. ft. to provide space for reading rooms, special collections and offices and work rooms for the library staff; the conversion of the present building into a book stack; and the construction of additional stack space underground;

2. The development of a new library plant on a new site, presumably the site of the President's house, to consist of three units, an undergraduate library, a research library, and a rare book and special collection library, each unit to be susceptible of separate construction and operation but each unit also planned so that it could be integrated with the other units and thus finally form a single operating facility.

   As a third choice, the Ad Hoc Committee recommended a proposal which would convert the present library building into an undergraduate library and would construct a research library and a rare book and special collections library on another site.[3]

Because of a change in the university administration, the plan that had been approved by the Planning and Development Committee of the Board of Trustees the previous year now stood neglected.[4] However, in 1951, money was provided to renovate the existing library into a more comfortable, well-lighted, and well-ventilated place to study.[5]

Over the years there were many different plans proposed to solve the library building problem at Cornell. The elements of these eight plans were as follows:

I. 1. Convert present library to stacks
   2. Enlarge present library
   3. Off campus storage
II. 1. Convert Boardman[6] to undergraduate library
   2. Remodel present library to make research and rare book library

93

        3. Off campus storage
  III. 1. Convert Boardman to stack building
        2. Build new undergraduate library
        3. Remodel present library
  IV. 1. New undergraduate library
        2. Storage stack below undergraduate library
        3. Remodel present library
   V. 1. Addition to present library for undergraduates
        2. Remodel present library
        3. Off campus storage
  VI. 1. Convert present library to stacks
        2. Enlarge present library
        3. Underground storage stack
 VII. 1. Undergraduate library
        2. Research library
        3. Rare book and special collections library
VIII. 1. Convert present library to undergraduate library
        2. Research library on site of President's house
        3. Rare book and special collections library[7]

Although planning had gone through all of these stages, none of these proposals proved to be "the" plan for library development at Cornell. Money was the major problem in getting any program accepted. During the years of planning, the situation in the old library became worse. Finally, the Librarian, Stephen A. McCarthy, persuaded the president, the vice-president, and the provost of the university to visit the library. The building obviously needed immediate attention. Keyes D. Metcalf, Librarian of Harvard University, and Frederick C. Wood, consulting engineer, were brought in as consultants: Mr. Wood for the architectural considerations and Mr. Metcalf for library problems.[8]

On October 13, 1955, the Executive Committee of the Board of Trustees adopted the proposals of Mr. Metcalf and Mr. Wood, who had conducted a study of library conditions at Cornell in the spring of 1954.[9] Both Mr. Metcalf and Mr. Wood issued reports of their findings. Mr. Metcalf's solution was to convert the old library building into an undergraduate library and to erect a new research library on the site of Boardman Hall.[10] Mr. Wood's conclusions were similar.[11]

These reports contained two key features. Mr. Wood's was an economic analysis showing that Boardman Hall occupied one of Cornell's most valuable pieces of land, but that the building itself was among the most inefficient. "Mr. Metcalf, on the other hand, through his analysis of the situation was able to show quite clearly that the existing building could be made into a satisfactory undergraduate library without disturbing its exterior lines, whereas it could not be made into a graduate and research library without that change."[12] The plan finally adopted by the Library Board and the university administration on July 21, 1955, was for "a two building central library, consisting of a new Graduate and Research Library on the site of Boardman Hall and the present Library Building remodeled and converted into an undergraduate library."[13]

The existing library building determined, in part, the final decision: "it was not large enough, without an addition, to serve as the research library; it was adequate in size as the undergraduate library."[14] For sentimental and aesthetic reasons, the old building was retained without altering its exterior.

A careful analysis of the advantages and disadvantages of an undergraduate library had been undertaken during the long years of planning. Among the advantages of an undergraduate library, as seen at Cornell, were direct access to books selected to correspond to the needs and interests of the undergraduate and the "informal and simple organization of the library and its services designed to facilitate undergraduate use."[15] One disadvantage of an undergraduate library, as seen at Cornell, is that the intellectual challenge of a large collection is lost to the student. It is also difficult and in some ways undesirable arbitrarily to divide knowledge into two levels. Perhaps the main consideration to administrators is the considerable expense involved in duplication of books and staff. The inconvenience to the user which results in having to look in two places for material is considered a disadvantage.[16]

Cornell's undergraduate library was intended to serve students enrolled in courses in the College of Arts and Sciences. The undergraduate library was not to be a new department library, nor was it to conflict with the services given by the department and college libraries.[17]

> The plan recognizes that library service to a large university community involves several disparate elements and that, under certain circumstances, it is desirable to recognize these elements, to separate them and to make special provision for them as the best means of accommodating the number of books, readers, and staff that are involved.[18]

Actual planning began in 1956 with a preliminary program for the undergraduate library. One thousand to 1300 seats and 100,000 to 150,000 volumes were the original requirements. Objectives and functions for reference, periodicals, reserve books, audio materials, circulation, and bound newspapers and microtexts were part of the program. The reference collection was to consist of 2000 to 3000 volumes, supporting the chief teaching function of the library. About 150 current periodical titles with ten-year back files were to provide for the undergraduate's needs. An area accommodating 4000 to 6000 volumes on closed reserve was considered sufficient, as there was also to be an open-shelf reserve collection. Discs, tapes, and other recording media of speeches, poetry, and dramatic readings were to be provided. No bound newspapers or microtexts were to be housed in the undergraduate library.[19]

Nothing further happened regarding the planning of the undergraduate library until after the authorization for the taking of bids for the Olin Library, the new central research library, in October, 1958. At this point, the provost of the university appointed the Undergraduate Library Committee, a subcommittee of the Library Board, with Professor Robert M. Adams as chairman.[20]

First, the Undergraduate Library Committee reviewed the 1956 preliminary program for the undergraduate library. Recommended changes in the April, 1959, report were:

(1) that a group of small study rooms be provided,
(2) that every effort be made to provide adequate seating without introducing a second deck in the main reading room, and
(3) that additional carrel desks be provided in the existing multi-tier stacks.[21]

As a result, the committee drafted a new "Program for the Undergraduate Library" in July, 1959. The only change in the objectives and functions was to increase the capacity of the closed-reserve section from 6000 to 8000 volumes. The main differences in the plans were that the new plan called for more reading space.[22] There were no major changes planned for the building's interior dimensions. The southwest bookstack remained as the only actual bookstack, while the others were gutted and converted to reading areas. The only area to be left exactly as it was was the Andrew D. White Library, which serves as "a permanent memorial to its donor and its period."[23]

FINANCING

Once the general program of library development had been determined and the planning program begun, the next task was to undertake a fund-raising drive to make the new library a reality. When John M. Olin gave $3,000,000 for a new research library in 1957, part of the problem was resolved, but funds were still needed for the renovation of the old library building.[24]

In April, 1961, working drawings were completed and bids were let for the undergraduate library building. The resulting bids were higher than had been anticipated and were, therefore, rejected. Revised plans made changes where possible to bring the costs down to a more realistic level. The total cost was $1,250,000.

Completion of the project came closer to reality by the generous and timely gift of $200,000 by Arthur H. Dean, Chairman of the Board of Trustees, in June, 1961.[25] In August, 1962, Harold D. Uris and Percy Uris, of New York City, gave $1,000,000 for the support of the undergraduate library. These two gifts financed the renovation and furnishings of the undergraduate library. In recognition of the Uris gift, the undergraduate library became the Uris Library.[26] There were other small gifts which the university had been accumulating for several years that were allocated for the Uris Library. The remainder of the necessary money came from the General Alumni Fund of unrestricted gifts to the university.[27]

THE BUILDING

Description

Unlike the other undergraduate libraries considered here (except Indiana), the Uris Library at Cornell was not housed in a new building designed to meet the needs of the undergraduate student. To retain the original flavor of the building, many of its unusual features were preserved, but not the crowded, musty, and congested aspects of the old building. In their place are light, air, and plenty of room. The architectural firm of Warner, Burns, Toan and Lunde, of New York, served as architects. Its job was to convert the old, drab, overcrowded building into a modern functional one.

Most of the renovation work was "resurfacing of walls, ceiling, and floors," although some walls were knocked out and others put up in order to make the building functional.[28] After completion of the work, the transformation was somewhat of a shock to the faculty and students. The library opened on September 19, 1962.[29]

Dean reading room, Uris Library

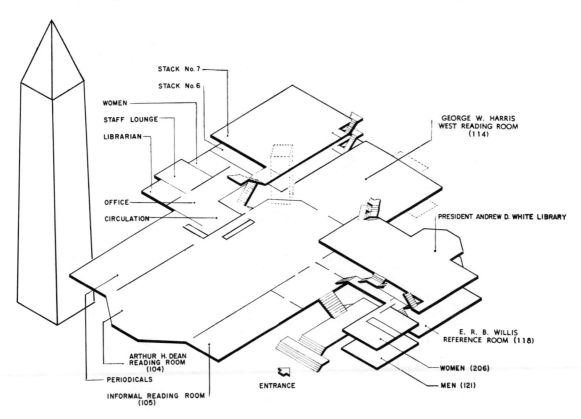

Fig. 26. First floor, Uris Library

The renovated building consists of three main floors containing 50,000 square feet, but in actuality there are thirty-two different floor levels. On the main level are the lobby, an informal reading room, the Arthur H. Dean reading room, the circulation desk, the librarian's office and staff lounge, the periodical desk and alcove, stacks, the west reading room, the reference room, and the President Andrew D. White Library (Fig. 26). The informal reading room, the former reference room, is a smoking room where conversation is permitted. Furnished primarily with lounge furniture, it has some small reading tables and some carrels.

The lobby, which is rather small, contains only an exit inspection station. The Arthur H. Dean reading room remains much the same as it was in the old building. A new acoustical ceiling was installed, and the circulation desk was moved from the west end of the room to the south side. The large fireplace and an arch directly across the room from it were uncovered and restored. Refinished reading tables which had been in use since the library opened in 1891 were put back in the room. The card catalog is in the west end of the room where the circulation desk used to be. The circulation desk and work area are in what was formerly a stack area. Directly behind the circulation desk is the librarian's office. Next to this is the staff lounge and in front of that a work area. The periodical desk and alcove occupy the former reserve-book reading alcove which houses the unbound periodicals, college catalogs, and the newspaper collection. The George W. Harris west reading room was created by gutting the west eight levels of book stacks. The furniture in the room features some of the old slant-top tables from the original building and new Douglass carrels. The E. R. B. Willis reference room occupies the former catalog room on the north side of the building off the main lobby. It has shelving for 3000 volumes and seating for forty-six readers.

Only one stack area was retained for its original purpose. The southwest stack, added to the building in 1937, provides shelving for the book collection — exclusive of reserve and

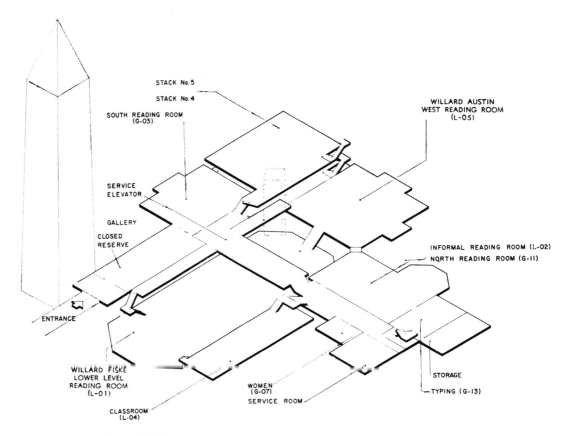

STACK No. 5

STACK No. 4

SOUTH READING ROOM
(G-03)

WILLARD AUSTIN
WEST READING ROOM
(L-05)

SERVICE
ELEVATOR

GALLERY

CLOSED
RESERVE

INFORMAL READING ROOM (L-02)

NORTH READING ROOM (G-11)

ENTRANCE

WILLARD FISKE
LOWER LEVEL
READING ROOM
(L-01)

STORAGE

TYPING (G-13)

WOMEN
(G-07)
SERVICE ROOM

CLASSROOM
(L-04)

Fig. 27. Lower floor, Uris Library

reference books and current periodicals. Only the top seven levels house the collection; levels one and two, which are both underground, are only for storage.

The turn-of-the-century charm of the library was retained in the President Andrew D. White Library which honors the university's first president. The ornate three tiers of stacks were regilded. At present, the room has no specific purpose except to serve as a secluded reading area. The desks on the upper tiers of stacks are equipped for individual listening from the listening rooms.[30]

The lower level consists of the McGraw Tower entrance, the reserve desk, the lower south reading room, a classroom, the north reading room, and a typing room (Fig. 27). The reserve desk is on a newly constructed level in the upper portion of the old periodical room. All closed-reserve books are behind this desk. The lower south reading room is one level of the old south stacks. Part of the room has been taken over for the reserve librarian's office and another area houses the Xerox machine. The room is for students studying together or for students who wish to study out loud. The Willard Austin west reading room is a former stack area and contains slant-top tables, regular tables, and some Douglass carrels. The Willard Fiske lower-level reading room is found in the former stacks areas known as crypts 1 and 2. Divided into two sections, the smaller, closed-off section is a reading room in which smoking is permitted. There are more of the old divided tables in the larger area along with lounge furniture and individual carrels. The present classroom, which seats about 70 persons, occupies the former documents area and is used primarily for the orientation lectures given by the staff to all new freshmen each fall. It is also hooked up to the listening rooms so that large classes can listen as a group. A movie screen is provided. The former Acquisition Department, now the north reading room and a typing room, is immediately below the reference room. Beyond the reading room, is a small typing room equipped with coin-o-matic typewriters. Behind that is a small storage area.

The upper level of the library consists of the listening-room complex, the second and third tiers of the White Library stacks, the Otto Kinkeldey west reading room, two levels of stacks, a seminar room, and the south reading room (Fig. 28). The listening-room complex contains the audio-control room, the group listening room, and an individual listening room. The audio-control room is in the former office of the assistant director for readers services. The group listening room occupies the former classics seminar room, and the individual listening room is in the former American history seminar room. The Otto Kinkeldey west reading room, a part of the converted stack area, has reading tables for eight, Douglass carrels, and a few lounge chairs. The south reading room is similar to the Kinkeldey west reading room in arrangement and appearance.

Before the renovation in 1961, there was no elevator in the building, but one was installed in the stack area during the renovation.[31]

Furnishings

The total seating for the library is 1067 (Table 23): 245 lounge seats, 363 individual carrels (about one third of the total seating), and 459 places at tables that seat from four to twelve readers.[32] There are 608 individual seats, which is 57 percent of the seating capacity.

One distinguishing feature about the seating in the Uris Library is the use of Douglass carrels. The Douglass carrel is a double- or triple-staggered series of carrels placed side by side. The readers face in opposite directions and are separated by a partition (Fig. 29).[33]

The furniture found throughout the building is of three different types. First, there is the old furniture from the original library, including 16 divided-top tables, 8 slope-top tables, and some refinished bookcases.[34] Second, 300 blond birch chairs, added to the library in 1951, were retained for use. Third, all the new furniture (tables, chairs, and carrels) is walnut. There was hesitation about combining the three styles, but the overall effect has been pleasing.[35] The dark furniture helps maintain the old character of the building. The muted tones used in the lounge furniture—black, orange, and tan—were

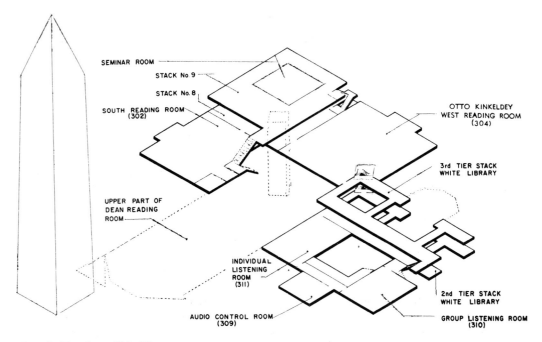

Fig. 28. Top floor, Uris Library

TABLE 23

SEATING IN THE URIS LIBRARY[a]

Dean reading room	142
Periodical alcove	47
Reference room	43
Informal reading room	44
Harris west reading room	59
White Library	29
Kinkeldey west reading room	65
Upper south reading room	53
Carrels in stacks	188
Seminar room (9th level)	12
North reading room	44
Typing room	15
Fiske reading room	107
Lower-level informal room	41
Austin west reading room	60
Lower south reading room	29
Classroom (as a reading room)	57
Listening rooms	32
Total	1,067

[a]"Seating Capacity in the Undergraduate Library," Dec. 23, 1964 (in the files of the Uris Library).

chosen for the same reason.[36] The furniture has been so arranged that there is a variety of seating in each of the many reading rooms. In the stack area, there are only carrels. In the larger reading areas, small islands of lounge chairs break up the blocks of tables. Bookstacks are not used for this purpose.

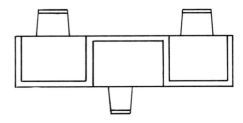

Fig. 29. *Douglass carrel*

New lighting was installed in all areas of the building with the exception of the Dean reading room and the periodical alcove, which had new lighting installed in 1951. Since this lighting provides 40 to 50 footcandles, it seemed sufficient.[37] This room has fluorescent lighting with egg-crate troffers. In the areas where new lighting was installed, recessed fluorescent lighting was used, except in the reference room where the ceiling was not thick enough to accommodate it. Seventy-footcandle lighting was provided for all reading and work areas.[38] A proposal for a luminous ceiling for the Dean reading room is being considered.[39]

Floor covering throughout the building is vinyl tile, which has proven satisfactory everywhere except in the Dean reading room where the high ceiling and heavy traffic cause excessive noise. Because it is the largest reading room and because the circulation desk, the periodical alcove, and the main entrance to the stack area are on this floor, there is a considerable amount of traffic. An acoustical engineer was consulted about the problem, and at his suggestion, nylon carpeting was installed in this area in December, 1965. Carpeting was also put in five of the smaller rooms on the main level.[40]

BOOK COLLECTION

General Collection

Planning the book collection for the Uris Library at Cornell began about four years before the library opened. The book-selection process consisted of four steps:

> definition of the kind of book we want; compilation of a comprehensive list of titles which might be this kind of book; determination of those titles on this list which actually are this kind of book; and the purchasing and processing of the titles selected with the amount of duplication determined.[41]

Several answers were suggested for the first of these problems: the definition of an under-graduate book. It might be a book that a member of the faculty considers an undergraduate book, i.e., one put on a reading list. It might be a book that will or should be used two or three or four times a year. An undergraduate book would also be a book placed on re-serve for an undergraduate course. It might be a "best book" or a standard title that every undergraduate should be exposed to. It might also be a book that would be an "invitation to learning" for the student.[42]

In trying to define an undergraduate book, several factors had to be considered, such as the relationship of the Uris Library to the Research Library, the clientele the Uris Li-brary would attempt to serve (all undergraduates, only freshmen and sophomores, only students in the College of Arts and Sciences), and the extent to which the library was to be an open-shelf collection. Only after answering these questions and others could the next step—the compilation of a list of titles—be undertaken.[43]

Tentative general policies for book selection were finally compiled. The collection was to include books for use below the extensive research level. In other words, the student would be able to find materials in the Uris Library to write a freshman theme but not a senior seminar paper. The collection would exclude specialized works, "less-used" books, and poor or unreliable works. Duplication would be emphasized as a policy for the under-graduate library. Foreign language works and browsing titles would be considered ques-tionable materials for inclusion.[44]

The preliminary conception of the Uris Library collection delineated one which would create a "thoroughly informed and cultured modern person."[45] The book collection of the undergraduate library was based on the needs of the undergraduate student in courses and the instructional program, and provided books for exploration, recreation, and stimu-lation. In a general letter to the faculty of the College of Arts and Sciences, Robert Adams described the essence of the undergraduate collection:

> Our preliminary conception of the undergraduate collection is that it will contain as a core the books essential to the routine instructional program of the College of Arts and Sciences. It will contain these books in a number of copies, to be determined as far as possible according to the succinct formula E + 1 (Enough plus 1). In addition it will contain the best of those books which in the judgment of the university faculty are requisite to create a thoroughly informed and cultured modern person. . . . Our aim is to provide a library large enough so that the undergraduate has plenty of elbow room for exploration, selective enough so that exploration is in effect directed, and not so large that it will bewilder or discourage him.[46]

The Uris Library collection was to be a 100 percent duplication of titles in the Olin Library. Only under unusual circumstances would a book be found only in the Uris Library. Although the undergraduate student was to have his own collection, he would by no means be restricted to use of the Uris Library collection. In fact, for extensive papers he was urged to use the facilities of the Research Library, just as any graduate student or faculty member was welcome to avail himself of the ready accessibility of the books in the Uris Library.[47]

In order to compile a comprehensive list of books, the staff used many different sources. The two lists used most extensively were the shelf list of the Undergraduate Library of the University of Michigan and the catalog of the Lamont Library. The Goldwin Smith Library was the predecessor of the Uris Library in that it was the department library for the College of Arts and Sciences, and its collection served as the core collection for the undergraduate library.[48] To supplement the previous sources, the Librarian of the Goldwin Smith Library, Charles A. Carpenter, Jr., compiled a list of approximately 11,000 titles, many of which (about 5000) were in English and American literature.[49]

In February, 1959, the University Library purchased the stock of the Pyetell Bookshop in New York City "to serve as the nucleus of the Undergraduate Library book collection."[50] The collection contained many standard literary, historical, biographical, and general materials. Cards were made for 50,000 titles to be included in the initial selection. The library staff selected the titles suitable for the collection.[51] Reserve lists, syllabi, recommended-reading lists, and University Library duplicates formed a basis for the collection.[52]

In actuality, only cards for the University of Michigan shelf list were submitted to the faculty. In the fall of 1959, the library purchased two photocopies of the University of Michigan Undergraduate Library shelf list—one in bound book form and the other cut into 3-inch by 5-inch slips. The slips were then sorted into subject areas by Library of Congress classes and departments at Cornell.[53]

The participation of faculty members in the selection process was considered essential, because their value was "in their knowledge of books, in their ability to describe and evaluate books."[54] But to use this knowledge to best advantage, a preliminary list was necessary as a beginning point.

In the final selection of the book collection, several considerations were kept in mind. The books selected were to be relevant to this kind of collection. There was to be some balance in the collection. The question "of editions, duplicates, popularizations, recreational reading, textbooks and texts which students are required to purchase, books available in paperback, books written in foreign languages, and books which might be on reserve for years" were also weighed in the final selection process.[55]

The packets of cards sent to the departments in September, 1959, contained about 50,000 titles. The faculties were to rate these in three categories:

    1 equals Must have; strongly advise; get by all means
    2 equals Nice to have but not essential
    x equals Don't bother; it isn't worth having for undergraduates.[56]

The faculties were also to indicate desirable editions and the number of copies they felt necessary.[57] The academic departments did not select in all subject areas. The library staff checked areas which were outside specific departmental interests.[58] The Undergraduate Library Subcommittee also reviewed some of the cards.[59]

By the end of the Spring Semester, 1960, all cards were to be returned. Upon receipt, the cards were sorted by the ratings. The master purchasing list consisted of the 1's and additional titles recommended by the faculty.[60] After the faculty and the library staff checked the cards, the selections were checked against the holdings of the Goldwin Smith Library and the Pyetell collection to see which titles were already available and which would have to be purchased.[61]

Of the University of Michigan shelf list cards checked, "50% of the total titles were rated 1; 20% were rated 2; 25% were rated x; and 5% not rated at all."[62] Because the Michigan shelf list included publications only up to 1958, the Goldwin Smith librarian checked *Publishers' Weekly, American Book Publishing Record,* and the *Technical Book Review Index* from 1958 to 1961.[63]

The assembled cards were put in two files: one for the Michigan and faculty list and another for the reserve books and the selections made by Charles Carpenter. The books in the first category were automatically ordered, while those in the second group were checked against the holdings of the Research Library. If there was only one copy, another copy was ordered. If there were multiple copies, a decision based on condition and use determined whether to transfer the copies or to order new ones.[64]

After the departments returned the cards, an estimated 25,000 titles remained to be purchased. Based on a sampling of 1000 titles, it was determined that 4000 titles would be transferred from Olin Library, that 11,500 titles were in print and would be ordered from dealers and publishers, and that 9000 titles were out of print.[65] The 6200 titles (approximately 8000 volumes) in the Goldwin Smith Library were to be moved *in toto* to Uris.[66]

In acquiring the collection, the purchase of in-print items and the transfer of books from Olin received priority. The staff of the Olin Acquisition and Cataloging departments processed the books and periodicals, with one exception. In February, 1961, a special staff of sixteen persons worked on the sorting, searching, cataloging, and processing of the books that were in the Pyetell collection which were to be added to the Uris Library book collection.[67]

In addition to those books purchased for the Uris Library, some books and a large number of back files of periodicals were received as gifts from friends and faculty of Cornell.[68] A list of the desired titles given in a general letter to the faculty and an article in the *Cornell Alumni News* prompted most of the gifts. A plea was made largely because there was not a sufficient budget to provide extensive runs of back files of periodicals.[69]

The Uris Library opened with a book collection of 42,722 volumes—nearly equal in size to the proposed opening collection of 50,000 volumes (Table 24). In the three years during which the library has been open, the collection has grown to 57,103 volumes, an increase of 14,381 volumes, or 33 percent. In a count taken from the shelf list, the collection shows 38,998 titles, with the heaviest concentration being in literature and the social sciences (J's).[70]

TABLE 24

GROWTH OF THE BOOK COLLECTION, URIS LIBRARY

	INCREASE	TOTAL	PERCENT INCREASE
1961–62		42,722	
1962–63	3,876	46,404	8
1963–64	6,200	52,032	12
1964–65	5,386	57,103	9

The collection is strong in literature (American, English, Russian) and history. Philosophy, drama and speech, economics and government are also strong areas. Weaknesses are in areas in which there are college or department libraries, as in fine arts, physics, chemistry, and education. The collection is also weak in the area of out-of-print books. Overall, the humanities are stronger than the social sciences, and the sciences are the weakest of the three.[71] An effort is being made to build up the collection in areas of weakness. In the sciences, general titles are being purchased to round out the collection.

Because of the lack of sufficient funds to purchase multiple copies of recent books for the general collection, duplicate copies are purchased only when extensive use of a title is anticipated.[72]

Fortunately, some of the problems created by an insufficient budget can be corrected, or at least partially corrected. A donor gave $100,000 to the Uris Library for a "book endowment as a memorial to his brother." Only the yearly interest—$6000 to $7000— will be used for the purchase of books "in the fields of American history, sociology, and economics."[73] The endowment will enable the library to spend its regular book budget in areas in which the collection needs strengthening and to purchase the needed duplicate copies for the general collection.

Some weeding of the collection has already been done. Primarily, two types of materials are being removed. Unused multiple copies, mainly of reserve books, are an obvious target for weeding.[74] The other category of books being weeded consists of those which originally should not have been included in the collection. Because there were collections available to draw from when the Uris Library collection was begun, there was a tendency to include some books in the collection merely because they were readily available. There are also always some mistakes in purchasing which have to be weeded out. The weeded books are usually incorporated into the research collection.[75]

To keep the collection in the best possible condition, there is an annual inventory of the entire collection (Table 25). Not only is the book collection kept under close scrutiny by an annual inventory, but it is also possible to keep the catalog and the shelf list in correct order. The number of missing books per year has been kept relatively low, particularly in view of the heavy use of the library and the collection.[76]

TABLE 25

RECORD OF INVENTORIES, URIS LIBRARY

	MISSING TITLES	MISSING VOLUMES	PERCENT OF COLLECTION
1962–63	630	Not recorded	1
1963–64	549	599	1
1964–65	541	581	.9

The present philosophy of book selection is based on the curricular needs of the undergraduate student. Exclusions include such things as best sellers unless the book is, in addition, a book of literary merit. Because there is a limited amount of money, book selection is an exacting task. To select what is going to be needed, the book selector has to be aware of what the faculty requires of the student and what interests the students themselves have.

The initial periodical collection of about 250 titles (presently 282) for the Uris Library was selected primarily by the Olin Library Reference Department staff. Titles from the Michigan shelf list and those suggested by Cornell faculty members formed the basis of the list. Only those titles most needed by undergraduate students were to be included. It was decided to include back files for only ten years, but many exceptions were made to provide important materials for undergraduate students.[77] Back files were not provided for all periodicals. In some cases, they were not needed, and in some cases, they were unavailable or there were no funds with which to purchase them.[78]

Due to lack of funds, some back files of periodicals have yet to be acquired. These files are needed, because more and more use is being made of periodicals as the staffs of both Olin and Uris libraries train the undergraduate students to use the periodicals in Uris, where they have easier access to them.[79]

The arrangement of materials in the stacks was determined by a study of the subject areas of heaviest circulation in the Olin Library. The sixth level, which is on the same level as the Dean reading room, houses the bound periodicals, which are arranged alphabetically by title.[80] Literature is on the seventh and eighth levels; the sciences, classes Q–Z,[81] are on the ninth level; the social sciences, G–N, are on the fifth level; history (except American, class D) is on the fourth level; and the third level contains classes C, E, and F.[82]

The collection for the listening rooms consists solely of phonograph recordings and tapes of the spoken arts to supplement class readings and for recreational listening. No music is provided, because two music collections were already available on the campus.[83] The library also has a policy of taping literary lectures and poetry readings that take place on the campus for inclusion in the collection.[84] In June, 1964, the collection contained 317 tapes. A budget of $2000 is available to purchase materials for the collection.[85] All materials are for building use only.[86]

Reference Collection

The reference staff of the Olin Library selected the reference collection for the Uris Library. They pulled from the Michigan shelf list cards the reference titles which the Cornell faculty rated as 1 choices. To these were added reference titles from other bibliographic sources.[87]

The reference collection contains about 2653 volumes. The reference room has a capacity of approximately 3000 volumes. All materials in the collection are in English with the exception of French, German, and Italian dictionaries and encyclopedias. "The collection has been selected to meet the needs of the first two years of instruction in the social sciences and humanities."[88]

Reserve Collection

Reserve books, purchased at a general ratio of one copy to ten students, seem to be sufficient except in times of extreme pressure.[89] One copy for fifteen students is used for supplementary reading. Although these figures constitute guidelines, they do not imply rigid rules to be strictly adhered to. The reserve librarian has to be able to determine what the use of any individual title will be by talking with the instructor and then deciding if the ratio applies or not.[90]

Most of the books now placed on reserve are Uris Library books (in 1964, 4451 volumes belonged to Uris Library, 4075 to Olin, and 344 to other libraries, but in 1965, 5921 volumes belonged to Uris Library, 1964 to Olin, and 544 to other libraries).[91] About 30 percent of the books are borrowed from other libraries—primarily Olin—and 70 percent belong to the Uris Library. When the library opened, this percentage was just the reverse. Some of the borrowing is necessitated by a budget insufficient to purchase all that is needed, although about $10,000 a year is now being spent on reserve books, which is about a third of the total book budget.[92]

Open Access to the Collection

The planning of the undergraduate library centered on two important principles:

> First, books and students must be brought as close together as possible. Second, it is desirable to have as many different kinds of study location and seating arrangements as possible.[93]

To fulfill the first principle, students have access to the whole building. Books and reading accommodations are side by side. There are carrels in the stack area and books in most reading rooms.[94] The majority of the books, with the exception of those on closed reserve, are to be on open shelves. Seating provisions emphasize single desks and individual carrels in addition to smoking areas, a general reading room, and several smaller reading rooms.[95]

The undergraduate library was to be more than just additional space for readers and books. It was to provide the means whereby instruction could be improved "by requiring greater use of library materials."[96] The introduction of honors courses and individual study projects required the student to abandon the textbook and reserve book and seek out materials on his own initiative. In order to do this, the student needed access to books, not merely to a card catalog.

Free access to books is necessary to encourage reading habits in students who have not acquired them by the time they come to college. To do this, the students should become familiar with a small collection.[97] Summed up briefly, the problem was this:

> The College of Arts and Sciences provides the central core of liberal instruction in the University; books are the medium for most of our teaching, and reading is our principal instrument, but all undergraduates who take courses in the humanities and the social sciences in the College must use a library which has too little room, which contains too many unselected titles, and which interposes too many obstacles between the reader and his books.[98]

SERVICES

Reference

The reference staff consists of the reference librarian and three professional assistants. However, each of the other members of the professional staff spends some time—usually ranging from ten to fifteen hours a week—at the reference desk, depending on the pressure of his other duties. The professional assistants in reference are also responsible for catalog maintenance, preparation of general collection orders, and "maintenance of the Reference Collection and preparation of reserve books orders."[99]

Reference questions have not been as numerous as expected, nor did the additional service point relieve the pressure on the Olin Reference Department. There has been a steady increase in the number of general questions (41 percent), a decrease in the number of informational or directional questions (9 percent), but an increase in the number of search questions (Table 26). The totals, however, show a general decrease. Cornell defines a general or information question as one which takes less than fifteen minutes to answer; a search question takes fifteen minutes to an hour.[100]

TABLE 26

REFERENCE STATISTICS, URIS LIBRARY

	GENERAL QUESTIONS	SEARCH QUESTIONS	INFORMATIONAL QUESTIONS	PROBLEM QUESTIONS	TOTAL
1962–63	2,800	17	3,792	0	6,609
1963–64	3,830	55	2,446	4	6,335
1964–65	3,957	48	2,423	0	6,428

In order to avoid duplication of effort on some of the more difficult questions and for those that occur repeatedly, a list of reference questions and the answers is maintained. An examination of this record shows that most of the questions are course related, the majority being in the area of literature.[101] Reference service reaches peaks about the first of October and the end of May. "The most used materials in the Reference Collection are the indexes to literary criticism, mathematical tables and language dictionaries."[102]

Circulation

A McBee Keysort charging system is used for all stack collection books. The loan period is four weeks, but books may be recalled after two weeks if there is a request by another borrower. Graduate students and faculty do not have extended loan privileges.

Beyond the regular routines of charging and discharging books, the staff of the circulation desk is also responsible for the periodical collection, the college catalogs (both are noncirculating), and searches of titles recommended for purchase.[103]

One feature of the circulation desk is the lack of stationary shelving for books waiting to be shelved. Instead of stationary shelves, book trucks are used. Diagrammed areas on the floor show the various Library of Congress classes, and book trucks are placed at each location. Returned books are placed on these trucks in classified order. After one truck is filled, it is removed and replaced by an empty truck, allowing the books to be shelved from the truck on which they are placed. Such a system reduces the number of handlings for each volume.[104]

Another unusual feature is the lack of student shelvers. The stack supervisor does all shelving and searching for missing and lost books.[105]

Reserve

Reserve procedures in Uris Library are centered at the reserve desk. There are two kinds of reserve materials: open reserve and closed reserve. All required reading is on closed reserve; supplementary and suggested materials are on open reserve. At the outset, the library recognized the value of advertising books by duplication. It was hoped that there would be little need for reserve books, because of the degree of duplication that would be possible. However, this has not been the case.[106]

Open reserve books are located in the lower-level reading room, the north reading room, and the lower south reading room.[107] Closed-reserve books circulate for two hours and can be renewed. Open-shelf reserve books circulate for one, two, or three days as indicated on the books on colored bands.[108] An open-shelf reserve, which limits books to room use until 10:00 P.M., was initiated to keep all the books together but allow the student to browse through them.[109]

For the Fall Semester, 1962, there were approximately 7500 volumes (from 165 lists) on reserve, whereas in the Spring Semester, there were only 6500 (from 160 lists).[110] In the Spring Semester, there were 4500 volumes (1779 titles) on closed reserve and 4460 volumes (2951 titles) on open reserve, making a total of 8960 volumes on reserve.[111] During the Spring Semester, 1965, there were 5293 volumes (1669 titles) on closed reserve and 3136 (3351 titles) on open-shelf reserve, totaling 8429 volumes (5020 titles) on reserve.[112] For the Fall Semester, 1965, there were approximately 6000 volumes on closed reserve and 3000 volumes on open reserve. The main entry in the card catalog has a plastic jacket indicating the title is on reserve.[113]

Probably Uris Library's major problem has been reserve books. Two factors account for most of the problems. First, it once took about twenty days to acquire a new reserve book on a rush basis. Beginning in January, 1966, all "Rush Reserve" books are ordered through a local book shop, reducing the delay to 11.5 days.[114] The second problem arose because of the time it took to process a book for the reserve collection (ten days if it is in the Uris Library and longer if it has to be borrowed from another library). If the lists do not arrive far enough in advance—which is often the case—an assignment may be made before the books have reached the reserve shelves. A third problem was the lack of sufficient duplicate copies of reserve titles.[115]

Special Services

The classroom is one special feature of the Uris Library. If the need arises, the room can quickly be transformed into a reading room by using folding tables. Providing fifty-seven seats, this room is used primarily for orientation lectures each October for all freshmen English classes.[116] Members of the Uris Library staff give the lectures. When the lectures began, each was approximately fifty minutes long, providing general information on the library system with some details about the Olin Library. A major portion of the lecture dealt with the services and operations of the Uris Library. The card catalog, the Library of Congress Classification scheme, reference service, and loan regulations were part of the discussion.[117]

Until the Fall Semester, 1965, a brief tour of the building followed the lecture. The tour was discontinued, because of the short time available for it and the ineffectiveness of trying to talk to such a large group while showing them the building.[118] Approximately 2300 students are introduced to the library in this fashion each October.[119]

The listening-room complex includes a control room, a group listening room, and an individual listening room. At present, there are eight channels: one AM-FM radio channel, two channels for phonograph players, and five channels for tape-recorder players.[120] The system can be expanded to include twenty-five channels.[121]

There are forty stations wired for individual listening: sixteen in the individual listening room, sixteen in the group listening room, and eight in the White Library. If the seats in the classroom are included, this number would be greatly increased, although those are not equipped for individual listening.[122]

There is a special catalog located in the listening-room complex which lists all of the recordings in the library. A main entry for each recording is filed in the Uris public catalog and in the Olin union catalog.[123]

Other special services included assigning carrels to honors students in the College of Arts and Sciences. Only those students who were actually working on their honors papers were eligible. During 1962–63 and 1963–64, the students could charge books to their carrels, but this policy has since been discontinued.

Simplification and Centralization

The Uris Library made it possible to bring together sufficient study seats and a collection chosen to meet the undergraduate's academic needs in the College of Arts and Sciences, thereby simplifying use of the library. Centralization, therefore, contributed to the simplification of library service. Efforts were also made to simplify library use by means of a less complicated card catalog, ease of access to books, etc.

Instruction in Library Use

One purpose of the Uris Library was to serve as a teaching laboratory. In conjunction with the English Department, library orientation lectures are given to all freshman English classes by members of the Uris staff. The reference staff assists in helping individual students to learn how to use the library, as their needs arise.

STAFF

To administer the collection and the library, the Librarian of the Goldwin Smith Library, Charles A. Carpenter, was designated as the librarian-elect of the undergraduate library. When Mr. Carpenter resigned from the staff in 1961, Billy R. Wilkinson of the Olin reference staff was appointed in his place.[124]

The library opened with a staff of nine professional librarians, thirteen nonprofessional full-time employees, and student assistants. Each of the professional staff has a specific area of responsibility in addition to doing reference work. The positions are: librarian, reference (4), circulation, reserve (2), and listening rooms. All the professional staff do reference work and book selection, with the final decision for the latter being made by the librarian.[125]

The staff of the Uris Library has largely been young. In some instances, it is felt that a younger person can better understand and develop a better rapport with the students.

Originally, professional staff members were on duty whenever the library was open, which was from 8:00 A.M. to 11:30 P.M. In 1965, this was altered, and professional service stopped at 10:00 P.M. because there was not sufficient demand for it after that hour.[126] There is no professional service on Saturday night, but since 1962, it has been provided on Sunday night.

The professional staff of Uris Library is a flexible one. The summer school at Cornell is small, and, as a result, the Uris Library closes except for limited reserve service. During this time, the Uris staff—professionals and nonprofessionals—work in the Olin Library or in one of the department libraries. The interchange of staff also takes place during the regular terms. Such an interchange aids the service provided in those libraries and adds "to the experience and knowledge of the Uris staff."[127]

Administratively, the Uris librarian reports to the assistant director for readers services, as do the other school and college librarians. Within the Uris Library, the administrative structure is a simple one (Fig. 30).

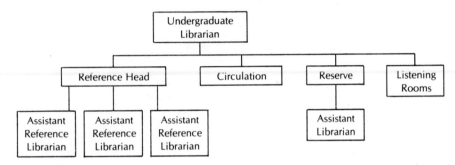

Fig. 30. Organization chart, Uris Library

LIBRARY USE

When the Uris Library first opened, there was some apprehension about how the undergraduates would react to the building. During the previous year, they had become accustomed to the Olin Library. When Uris opened its doors in September, 1962, only a few students came to see what the new library was like. But those who came liked what they saw and stayed. In contrast to Olin, the undergraduate had free run of the library; he could go anywhere in the building. Perhaps it satisfied his "urge for greater freedom."[128] By the time classes began, the Uris Library had "caught on," as the attendance figures show (Table 27). Within a month, circulation increased from 50 books per day to 150 per day.

TABLE 27

ATTENDANCE IN OLIN AND URIS LIBRARIES,
SEPTEMBER 19–23, 1962

	URIS	OLIN
September 19	1,497	1,195
20	2,854	1,691
21	3,067	2,230
22	2,808	1,142
23	2,673	901

One interesting fact about the use of the Uris Library is that attendance increased by 50 percent over what it was when the building served as the University Library. "The new Olin Library is used by approximately the same number that formerly used the old building, so that there is a net increase in the use of over 150 per cent."[129]

Even though total use of the two libraries has increased dramatically, attendance in the Uris Library has not risen much since it opened: 1962–63, 705,251; 1963–64, 758,331; 1964–65, 752,583. In fact, there was a decrease in use of .7 percent in 1964–65 compared with the use in 1963–64, although there has been an overall increase of 6 percent since the library opened. This is, however, less than the increase in undergraduate enrollment. It should be pointed out that attendance is kept manually by using hand tickers, allowing more possibility of error than an automatic device.

As the loan statistics show, regular circulation has increased by 72 percent (Table 28). The increase was more marked in 1963–64 than in 1964–65 partly because the figures for 1962–63 are only for a ten-month period. Reading room loans (which are actually stack books used in the building) are increasing more rapidly than are home loans. Circulation should be fairly stable because the enrollment (it increased 8 percent from September, 1962, to September, 1965) is limited. The increase in enrollment is, therefore, much less than the increase in circulation.

TABLE 28

CIRCULATION STATISTICS, URIS LIBRARY

	HOME LOANS	READING ROOM LOANS[b]	CARREL CHARGES	TOTAL	PERCENT INCREASE
1962–63[a]	34,268	14,812	205	40,285	
1963–64	41,644	22,224	172	64,040	58
1964–65	41,662	27,836	[c]	69,498	8

[a]Sept. – June 30, 1963.   [b]These are unofficial figures.   [c]Books are no longer charged to carrels.

In November, 1963, a study was made revealing that literature and the social sciences constitute the major areas of home circulation (Table 29). This is a predictable pattern since these are areas of concentration in the College of Arts and Sciences. The subjects that received the smallest use are those represented by department or college libraries.

Reserve statistics (Table 30) show an increase of 17 percent in the circulation of reserve books, which may indicate less reliance on closed-reserve materials in teaching methods. Although reading room use and overnight use have increased about the same amount (15 percent and 13 percent respectively), the use of open-shelf reserve books

TABLE 29

USE OF HOME CIRCULATION BOOKS, URIS LIBRARY[a]

SUBJECT	PERCENT OF TOTAL COLLECTION
Literature	32
Social Sciences	24
History	14
Religion, Philosophy, Psychology	14
Science	6
Mathematics	4
Arts	4
Other (R–Z of LC classes)	2

[a]Taken from the Uris Library *Annual Report*, 1963–64, p.13.

TABLE 30

TABLE 30

RESERVE STATISTICS, URIS LIBRARY

	READING ROOM USE	OVERNIGHT USE	OPEN-SHELF USE	TOTAL	PERCENT INCREASE
1962–63	111,676	8,515	24,289	144,480	
1963–64	107,901	9,682	35,683	153,266	6
1964–65	128,760	9,690	31,925	170,375	11

has increased 31 percent, which may indicate the students' preference for the open-shelf system. Books placed on open reserve are required reading only in the sense that an instructor placed a reading list on reserve for the student to choose the book or books he wants to read instead of assigning one specific title for the whole class.

The use of the listening rooms has risen more spectacularly than that of other facilities in the library. Since the complex opened, circulation has increased from 2247 to 6710, or 198 percent. During the first year of operation, little use was made of the facility mainly because students did not know about it. This is no longer the case as the increase in circulation indicates.

When the Uris Library opened, it was a quiet place to study. This continued to be true with few exceptions until 1962. Since then, study conditions have become somewhat less than desirable during the evening hours.

> It is an impossible place to study from 8 o'clock until 10 P.M. on some nights of the week. Usually, there is just too much activity, too much coming and going, too much socializing. In short too many lively and restless undergraduates. The good study conditions are shot down by the students themselves.
>
> Around 7 P.M. or a little earlier, the great entrance begins. It takes the next hour for everyone to settle down. When this is almost accomplished, it's time to wander around, smoke and talk in the lobbies and stairways, go to the Straight, etc., etc. This is the agenda for the next hour. We finally go through the settling down period again.
>
> From 10 P.M. until 11:30 P.M., the library is a good study place again.[130]

That is not to say that this routine is a nightly occurrence. Some evenings the library is a quiet, pleasant place. Some measures have been taken to reduce the noise, such as the installation of carpeting and the complete enclosure of one reading room, but they do not eliminate noise.

Although the undergraduates use the Uris Library, many of them also use Olin Library. Their use of Olin Library is justified if they have first exhausted the resources of the Uris Library. In January, 1965, a study was made on the use of books from the Olin circulation desk by undergraduates. The charges for an eighteen-day period were saved and then checked against the holdings of the Uris Library. Of the 3532 copies of monographs requested by undergraduates, Uris Library had 1039, or 29.4 percent. Several areas of deficiencies in the Uris Library holdings were also brought to light. Perhaps more serious was the use of periodicals in Olin by undergraduates when the Uris Library had the titles (especially since Olin Library has closed stacks). Of a total of 323 periodical titles requested, Uris had 98, or 30.3 percent; it had 32.8 percent of the volumes requested.

Efforts are being made to entice the 30 percent of the students who use Olin back to Uris. Added copies of material for which there are requests or recalls are being acquired. For periodicals, a list of frequently used titles found in Uris has been made available to the students. Olin Reference and Circulation departments try to refer undergraduates to the Uris Library for the use of these titles.[131]

Although a study was made of undergraduate use at Olin, it was not extended to other campus libraries. It seemed clear and reasonable that students in areas with departmental or college libraries use these libraries, since they are intended for the undergraduate, the graduate student, and the faculty member. But even though the undergraduate does use one of the departmental or school libraries, he also has to use the Uris Library for the courses he takes in the College of Arts and Sciences.[132]

In May, 1965, a survey was made to determine who the users of the Uris Library are.

> Just as would be expected, Uris Library is an undergraduate library: undergraduates accounted for 96% of the activity at the Reference Desk, the Reserve Desk, and in the Listening Rooms. At the Circulation Desk, undergraduates charged out 89.6% of the home use loans.[133]

The present generation of students makes one of the main uses of the library that of a study hall. At Cornell, this seems to stem from several factors. Many students feel that they cannot study in their living quarters: first, because of the socializing that is often prevalent, and second, because many of the new dormitories are built without sufficient attention to acoustics. Then "there is a long, long standing tradition at Cornell that boy meets girl at the library in the evening."[134]

Circulation and attendance figures support this view. In 1964–65, 752,583 persons entered the library, but total circulation (home and in building), including the listening rooms, was 246,583, indicating that about one out of every three persons who entered the library either checked out a book or listened to a recording. When it is considered that most students check out more than one book at a time, the ratio becomes even less.

SUMMARY

Even though use is not as high as might be desired, Billy R. Wilkinson feels that Uris has succeeded in becoming the undergraduates' own library. Uris Library is not sleek and new like the Olin Library, but it has a distinct character all its own which the students seem to like. They can find a variety of places to study, and books are readily accessible. Uris Library may not have attained all the goals set for it, but it is meeting the everyday needs of the undergraduate student.

The book collection was carefully planned to include a core collection centered in instruction in the humanities and the social sciences. The collection is weak in areas in which there are department libraries. Systematic weeding is being carried on to keep the collection up to date. The reserve collection contains required reading (on closed reserve) and supplementary or recommended reading (on open reserve). To bring books and students together, the majority of books are on open shelves.

As elsewhere, demand for reference service is not as great as anticipated. McBee Keysort circulation control is used and found satisfactory for the library's needs. The special services in the library include a classroom, listening rooms, and some smaller services. The listening rooms were slow to catch on but now receive heavy use. Instruction in library use is mainly in the form of a lecture to all freshman English classes.

The staff has been stable and has been, for the most part, a young one for a young clientele. Each staff member is responsible for one area besides doing reference work.

Although attendance has not increased greatly, circulation has. Use of the library has been hampered to a small extent by the noise created in the library. Carpeting of some areas has decreased this somewhat.

NOTES

[1]Cornell University. Library, *Report of the Director*, 1949–50, p.13.

[2]The Library Board at Cornell sits as an advisory group to the director of the library. It is composed of twelve to fourteen members of the faculty which are representative of the campus. (Interview with Mr. G. F. Shepherd, Assistant Di-

rector for Readers Services, Cornell University Library, Oct. 20, 1965.

[3]*Report of the Director*, 1949–50, p.13–14.

[4]*Ibid.*, 1950–51, p.10.

[5]*Ibid.*, 1952–53, p.8.

[6]Boardman Hall was an old classroom building which engineers and architects concluded had

more unusable space than usable space and considered it uneconomic to let it stand on such valuable property. (Interview with Billy R. Wilkinson, Librarian, Undergraduate Library, Cornell University, Oct. 21, 1965. Mr. Wilkinson has since left this position to work toward a doctorate at Columbia University.)

[7]Cornell University. Library, "The Library Building Program" (Ithaca: 1950), p. [85–87] (in the files of the University Library).

[8]Interview with Stephen A. McCarthy, Director of the University Libraries, Cornell University, Oct. 20, 1965.

[9]*Report of the Director*, 1955–56, p.[1]

[10]Keyes D. Metcalf and Frederick C. Wood, "Central Library Facilities: The Wood Report. The Metcalf Report" (Ithaca: Cornell University Libraries, 1955), p.6.

[11]*Ibid.*, p.19.

[12]Interview with Stephen A. McCarthy.

[13]*Report of the Director*, 1955–56, p.[1].

[14]Stephen A. McCarthy, "The Cornell Library System," in Cornell University. Library, *The Cornell Library Conference; Papers Read at the Dedication of the Central Libraries, October, 1962* (Ithaca: Cornell University Library, 1964), p.27.

[15]Cornell University. Library, "The Library Building Program," p.[1–2] (in the files of the University Library).

[16]*Ibid.*

[17]Minutes of the Meeting of the Ad Hoc Committee, Feb. 14, 1950 (in the files of the University Library).

[18]McCarthy, *The Cornell Library Conference,* p.27.

[19]Cornell University. Library, "Program for the Undergraduate Library," March 26, 1955 (in the files of the University Library).

[20]*Report of the Director*, 1958–59, p. 2, 4.

[21]*Ibid.*, p.4.

[22]Cornell University. Library, "Program for the Undergraduate Library," July 13, 1959 (in the files of the University Library).

[23]William R. Keast, "What about the Undergraduates," Oct. 10, 1959 (in the files of the Uris Library).

[24]*Report of the Director*, 1956–57, p.[1].

[25]*Ithaca Journal*, Aug. 30, 1962, p.5.

[26]Interview with G. F. Shepherd.

[27]*Ibid.*

[28]*Cornell Daily Sun*, Sept. 18, 1961.

[29]Interview with Billy R. Wilkinson.

[30]Although no solution has been found to the problem of a use for the White Library, it is presently being used—but only on a temporary basis—to house the *Congressional Globe* and the *Congressional Record*. A proposal has been made to use the White Library to house a collection of Cornelliana, but as yet no final decision has been made. (Interview with Billy R. Wilkinson.)

[31]"Uris Library—Data Sheet" (in the files of the Uris Library).

[32]"Uris Library—Seating, Individual," Oct., 1963 (in the files of the Uris Library).

[33]Keyes D. Metcalf, *Planning Academic and Research Library Buildings* (New York: McGraw-Hill,

1965), p.327. Cited hereafter as *Planning Academic . . . Buildings*.

[34]Letter from John Jordan, Jr., Senior Purchasing Agent, Cornell University; to Loveless & Zeissig, Ithaca, N.Y. (in the files of the University Library).

[35]Interview with Billy R. Wilkinson.

[36]*Ibid.*

[37]Memorandum from Warner, Burns, Toan & Lunde to Cornell University, Undergraduate Library, July 17, 1962 (in the files of the University Library).

[38]"Outline Specifications—Cornell University—Undergraduate Library," Dec. 10, 1959 (in the files of the University Library).

[39]Interview with Billy R. Wilkinson.

[40]*Ibid.;* letter from Billy R. Wilkinson to the author, March 11, 1966.

[41]Memorandum from Charles A. Carpenter, Librarian, Goldwin Smith Library, Cornell University, to G. F. Shepherd, Jan. 6, 1958 (in the files of the Uris Library).

[42]*Ibid.*

[43]Memorandum by [Charles A. Carpenter] (in the files of the Uris Library).

[44]Memorandum by [Charles A. Carpenter] (in the files of the Uris Library). Thirty-four faculty members were asked about the inclusion of foreign language titles in the undergraduate library and a decisive majority said no. (Memorandum from Charles A. Carpenter to G. F. Shepherd, Jan. 14, 1958 [in the files of the Uris Library].)

[45]Cornell University. Libraries, *The Central Libraries* (Ithaca: Cornell University, [1962], p.[11].

[46]Letter from Robert M. Adams, Chairman, Committee on the Undergraduate Library, to the Faculty of the College of Arts and Sciences, May 29, 1959 (in the files of the University Library).

[47]Memorandum from Robert M. Adams to the Subcommittee on the Undergraduate Library [May, 1959] (in the files of the University Library).

[48]The Goldwin Smith Library served a dual purpose: "a reading room for undergraduates with a small select book collection strong in literature, philosophy, and drama; and the reserve book desk of the University Library for courses in the departments of English, Literature, Speech and Drama, Philosophy, Romance Literature, German Literature, and Classics." (Billy R. Wilkinson, "The Goldwin Smith Library, July 1962" [in the files of the Uris Library].)

[49][Charles A. Carpenter] "Sources of Titles for the Undergraduate Library—Possible Inclusions" (in the files of the Uris Library). Cited hereafter as "Sources of Titles."

[50]*Report of the Director*, 1958–59, p.8.

[51]*Ibid.;* interview with Stephen A. McCarthy.

[52]"Sources of Titles."

[53]"Brief History of the Processing of the Michigan Undergraduate Library Shelf-List" (in the files of the Uris Library). Cited hereafter as "Brief History of the Processing."

[54]A preliminary study was made to test how to use faculty members and how adequate they would be as book selectors. An identical list of books was given to four faculty members teaching in the same area asking them to indicate their evaluation of these titles. The following symbols were used:

1+ More than one copy should be in the collection.

1 One copy should be in the collection.

0 The book should not be in the collection.

− I do not wish to express an opinion.

I do not know enough about this book to evaluate it.

The results, in percentages, were as follows:

	1+	1	0	−blank
A	25	55	3	17
B	6	29	25	39
C	5	29	49	18
D	16	71	17	0

(Charles A. Carpenter, "An Experimental Study of Book Selecting for an Undergraduate Library by Faculty Members" [in the files of the Uris Library].)

[55]Charles A. Carpenter, "The Undergraduate Library Book Collection: Observations and Considerations" (in the files of the Uris Library).

[56]Letter from Robert M. Adams [for the Subcommittee on the Undergraduate Library] to the Departments, Sept. 14, 1959 (in the files of the University Library).

[57]Memorandum from Robert M. Adams to the Heads of Departments, Oct. 12, 1959 (in the files of the University Library).

[58]*Report of the Director*, 1959–60, p.20.

[59]*Ibid.*, 1958–59, p.4; "Brief History of the Processing."

[60]"Brief History of the Processing."

[61]*Report of the Director*, 1959–60, p.20.

[62]"Brief History of the Processing."

[63]"Program for the Undergraduate Library Book Collection," June 7, 1961 (in the files of the Uris Library).

[64]*Ibid.*

[65]Memorandum from Stephen A. McCarthy to Felix Reichmann, Assistant Director for Technical Services; Billy Wilkinson; G. F. Shepherd; and Hal Schell, Nov. 24, 1961 (in the files of the Uris Library).

[66]Interview with G. F. Shepherd.

[67]*Report of the Director*, 1960–61, p.7.

[68]*Ibid.*, 1962–63, p. 12.

[69]An open letter to all faculty from Billy R. Wilkinson (in the files of the Undergraduate Library); Billy R. Wilkinson, "New out of Old; A Look at Plans for the Undergraduate Library," *Cornell Alumni News*, LXIV (Jan., 1962), 13.

[70]"Titles Held at Uris Library Determined by a Count Taken from the Shelflist" (in the files of the Uris Library). As of Aug. 31, 1965, there was a total of 39,042 titles out of 58,524 volumes. (Memorandum from Billy R. Wilkinson to Stephen McCarthy, G. F. Shepherd, and Leo Cabell; Aug., 1965, Monthly Report Supplement, Uris Library, Sept. 2, 1965 [in the files of the Uris Library].)

[71]Interview with Billy R. Wilkinson.

[72]Memorandum from Billy R. Wilkinson to Stephen A. McCarthy and G. F. Shepherd, July 19, 1965 (in the files of the Uris Library).

[73]Letter from Billy R. Wilkinson to the author, March 11, 1966.

[74]Memorandum from Billy R. Wilkinson to Stephen A. McCarthy and Felix Reichmann, Aug. 9, 1963 (in the files of the Uris Library).

[75]Interview with G. F. Shepherd.

[76]Cornell University. Libraries. Uris Library, *Annual Report*, 1964–65, p.35.

[77]Memorandum on Bound Files of Periodicals for the Undergraduate Library, Sept. 22, 1959 (in the files of the Uris Library).

[78]Interview with Billy R. Wilkinson.

[79]Memorandum from Billy R. Wilkinson to G. F. Shepherd, May 24, 1965 (in the files of the Uris Library).

[80]The periodicals are shelved alphabetically by main entry which is usually by title.

[81]The books in the Uris Library are classified according to the Library of Congress Classification scheme.

[82]Interview with Billy R. Wilkinson.

[83]Cornell University. Libraries. Uris Library, *Basic Library Handbook* (Ithaca: 1965), p.31.

[84]Cornell University. Libraries. Uris Library, *Annual Report*, 1962–63, p.13.

[85]Interview with Billy R. Wilkinson.

[86]Cornell University. Libraries, *Handbook of the Libraries for Graduate Students and Faculty* (4th ed.; Ithaca: 1962), p.47.

[87]Memorandum from Charles A. Carpenter to Stephen A. McCarthy, June 16, 1961 (in the files of the Uris Library).

[88]Letter from Miss Frances Lauman, Reference Librarian, Uris Library, Cornell University, to Miss Annette Liles, Chairman, Department of Reference and Bibliography, University of Florida, July 23, 1965 (in the files of the Uris Library).

[89]Interview with Billy R. Wilkinson.

[90]Interview with G. F. Shepherd.

[91]Interview with Billy R. Wilkinson.

[92]Cornell University. Libraries. Uris Library, *Annual Report*, 1963–64, p.16; 1964–65, p.23.

[93]Keast, "What about the Undergraduates," p.5.

[94]*Ibid.*

[95]Letter to the Faculty of the College of Arts and Sciences.

[96]"The Cornell Undergraduate Library," Dec. 2, 1959 (in the files of the Uris Library).

[97]*Ibid.*

[98]Keast, "What about the Undergraduates."

[99]Letter from Frances Lauman to Annette Liles.

[100]Interview with Billy R. Wilkinson.

[101]Interview with Miss Frances Lauman, Oct. 22, 1965.

[102]Cornell University. Libraries. Uris Library, *Annual Report*, 1964–65, p.19.

[103]Interview with Billy R. Wilkinson.

[104]Memorandum from Billy R. Wilkinson to Stephen A. McCarthy, July 21, 1961 (in the files of the Uris Library).

[105]Interview with Billy R. Wilkinson.

[106]Memorandum from Robert M. Adams to the Subcommittee on the Undergraduate Library (in the files of the University Library).

[107]*Basic Library Handbook,* p.23.

[108]*Ibid.*

[109]Memorandum from Billy R. Wilkinson to Stephen A. McCarthy and G. F. Shepherd, March 15, 1965 (in the files of the Uris Library).

[110]Cornell University. Libraries. Uris Library, *Annual Report*, 1962–63, p.12.

[111]*Ibid.*, 1963–64, p.15.

[112]*Ibid.*, 1964–65, p.23.

[113]Interview with Billy R. Wilkinson.

[114]Interview with Gary Menges, Reserve Librarian, Uris Library, Cornell University, Oct. 22, 1965.

[115]Letter from Billy R. Wilkinson to Richard Levy, Chicago, Ill., July 16, 1965 (in the files of the Uris Library).

[116]Interview with Billy R. Wilkinson.

[117]Cornell. University. Libraries. Uris Library, *Annual Report*, 1962–63, p.18.

[118]Interview with Billy R. Wilkinson.

[119]Cornell University. Libraries. Uris Library, *Annual Report*, 1964–65, p.31.

[120]*Basic Library Handbook*, 31.

[121]Memorandum from Billy R. Wilkinson to Stephen A. McCarthy, Felix Reichmann, and G. F. Shepherd, Dec. 6, 1961 (in the files of the Uris Library).

[122]*Basic Library Handbook*, 31.

[123]Cornell University. Libraries. Uris Library, *Annual Report*, 1962–63, p.13.

[124]*Report of the Director*, 1960–61, p.20.

[125]Interview with Billy R. Wilkinson.

[126]Interview with Billy R. Wilkinson.

[127]Cornell University. Libraries. Uris Library, *Annual Report*, 1964–65, p.7.

[128]Letter from David Koren to Billy R. Wilkinson, Sept. 21, 1962 (in the files of the Uris Library).

[129]Metcalf, *Planning Academic . . . Buildings*, p.48.

[130]Memorandum from Billy R. Wilkinson to Stephen A. McCarthy, G. F. Shepherd, and Leo Cabell, Jan. 18, 1965 (in the files of the Uris Library).

[131]Memorandum from Billy R. Wilkinson to Stephen A. McCarthy; G. F. Shepherd; Felix Reichmann; Arthur Kulp, Head, Circulation Department; and Mrs. Caroline T. Spicer, Reference Librarian, June 1, 1965 (in the files of the Uris Library).

[132]Interview with Stephen A. McCarthy.

[133]Cornell University. Libraries. Uris Library, *Annual Report*, 1964–65, p.43.

[134]Interview with Stephen A. McCarthy.

The Undergraduate Library,
The University of Texas

The background of the Undergraduate Library at the University of Texas is different from that at the other institutions already discussed. At Texas, the impetus for a separate undergraduate library building came not from the librarian but from the Chancellor of the University, Harry H. Ransom (then Main University Vice-President and Provost).[1] Dr. Ransom first voiced the idea, but it was soon taken up by the students. In March, 1958, several thousand students signed a petition urging that an undergraduate library be built. The petition read:

> We, the undersigned students, do hereby petition the Administration and the Board of Regents of the University of Texas of our acute awareness of the startling need for adequate library facilities for the undergraduate students . . . we call attention to the antiquated, inefficient, unavailable, and completely uninviting nature of our present library facilities for undergraduate reading—pointing to far superior facilities at many other colleges and universities in Texas and across the nation.[2]

Later that same month, the Board of Regents of the University of Texas authorized an undergraduate library and academic center to be housed in a central campus location. The complex was to be part of "an accelerated library development program."[3] A subcommittee on the undergraduate library consisting of faculty and staff[4] was appointed to study the idea of the undergraduate library and to help in planning a new building. It outlined the problem as follows:

> In this one location we hope to have not only books and journals, but all types of library materials needed by the student in the preparation of his daily assignments. No barriers will be placed between the student and the selection of books he wishes to use. It is thought that in selecting specific books the student will be led to reading titles surrounding those books to which he has been directed thus gaining a deeper understanding of the subject investigated and in developing an acquaintanceship with the new fields. We hope that use of the library will not only meet the needs for specific courses, but will also make it possible for the student to further his general education.[5]

In addition, a student committee on the undergraduate academic center made recommendations for the new library similar to those of the subcommittee.[6]

Dr. Ransom called the new undergraduate library the Academic Center to show that the scope of the library was to be broader than was ordinarily the case. As he envisaged the new library, it would have rooms for students who wished to study only their own books; rooms where students could discuss books; rooms for listening to records and tapes and for watching slides and films; and exhibition corridors for the display of books not circulated. Besides, the Academic Center was to contain space for some of the university's special collections.[7]

Dr. Ransom pointed out that none of the educational solutions provided by the undergraduate library would be final:

Its planners have resisted all influences to make the place a mausoleum of dead ideas attended by the undertakers of polite scholarship. No amount of planning can anticipate the opportunities and obligations which a dynamic educational program will produce from year to future year. Equally important inhabitants of the mere building, of course, will be both the immortal words and the growing, mortal minds. The really significant changes that lie ahead will therefore be mental rather than architectural.[8]

The actual planning of the building began even before the Board of Regents approved the idea. In order to have a plan to show the Board of Regents, Dr. Ransom had Mr. George L. Dahl, of Dallas, later appointed associate architect, draw up a set of sketches to embody as nearly as possible Dr. Ransom's ideas. He wanted a building where groups of students could work together, where others could study in solitude, or where a blind student could listen to his talking book. Although the main idea was openness and a feeling of spaciousness, there had to be some privacy in the building, which the small study rooms were to provide. Dr. Ransom also wanted a place where students could come and listen to music or spoken arts, smoking rooms, and "space and books and reasonably comfortable chairs"; in short, a place which would combine students, books, and comfort.

In planning the building, he wanted no intruding elements to distract the students' attention from their books. Hence, a scheme of quiet, unassuming colors was used throughout the building. The colors of the books and of the students' clothes would provide all needed color. There were also plans to use paintings and art objects (a $90,000 budget was set aside for this purpose, i.e., for the whole building) to add some color to the rooms.

After Mr. Dahl's basic plan was approved by the Board of Regents, the consulting architects, Jessen, Jessen, Millhouse and Greven, of Austin, assumed the duties of carrying the design and supervision of the building to completion.[9] Once the exterior of the building was decided upon, Mr. Dahl made final detailed drawings of the interior. After many consultations among the architect; Mrs. Frances Hudspeth, Associate Director of the Humanities Research Center; Mr. Fred Folmer, Associate Director of the University Library; and Mr. Alexander Moffit, Director of the University Library, final plans were agreed upon.[10]

Dr. Frederick Wagman came to Austin in March, 1958, as a consultant to give further help with the planning of the building. During a two-day visit, he went over the plans for the building and made suggestions and recommendations. "The Michigan building and philosophy were used as guidelines in planning this building."[11]

FINANCING

Financing of the Undergraduate Library at Texas took a different form from that of the other undergraduate libraries, which got their money either by gifts or by legislative appropriations. Buildings at the University of Texas are not put up with tax money but with money in the university's Available Fund. Royalties from university-owned lands go into a permanent endowment fund, and the interest on these royalities or endowment comprises the Available Fund, which is used for the erection of buildings.

The total cost of the building and furnishings was $4,700,000. The cost per square foot was only $17, "a remarkably low figure compared with other academic buildings."[12]

THE BUILDING

Description

After the money was obtained and the planning finished, the construction of the Undergraduate Library and Academic Center building began in December, 1960. On September 23, 1963, the new library was opened for use. Fortunately, a convenient, centrally located site became available just before reaching the planning stage of the building.[13] The site chosen was adjacent to the Main Library and to the Student Union.

The architectural style of the building is contemporary. Native limestone, shellstone, and granite provide an exterior to match that of most other campus buildings. Pierced stone screens conceal the windows on the second and third floors. The glass used around the perimeter of the building on the first floor is tinted and heat absorbing.

The Undergraduate Library occupies three floors of the five-story Undergraduate Library and Academic Center building. The building is basically a modular building (28-foot modules). The reading areas are open, but all other areas are fixed by walls, although they are not load bearing and could, therefore, be changed. In contrast to some of the other undergraduate libraries, there is no basic floor design.[14]

The first floor contains the exhibit area, the lobby, offices, circulation desk, reserve desk, and the reference and periodical collections. The exhibit area runs across the whole

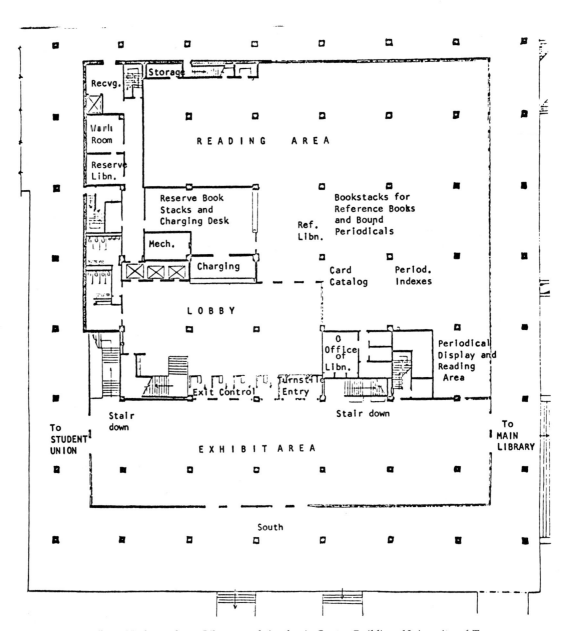

Fig. 31. First floor, Undergraduate Library and Academic Center Building, University of Texas

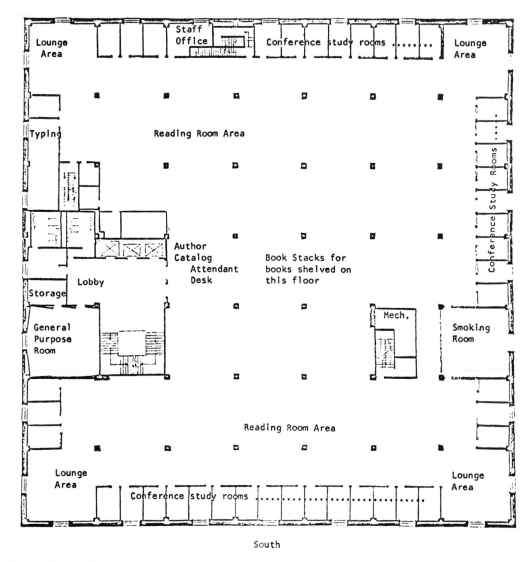

Fig. 32. Second floor, Undergraduate Library and Academic Center Building, University of Texas

front of the building, comprising about one fifth of the total area of the first floor. Entrance into the library from the exhibit area is through two turnstiles which enter directly into the lobby (Fig. 31). The circulation desk is the only function located in the lobby. Glass-encased walls and doors close off the lobby from the reading area on all floors. To the rear of the charging desk but facing into the reading area is the reserve bookstack and charging desk. The reserve desk can be closed by means of a folding screen when the desk is not open but the library is.[15] Behind the reserve-book area is the reserve librarian's office, a workroom (which the Card Production Division of the Main Library now uses), and the receiving room. Also on this floor, inside the doors from the lobby, are the reference desks, reference collection, and card catalog. Behind the card catalog are the librarian's office and microfilm rooms. The periodical display and newspaper reading area are in the southeast corner of the room in conjunction with a lounge area.[16]

The second floor has conference rooms all along the north, south, and east walls (Fig. 32). On the east wall, there is also one smoking room. In each of the four corners of the room, there is a lounge area. Along the west wall are three rooms for the blind, a typing room, a general-purpose room, and the lobby. The bookstacks form two rows down the center of the floor. At the front of the stacks just inside the entrance from the lobby are an

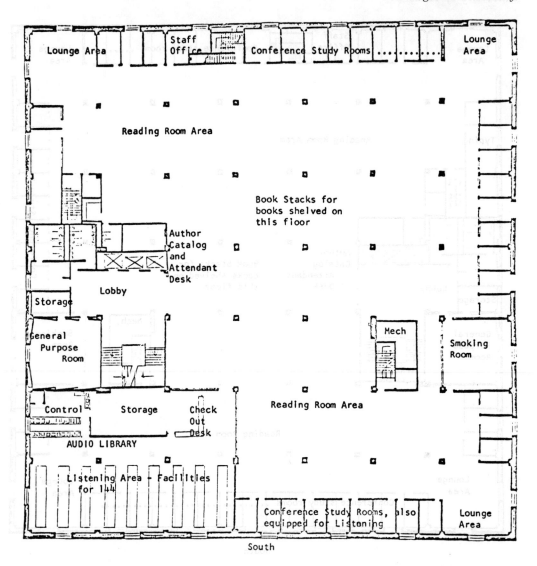

Fig. 33. Third floor, Undergraduate Library and Academic Center Building, University of Texas

author catalog and the attendant's desk. The remainder of the floor area contains reading tables, most of which run parallel to the bookstacks.[17]

The third floor is the same basic design as the second except for the Audio Library which occupies the southwest corner of the floor (Fig. 33). Off the lobby on this floor, there is a general-purpose room, but it has been taken over by the Humanities Research Center to house the Ruth Stephan Poetry Center. The conference rooms on the south wall have equipment for listening through the Audio Library. The Audio Library has facilities for 144 listeners, a storage area, and the control room. The Education-Psychology Library, consisting of approximately 26,500 volumes, occupies the north part of the third floor. In August, 1964, it was moved from Mezes Hall to the Undergraduate Library.[18]

The fourth floor houses the Humanities Research Center and some of the special collections of the University Library. There are a reading terrace and a terrace garden, which are popular study places with the undergraduates (Fig. 34).

The Humanities Research Center and special collections occupy most of the basement level. However, the Undergraduate Library Catalog and Acquisitions departments are located here. The staff room is adjacent to the Catalog Department (Fig. 35).

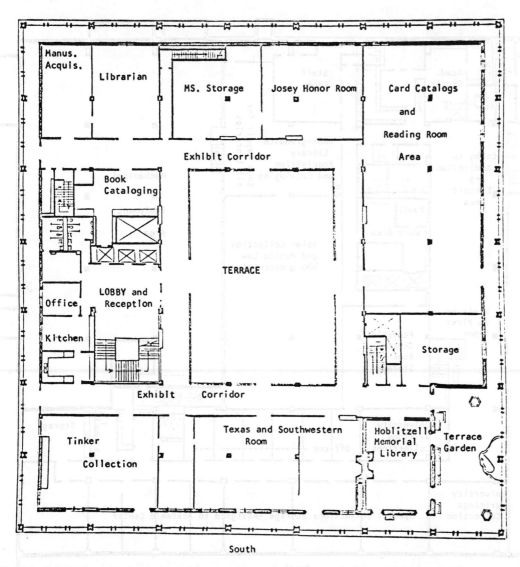

Fig. 34. Fourth floor, Undergraduate Library and Academic Center Building, University of Texas

The Undergraduate Library portion of the building consists of 100,400 square feet. The high ceilings add to the sense of spaciousness of the building. Much space in this building is nonassignable space.[19]

Furnishings

There are two different kinds of seating, at tables and in lounge furniture. The lounge furniture is placed systematically in a corner on each floor. There are eight lounge areas: one on the first floor, four on the second floor, and three on the third floor. Arranged in a similar pattern, each lounge area seats about twenty-one persons on lounge chairs and sofas.

The reading tables seat from four to sixteen persons. All of the reading tables seating more than four persons have divided tops, with a 2-foot by 3-foot working space. The dividers are 8 inches high. The tables all have light, glare-free Formica surfaces. It is felt that the divided-top tables serve the same purpose as individual carrels found in most of

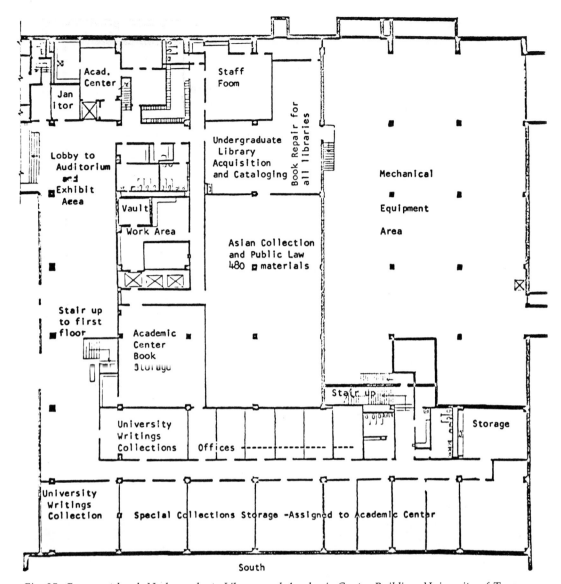

Fig. 35. Basement level, Undergraduate Library and Academic Center Building, University of Texas

the other undergraduate libraries.[20] Because of the table dividers, students occupy every seat at a table instead of leaving some of them unoccupied as is usually the case with large reading tables. The dividers seem to provide enough privacy so that people do not bother one another.[21] By using divided-top tables, more seating can be put in an area than would be possible by using individual carrels.[22]

The seventy small conference rooms that line the outside walls on the second and third floors seat four persons each and are the most popular type of seating because of the privacy and because smoking and talking are allowed. Although popular, these rooms are not an economical type of seating. There are smoking rooms on the second and third floors of the library to accommodate persons who want to smoke while studying. Each of these rooms seats twenty-eight persons. In the original plans, smoking was to be allowed all over the building, but this plan was later rejected.[23]

Seating capacity for the building was originally 1901 (Table 31). Since the Undergraduate Library lost the use of Room 300 it is only 1885.

Except for the colors, all the reading table chairs in the building are identical. The chairs, covered with nylon upholstery, have an aluminum frame and were chosen for

TABLE 31

SEATING CAPACITY IN THE UNDERGRADUATE LIBRARY,
UNIVERSITY OF TEXAS[a]

First floor	260
Second floor	811
Third floor	678
Audio Library	90
Room 200	46
Room 300	16
Total	1,901

[a]"Seating Capacity of the Undergraduate Library" (in the files of the Undergraduate Library).

their comfort and to make the library as attractive as possible. The frame of the chair is vertical to the seat, preventing the chair from being tipped back. Two problems have arisen in connection with the chairs. First, because the chairs have soft fabric coverings, there has been some tendency for the upholstery to pull out at the seams. Second, because

First floor reading area, Undergraduate Library, University of Texas

the legs are straight and attached only at the top of the chair, they tend to vibrate when pulled back from the table. To reduce noise, larger glides have been placed on the chairs.[24]

The chairs in one of the smoking rooms and in the Audio Library are light yellow and after only two years of wear have already required cleaning. Some additional chairs have been purchased, but they have a vinyl cover which appears to be better suited to heavy use than fabric coverings.[25]

The lighting in the building is of two different types. The first floor has a luminous ceiling in the reading area; on the second and third floors, there is recessed-troffer, high-intensity fluorescent lighting on 6-foot centers. All lighting has 70-footcandle power.

The flooring throughout the Undergraduate Library is vinyl tile (except the Humanities Research Center on the fourth floor). This type of flooring is rather noisy, especially where acoustical tile was not used or was limited because of light fixtures. The noise is most noticeable on the first floor where there is no acoustical tile on the ceiling. In planning the building, carpeting was considered, but because of the cost and because at that point there was to be smoking throughout the building, the idea of using carpeting was abandoned.[26]

BOOK COLLECTION

General Collection

The basic book collection for the Undergraduate Library at the University of Texas was conceived as consisting of 60,000 volumes, while the maximum size of the collection was set at 175,000 volumes.[27] The collection is intended not only "to serve curriculum and reserve book needs of the undergraduate, but to stimulate lifetime reading interests in fields outside the specific discipline of the student's major field."[28] The collection is not for the graduate student or faculty members and does not even fully serve the needs of the advanced undergraduate student. The collection basically meets the needs of the students enrolled in courses in the College of Arts and Sciences. No effort was made to provide extensive coverage in areas where there were existing department libraries. In such areas, the library "provides only a minimum collection—a relatively few books on the layman's level."[29] However, in such areas as art and music, where there is a considerable amount of interest on the layman's level, some effort was made to provide a more complete inclusion. The Undergraduate Library was thought of as an enlarged "gentleman's library" with books in the arts, letters, and sciences aimed at the level of the layman. "Emphasis is on fine biography and history, contemporary *belles lettres*, literary criticism and reliable interpretation of science for the non-scientist."[30]

Actual selection of the book collection for the Undergraduate Library at the University of Texas began in September, 1959, when Miss Jean Cassel was appointed as Academic Center librarian (this was later changed to undergraduate librarian). Even before Miss Cassel's appointment, the university librarian obtained four copies of the University of Michigan Undergraduate Library shelf list, two in book form and two in card form. Miss Cassel and her staff separated the slips from one copy of the Michigan shelf list "according to the University's departments of instruction."[31] Mr. Moffit met with academic department heads or their representatives to tell them about the nature of the collection and ask them to check the slips for their departments.[32]

Miss Cassel used an alphabetized copy of the University of Michigan shelf list as a selection tool. Because there was no budget for books when Miss Cassel began, she directed her first efforts at selecting titles from the resource collections of the University Library. When the undergraduate reading room in the Main Library closed in June, 1960, about 325 volumes were selected for inclusion in the Undergraduate Library.[33] About 30 percent, or 12,000 volumes, of the basic collection came from the resource collections.[34]

As titles were found in the resource collections, they were moved and stored in one location in the Tower.[35] Each was checked against the alphabetical file of Michigan cards, and its inclusion noted on the card. Faculty recommendations were also checked against the master file. If they were already on hand (through the resource collections), they were put in one file; if they were in-print titles, the price was added to the slip, and the slip filed by publisher; if the book was out of print, it was put in an out-of-print file; if it was a paperback, it was put in a reject file along with faculty rejects. Titles rejected by one person and recommended by another were considered for inclusion.[36]

The decision was made to order all books published from 1957 to 1960 (the period after which the Michigan list stopped and the Texas project began) from the contract dealer.[37] Earlier in-print titles were ordered directly from the publishers, and out-of-print titles were ordered from Barnes and Noble, Inc. British and foreign publications were held until the American selections were acquired.

Actual purchasing of the collection did not begin until June, 1960, when a book budget of $10,000 became available. The Undergraduate Library staff did the ordering, except for serials. The first appropriation was spent on university press books, thereby providing some of the basic materials for the collection.[38] In September, 1960, an appropriation of $50,000 became available for purchases for that fiscal year. Besides purchases, the library received a number of books (approximately 900 by the time the library opened) as gifts from various individuals and departments of the university.

Because faculty recommendations beyond the Michigan shelf list were not numerous, it was necessary to seek the help of individual faculty members to select current materials. Miss Cassel also checked many periodical reviews and secondhand catalogs for out-of-print items to keep selection current until the library opened.[39]

In addition to faculty selection from the University of Michigan shelf list, some specific persons prepared lists in such fields as Texana and Latin America which were not represented in the Michigan shelf list but which were imperative inclusions. Members of the Main Library staff selected the reference titles, using the University of Michigan shelf list as their basic guide.[40]

Besides the Michigan shelf list, some use was made of the Lamont Library *Catalogue* as a selection aid. Both of these tools were used as guides, not as rigid rules. The University of Texas collection was tailored to fit certain needs. To complete the collection, a list of 212 periodical titles was compiled from the Lamont *Catalogue,* the Michigan Undergraduate Library shelf list, and Farber's *Classified List of Periodicals for the College Library.*[41]

After selecting and ordering the initial list of periodical titles, it was decided to provide back files to 1950 for the more popular titles.[42] Most of the titles, however, began with 1960 when the actual selection of the collection began. The titles selected for inclusion were, for the most part, those indexed in *Readers' Guide, Social Sciences and Humanities* and *Public Affairs Information Service.* Most of the titles were general and unspecialized. Few foreign language titles were included.[43] When the library opened in September, 1963, there were approximately 2150 volumes of bound periodicals on hand.[44] About 250 titles are currently received.[45]

The last type of materials selected were the recordings for the Audio Library. "An attempt is made to cover the various periods and forms of music in the Western world. Attention is given to performer, quality of performance and technical excellence of the recording, with quality of performance being given first place."[46] Only a small number of the recordings are spoken records, mostly authors reading their own literary works.

The Audio Library collection is largely on tape. Records do not circulate to the students for home use. Three tape copies are made: one master copy, one for student use, and a control room tape. The collection contains music, spoken arts, and tapes made especially for class use. The music collection has all types of selections: classical, popular, jazz, folk, and show music.[47] Music accounts for 1433 of the 1587 selections in the collection.[48]

> The collection which the Audio Library is building may be considered a core collection of recognized musical classics, and it is in some ways an extension of the core collection of books for undergraduates which the Undergraduate Library contains. A representative and not an archival collection, it will not grow as rapidly in the future as it did during the Library's first months of operation now that it contains the basic phonodiscs.[49]

Besides purchases, two large groups of transfers were made to the Undergraduate Library. In the summer of 1963, 3701 volumes of Y collection books, which is a collection of young people's literature, were transferred from the Graduate School of Library Science to the Undergraduate Library (these volumes are not counted in the Undergraduate Library holdings).[50] The second group of books, those in the reserve book collection in the Main Library, were transferred in the summer of 1963 shortly before the Undergraduate Library opened. The reserve books were not transferred *in toto* — only added copies were transferred. If the book was the only copy that the Main Library owned, it was charged to the Undergraduate Library instead of being cataloged for it. The books transferred to the Undergraduate Library were reclassified when necessary to fit into the overall scheme of the Undergraduate Library collection.[51] Only those titles on reserve for undergraduate courses were transferred; those on reserve for graduate courses (which are also housed in the Undergraduate Library) were merely charged to the Undergraduate Library. About 5000 volumes were moved from the Main Library to the Undergraduate Library.[52]

The same principles which applied in selecting the basic collection also apply to current purchases. Since the library opened, efforts have been made to fill gaps in the collection, to buy current titles for the collection, and to buy multiple copies of titles which are in heavy demand. There are three ways to find gaps in the collection: the faculty call such omissions to the attention of the staff; reference questions often indicate particular subject or title omissions; and the acquisition librarian also examines the old charge slips to see what areas are in heavy demand.[53] Some departments such as history, government, and sociology take an active interest in current selection, while in other areas there is little or no faculty cooperation. The scope of the collection is growing, which is testified to by the fact that "this year (1964–65) even more graduate students and faculty remarked to the staff that they found books in the Undergraduate Library which are not available elsewhere on the campus."[54]

One guideline followed in building the collection that has since been maintained is the purchase of foreign language materials only in belles lettres. The only exception is art books in which the text may be incidental to the plates which led to the purchase. For current fiction, selective buying is done if the book appears to have some literary merit. The permanent value of the book is always kept in mind as a primary guide in selection.[55]

Even though science books in the Undergraduate Library receive heavy use and suffer a high rate of loss, no real effort is made to build up the collection in this area. Buying is for the needs of freshmen and sophomores, not advanced students served by the various department libraries.[56]

One change in policy has been in regard to foreign newspapers. When the library opened, it had only a few local newspapers. But now, because of demand and the library's longer hours, the Undergraduate Library has many foreign language newspapers. The papers are retained only a short while.[57]

There is an annual inventory which keeps the collection up to date and indicates which books need to be replaced. Less than 1 percent of the books is missing each year.[58]

TABLE 32

GROWTH OF THE BOOK COLLECTION, UNDERGRADUATE LIBRARY,
UNIVERSITY OF TEXAS

	INCREASE	TOTAL
1959–60		16,000
1960–61	2,319	18,319
1961–62	21,424	39,743
1962–63	10,656	50,399
1963–64	14,675	65,074
1964–65	6,345	71,419

The collection has grown at a steady pace (Table 32). The yearly increases are somewhat larger than at other undergraduate libraries. This is probably accounted for by the $50,000 book budget for the Undergraduate Library at Texas. The library opened with a collection of 50,399 volumes, which was close to the proposed 60,000-volume opening figure. Since opening, the collection has increased by 9 percent. The collection now contains 56,445 titles and 71,419 volumes.[59]

The arrangement of books by floor is as follows:

First floor: Reference books, periodicals, indexes, and the reserve books.
Second floor: Dewey Classification 000 (General Works), 100 (Philosophy), 200 (Religion), 300 (Social Sciences), 500 (Science), 600 (Technology), 900 (History and Biography), and the Y collection of literature.
Third floor: 400 (Language), 700 (Fine Arts), 800 (Literature), the Audio Library, and the Education-Psychology Library.[60]

History was placed on the second floor so that it could be near the other social sciences. The 500's and 600's were originally shelved on the third floor, but when the Education-Psychology Library moved in, they were moved to make room for the new library. The Y collection is housed at the rear of the room along with its own catalog. Because of their close subject relationship, the 400's are shelved near the 800's on the third floor. The three classes located on the third floor are there because of the proximity of the Audio Library and the relationship between literature and fine arts in both book form and recorded form.[61]

Reference Collection

The reference collection is relatively small—about 1500 titles—because the Undergraduate Library serves in large part as a referral library. No effort is being made to expand the collection, because it is not designed to serve research needs of undergraduates or graduate students. It is inevitable that the collection will grow and change, but it will never satisfy all the needs of the undergraduate.

Reserve Collection

Reserve books are purchased at a ratio of one copy to fifteen students for required reading. Exceptions are made when the use of the materials justifies the purchase of additional copies.[62] Fifty-four percent of the books placed on reserve come from other campus libraries. During 1964–65, 30 percent of the collection was borrowed from the Main Library, 7 percent from department libraries, and 17 percent were instructors' personal copies or photocopied materials. Not all of the materials borrowed were out of print or too specialized and therefore not suitable for the Undergraduate Library collection.[63] All books requested for reserve for undergraduate courses are not automatically purchased.[64]

Books are not ordinarily placed on reserve for courses in areas which have department libraries. Some exceptions to this are made in areas whose library facilities will not accommodate undergraduate reserves.[65]

The reserve librarian makes a conscious effort to keep the reserve collection active by securing from instructors terminal dates for all reserve lists. During the summer of 1964, the reserve collection was weeded and professors sent notification of books that had not circulated.[66] However, books are not automatically taken off reserve at the end of a semester. If, for instance, a reserve list is used in the Fall and Summer semesters the books remain on reserve for the Spring Semester to alleviate the work in taking the books on and off reserve.[67]

Open Access to the Collection

The Undergraduate Library supplies the student with a place to study with comfortable and conducive surroundings. It puts him in close proximity to books and makes them readily accessible, and it prepares him to use the research library.

The central idea of the Undergraduate Library was to eliminate barriers between the student and the materials he needed. Open access was to provide the student the opportunity to explore the collection for himself and to discover new areas of interest. The open-shelf collection was intended to help the student develop interest in areas outside his major discipline.

SERVICES

Reference

During the first year of operation, there was professional reference service on all three floors of the Undergraduate Library. It soon became evident that such service was unnecessary, and the desks on the second and third floors are now manned by subprofessionals. As has already been mentioned, the reference staff consists of three persons, each of whom has another specific duty.[68]

The reference statistics (Table 33) show the nature of reference service. During 1963–64, 62 percent of the questions were directional, while in 1964–65 only 35 percent were directional questions. In assisting students in the use of the card catalog, periodical indexes, and other reference sources, there was an increase from 22 percent to 29 percent.[69] The referral nature of the Undergraduate Library can be seen by the number of students that have been sent to other libraries, although this is still a small part of the total.

TABLE 33

REFERENCE STATISTICS, UNDERGRADUATE LIBRARY,
UNIVERSITY OF TEXAS[a]

TYPES OF QUESTIONS	1963–64	1964–65
Directional questions (places)	4,530	846
Directional questions (material)	21,552	18,331
Use of catalog, periodicals, etc., for location of subject information	7,090	8,788
Telephone	574	751
Referral questions	1,063	523
Search (15 minutes or more)	143	82
Total	34,952	29,321

[a]Taken from information desk tally sheets for 1963–64 and 1964–65.

Circulation

The circulation system employed by the Undergraduate Library at Texas is the same as that of the University of Michigan Undergraduate Library. "The Michigan circulation system was adopted because it permits rapid charging and discharging."[70] All loans are for two weeks. The aim of this policy is to give students first consideration and to make the books available at all times.[71]

The continued use of the present system has been questioned because of the amount of time spent in filing and discharging. With daily circulation ranging from 800 to 1200 items, a large part of the time of the circulation staff is spent in filing.

Reserve

The reserve collection at Texas is complicated because it contains materials for both undergraduate and graduate courses. Both functions remain as one unit because of space limitations and because there would be too much duplication of staff and books to provide two separate collections.[72] Because of the inclusion of graduate reserves in the Undergraduate Library, some special policies had to be adopted. For instance, books placed on reserve for graduate courses are not purchased by the Undergraduate Library but are simply borrowed from the Main Library. Furthermore, there is a special card catalog for the reserve collection so that students have a means of access to the books borrowed from other libraries.[73]

The reserve system at Texas is basically a closed-reserve system with provision for approximately 10,000 volumes. The closed-reserve system was retained because of the amount of stealing and hiding that seem to characterize most open-shelf reserve systems. However, when the reserve unit moved to the Undergraduate Library, all three-day reserve books were placed on the open shelves, leaving only two-hour and one-day books behind the reserve desk.[74] During 1964–65, another innovation changed some "Building Use Only" reserve books to "Open Shelf Building Use Only" books, thereby creating a new type of reserve.[75] The reserve books placed on the open shelves are in their regular order in the collection and indicated as reserve books with different colored date due slips.

The time it takes to put a book on reserve depends on three factors: (1) when the list is received. If the list arrives before the beginning of classes, it can be processed rapidly. If it arrives two weeks after classes begin, processing may take as much as a month; (2) whether the book has been on reserve before. Whenever a book is removed from the reserve collection, the cards made for it are retained for future use. If the cards are already available, it takes less time to put the book back on reserve; and (3) availability of the book in the Undergraduate Library. If the book is in the collection and does not have to be searched in the catalog in the Main Library and then borrowed, the book naturally is processed more quickly.[76] However, if the Undergraduate Library has to order the book, it borrows it from the Main Library and then returns that copy when the new one is received.

The time and work involved in processing the reserve collection are increased by the late receipt of many reserve lists and the high percentage of volumes borrowed from other libraries. In 1964–65, 2733 of 5021 volumes were borrowed.[77] Amazingly, out of a total of 7371 volumes on reserve in 1964–65, only 31 titles were missing at the end of the year (Table 34). Eleven were closed-reserve titles, and 19 were open-shelf reserve books.

TABLE 34

BOOKS PLACED ON RESERVE, UNDERGRADUATE LIBRARY,
UNIVERSITY OF TEXAS

	1963–64	1964–65
Volumes on closed reserve	6,184	5,021
Volumes on 3-day open reserve	3,323	2,350
Titles on closed reserve	5,199	1,965
Titles on open reserve	a	1,437

[a]Figure not available.

Courses in the social sciences make the greatest use of reserve materials, although the English Department submits the largest number of lists. The Government, History, Sociology, and Psychology departments also make heavy use of reserve materials.[78]

Special Services

The special areas in the Undergraduate Library consist of typing rooms, two general-purpose rooms, and the Audio Library. The typing rooms are on the second and third floors. When the building opened, there was space for twenty-four students and their typewriters. In November, 1964, the library installed new electric coin-operated typewriters which have proven popular. It is generally agreed that these rooms are larger than necessary.[79]

The two general-purpose rooms are on the second and third floors. These rooms are used to instruct students in the use of the library and for classes or groups that want to listen to a broadcast from the Audio Library.[80] Room 200 is furnished as a classroom and is used for most of the above-mentioned purposes. Room 300 was furnished as a lounge and was used mainly for leisure or pleasure listening during the hours the Audio Library was open.[81]

The Audio Library "serves the dual purpose of making audio materials and facilities available to students and faculty for class assigned and leisure listening."[82] The Audio Library has 144 listening stations, of which 120 have tape decks and 24 have turntables. The conference rooms adjacent to the Audio Library provide a total of 36 more listening stations, although these are not presently being used. The control room can channel anything that is being played into both general-purpose rooms.[83]

Technical Services

The Undergraduate Library at Texas is the only undergraduate library which has its own technical services unit. The pilot project for selecting and processing the initial collection for the Undergraduate Library had its own staff for technical processing of the collection. The original thought was to transfer these functions back to the Main Library when the Undergraduate Library began operation, but because of space problems the transfer has not yet been made. One advantage of having the technical services in the Undergraduate Library is the quickness with which a book can be added to the collection; the cost of such an operation is its main disadvantage.[84]

At the beginning of the pilot operation, standards were set for cataloging the collection.[85] The only exception made to regular routines was to classify biography in 92 instead of with the subject as is done in the Main Library.[86] Books in the Undergraduate Library were to be represented in the Main Library card catalog only by main entry cards.[87] Besides the complete catalog for the Undergraduate Library, which was to be a divided catalog (author-title and subject), there were to be author catalogs on the second and third floors.[88] Cataloging of periodicals was delayed as long as possible to have enough bound volumes on hand. For the periodicals, an abridged or simplified form of cataloging was adopted; the periodicals were not classified.[89]

Simplification and Centralization

The Undergraduate Library at Texas has tried to simplify procedures to facilitate use. A simplified floor plan, a simple card catalog, and a logical arrangement of books all contribute to ease of student use. The building itself is in a central campus location on one of the major student traffic routes. Services and the collection are centralized by bringing them together in one location.

Instruction in Library Use

Reference service in the Undergraduate Library has been more in the nature of teaching students how to use the library rather than in doing detailed bibliographic searching. The staff attempts to give individual instruction in library use when a student has a need for it. Some effort is made to anticipate this need by holding classes once a semester for interested students. However, the program has not met with much support from the students.[90]

STAFF

The Undergraduate Library opened with a staff of six professionals, sixteen nonprofessionals, and about 33,000 hours of student assistant help. This also describes the current staff except for student help, which has been cut to 25,000 hours. Originally, there were nine professional positions allocated for the Undergraduate Library, but that many are not currently needed.[91]

During the pilot operation, the constant problem of turnover in the clerk-typist group caused some disruption of work. This same problem has persisted since the library began operation. Two factors seem to account for some of the turnover. Many of the subprofessionals in the library are students in the Library School who go on to other jobs when they have completed their degrees. The staff is young and are not inclined to remain in one place.

The six professionals are the librarian, the acquisition librarian and assistant librarian, a cataloger, 2.5 reference librarians, and one person half time in circulation. The duties of the librarian consist mainly of the overall administration of the library. She spends some time at the reference desk and the circulation desk.[92] The acquisition librarian is responsible for all book selection and order routines. She does not actually do all of the selection (the rest of the staff does some and the faculty does some), but she has the final decision. She also spends some time at the reference desk.[93]

None of the three reference librarians spends all of her time doing reference work. One person spends half time at circulation. The amount of time she spends in each varies with the pressures at the circulation desk. Another person spends part of her time cataloging records for the Audio Library. The third reference librarian is responsible for the periodical collection and devotes part time to that.

The library uses one senior clerk to patrol the building in the evenings. He is an older man, and it is thought useful to have him in the building after ten o'clock when the professionals leave. Although there have not been any incidents in the past, it is planned to keep someone of this nature on the staff to help eliminate the possibility of their occurring.[94]

Administratively, the undergraduate librarian reports to the associate librarian in

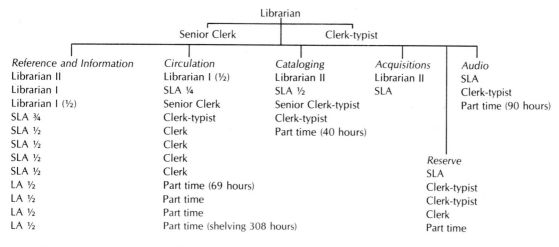

Note: Security guards who man the check-out stations are employed by the Security Departments.
    The audio technicians are employed by the Communications Department.

Fig. 36. Administrative structure of the Undergraduate Library, University of Texas

charge of the general service units. The administrative structure of the Undergraduate Library (Fig. 36) is a simple one of line and staff, each unit reporting directly to the undergraduate librarian. However, each unit of the library operates as a separate entity without much overlap.

LIBRARY USE

Before the Undergraduate Library opened, it was felt that it would decrease the use of the Main Library; much of the demand for seating space in the reading rooms would be diminished, as would be the circulation of books from the main stacks. This has been only partly true.[95] During the first year of operation of the Undergraduate Library, there was an overall increase in circulation of 16.25 percent, attributed mainly to the Undergraduate Library. While there was an overall increase in library use, there were decreases in Main Library circulation — in reference and in some of the department libraries — attributed to the presence of the Undergraduate Library.[96]

Circulation statistics (Table 35) show that the total circulation has almost doubled in two years. Of course, it must be taken into account that the circulation figures include those of the Education-Psychology Library for 1964-65. No separate record was kept for Education-Psychology books. However, during 1963–64, total circulation for the Education-Psychology Library was 66,575. (These statistics really are not comparable as the Education-Psychology Library was a closed-stack collection.)[97]

TABLE 35

CIRCULATION STATISTICS, UNDERGRADUATE LIBRARY,
UNIVERSITY OF TEXAS

	HOME USE	PERCENT INCREASE	BUILDING USE	PERCENT INCREASE	TOTAL	PERCENT INCREASE
1963–64	116,531		205,128		321,659	
1964–65	165,276	41	460,472	124	625,748	94

Reserve statistics (Table 36) show a marked increase in the use of reserve books since the Undergraduate Library opened. No valid comparison can be made with earlier figures because of the exclusion of three-day books from the present reserve statistics. The number of courses serviced for reserve has increased from 241 in 1962–63 to 377 (270 undergraduate) in 1963–64 to 424 (299 undergraduate) in 1964–65.[98] Although circulation of reserve materials and the number of courses using reserve materials is increasing, the number of books on reserve is actually decreasing.

TABLE 36

USE OF RESERVE BOOKS, UNDERGRADUATE LIBRARY, UNIVERSITY OF TEXAS

	1963–64	1964–65	PERCENT INCREASE
Home use	25,287	35,495	40.36
Room use	45,537	61,691	35.47
Total	70,824	97,186	37.22

During the second year of operation, use of the Audio Library (Table 37) showed a 52 percent increase in the number of earphones borrowed and a 95 percent increase in the

TABLE 37

AUDIO LIBRARY USE, UNDERGRADUATE LIBRARY, UNIVERSITY OF TEXAS

	1ST SEMESTER 1963–64	2D SEMESTER 1963–64	1ST SEMESTER 1964–65	2D SEMESTER 1964–65
Requests (includes sources)	7,025	11,528	21,130	19,696
Tapes checked out	465	1,818	6,842	6,679
Earphones checked out	16,684	14,747	26,276	22,108
Requests per day	75.5	115.2	a	a
Average room count	23.4	21.9	38.5	a

[a] Information not available.

number of requests.[99] The average number of requests per day was probably greater in 1964–65 than it was in 1963–64, although these figures are not available. The same is probably true for the average number of people using the Audio Library. Most listening on the channels is for course-related work. Two channels were originally set up as program channels for leisure listening, but limited channel space for required listening made it necessary to abandon this in April, 1964.[100]

Attendance figures show another increase in use: 1963–64, 1,473,048; 1964–65, 1,769,560. (The Michigan Undergraduate Library was open five years before reaching this latter figure.)

Opening-day reactions were interesting:

> After they [the students] had streamed through the turnstiles, some students wandered over the whole building, investigating every floor; some stopped at the open shelves, browsed and selected books for reading. Other students, surprisingly, went directly to a reading table and began to study before the first assignment had been made! All day they came and went. In midevening one had to search to find a vacant chair. By midnight 6,765 persons had entered the building.[101]

By the end of the week, 43,397 persons had entered the building, making it "clearly evident that the Undergraduate Library was meeting a long felt need."[102] Total items borrowed showed that every undergraduate used approximately eighteen books during the first year of operation.[103]

Since the library opened, there has been a continued demand for additional hours, and in April, 1964, the hours were extended to include Saturday nights. Because of further demands for additional hours (8:00 A.M. to midnight, Monday through Saturday; Sunday 1:00 P.M. to midnight are the regular hours) during the reading or examination period, an experiment was made in keeping the library open all night. There was considerable use of the building until about 2:00 A.M., but after that, there was a large drop in attendance. In the future, the library will not be open all night.[104]

The staff observed that students soon developed preferences for study places, to which they consistently returned. Some students were questioned about these habits but had no logical explanation either for their choice or their consistency.[105]

Heavy use of the collection falls mainly in the areas of literature, sociology, the sciences (particularly mathematics), and the Y collection. Use in the science fields is much heavier than anticipated, and as a result, unexpected pressures arose, even to the extent that book losses in this area were heavier than elsewhere.[106]

One major use of the library is as a study hall. A comparison of the total use figures with the attendance figures (Table 38) shows attendance is three to four times greater than circulation, indicating that students use the library more for its chairs than for its books.

The use of the library, as shown by attendance and by circulation, outstrips the increase in the enrollment. Enrollment of undergraduates in the College of Arts and Sciences has not varied greatly since the opening of the Undergraduate Library (from 8954 in the

TABLE 38

COMPARISON OF CIRCULATION AND ATTENDANCE, UNDERGRADUATE LIBRARY,
UNIVERSITY OF TEXAS

	TOTAL CIRCULATION	TOTAL ATTENDANCE
1963–64	423,475	1,473,048
1964–65	732,259	1,769,560

Fall Semester, 1963, to 8906 in the Spring Semester, 1965). The increase from September, 1963, to September, 1964, was only 792 students, or 9 percent, while circulation increased 72 percent and attendance increased 20 percent. There should be no doubt then that more students are using the library both as a study hall and for the resources of the library.

SUMMARY

The Undergraduate Library at the University of Texas was designed to provide for the needs of the undergraduate student in the College of Arts and Sciences. The degree of success achieved is partially seen in the total book use (724,934) and attendance (approaches the 2,000,000 mark). Considering that there are only about 9000 undergraduate students, the answer seems clear.

Although the planning of the Undergraduate Library at the university extended over a long time, the resulting structure is not completely satisfactory. Wasted space and the scattering of functions are major shortcomings. The use of divided-top tables allowed the best utilization of study space.

The general, well-rounded collection is based on undergraduate patterns of use. The reserve collection remains for the most part in a closed-stack area and is maintained at a fairly constant level. Open access is provided to all the collection with the exception of books on closed reserve.

Demand for reference service is on the decline as students become acquainted with the building and its resources. The referral nature of reference service remains a small part of the total service provided. As circulation of the collection grows, the suitability of the circulation system is being questioned. The reserve operation is not satisfactory, but steps are being taken toward improvement. The special services in the Undergraduate Library include the Audio Library and several smaller operations. The Audio Library has enjoyed a marked success.

The Undergraduate Library at Texas maintains its own technical services unit. This was a result of space shortages in the Main Library, although it does allow faster processing of materials. Procedures and physical layout were made as uncomplicated as possible to encourage use. Instruction in library use is done mainly through personalized reference service in instructing students to use the resources available to them.

The staff has been, for the most part, a young staff for a young clientele. Use of the library is heavier than anticipated, both in terms of attendance and circulation.

NOTES

[1]For about twenty years there had been discussion of adding to the Main Building to provide space for the undergraduates, but for various reasons it was never done. (Interview with Alexander Moffit, Director of the University Library, University of Texas, Dec. 20, 1965. Mr. Moffit is now Consultant for Library Development.)

[2]*Daily Texan,* Aug. 16, 1963, p.3A.

[3]"The University of Texas Undergraduate Library and Academic Center: A Summary," Aug. 15, 1963, p.1 (in the files of the University Library). Cited hereafter as "The University of Texas Undergraduate Library."

[4]The committee consisted of Esther Stallman, R. R. Douglas, Fred Folmer, William J. Hardy, A. E. Murphy, and Alexander Moffit, Chairman. ("Report

of the Sub-Committee on the Undergraduate Library," Nov. 14, 1958, p.5 [in the files of the University Library].)

[5]*Ibid.*, p.1.

[6]Jo Ann Walker Hawkins, "The University of Texas Audio Library" (unpublished Master's thesis, Graduate School of Library Science, University of Texas, 1966), p.5.

[7]Harry H. Ransom, "Arts and Sciences: The College Library," *Texas Quarterly*, II (Winter, 1959), ix–xii.

[8]*Ibid.*, p.xii.

[9]The university's supervising architect was Walter C. Moore. The interior designs were done by I.S.D., Inc., a division of Perkins & Well, Architects, New York City. ("The University of Texas Undergraduate Library," p.1.)

[10]Interview with Mrs. Frances Hudspeth, Associate Director of the Humanities Research Center, Dec. 22, 1965.

[11]Letter from Imogene Thompson, Librarian, Undergraduate Library, University of Texas, to the author, April 20, 1966; interview with Alexander Moffit.

[12]"The University of Texas Undergraduate Library," p.1. Hawkins cited the cost figures as $4,451,262 total and $20.71 per square foot.

[13]The building which had formerly occupied this site, the old Drama Building, burned down.

[14]Letter from Imogene Thompson to the author.

[15]The hours for the reserve desk are: Monday–Friday, 8:00 A.M. to 10:00 P.M.; Saturday, 8:00 A.M. to 1:00 P.M.; and Sunday, 1:00 P.M. to 10:00 P.M.

[16]"The University of Texas Undergraduate Library," p.3.

[17]*Ibid.*, p.4.

[18]*Ibid.*, p.5. Some problems have arisen because of this merger, especially since the Undergraduate Library charges out books for the Education-Psychology Library even though their loan policies differ in many respects from those of the Undergraduate Library. (Texas. University. Library. Undergraduate Library, *Annual Report*, 1964–65, p.2.)

[19]"The University of Texas Undergraduate Library," p.1.

[20]Interview with Miss Imogene Thompson, Dec. 21, 1965.

[21]Interview with Alexander Moffit.

[22]Interview with Mr. Fred Folmer, Associate Director of the University Library, the University of Texas, Dec. 21, 1965. Mr. Folmer is now Director of the University Library.

[23]Interview with Imogene Thompson.

[24]*Ibid.*; interview with Alexander Moffit.

[25]Interview with Imogene Thompson.

[26]Interview with Alexander Moffit.

[27]"Tentative Policy for Organization of Materials for the Undergraduate Library," p.1 (in the files of the University Library). Cited hereafter as "Tentative Policy for Organization of Materials."

[28]Jean Cassel, "The University of Texas Undergraduate Library Collection," *Texas Library Journal*, XXXIX (Winter, 1963), 123.

[29]*Ibid.*

[30]*Ibid.*, p.124.

[31]Texas. University. Library. Undergraduate Library, *Annual Report*, 1959–60, p.2.

[32]*Ibid.*

[33]Most of the books in the collection were moved to the browsing room in the Student Union and the rest were sent to the Main Library stacks. (Interview with Fred Folmer.)

[34]Texas. University. Library. Undergraduate Library, *Annual Report*, 1959–60, p.2–4.

[35]The Tower is the stack portion of the Main Building which houses the University Library.

[36]Texas. University. Library. Undergraduate Library, *Annual Report*, 1959–60, p.2–4.

[37]All state-supported institutions in Texas must purchase their current books from the dealer who obtains the contract by means of a bid.

[38]Texas. University. Library. Undergraduate Library, *Annual Report*, 1959–60, p.4.

[39]*Ibid.*, 1960–61, p.1.

[40]*Ibid.*, 1959–60, p.2.

[41]Cassel, *Texas Library Journal*, XXXIX, 125.

[42]*Ibid.*

[43]Interview with Jean Cassel.

[44]Memorandum from Jean Cassel [Aug., 1963] (in the files of the Undergraduate Library).

[45]Interview with Jean Cassel.

[46]Cassel, *Texas Library Journal*, XXXIX, 124.

[47]*Audio Library of the Undergraduate Library at the University of Texas* (Austin: The Undergraduate Library, n.d.), p.[1]. Cited hereafter as *Audio Library*.

[48]Texas. University. Library. Undergraduate Library. Audio Library, *Annual Report*, 1964–65, p.2.

[49]Hawkins, "The University of Texas Audio Library," p.16.

[50]Memorandum from Jean Cassel.

[51]Interview with Jean Cassel.

[52]Texas. University. Library, *Annual Report*, 1962–63, p.4.

[53]Interview with Imogene Thompson.

[54]Texas. University. Library. Undergraduate Library, *Annual Report*, 1964–65, p.5.

[55]Interview with Jean Cassel.

[56]Letter from Imogene Thompson to the author.

[57]Interview with Jean Cassel.

[58]Interview with Imogene Thompson.

[59]Letter from Imogene Thompson to the author.

[60]*A Guide to the Undergraduate Library of the University of Texas* (Austin: Office of Advisor to University Publication, University of Texas, n.d.).

[61]Interview with Jean Cassel.

[62]Interview with Imogene Thompson.

[63]Texas. University. Library. Undergraduate Library, *Annual Report*, 1964–65, p.3–4.

[64]Interview with Jean Cassel.

[65]Interview with Imogene Thompson.

[66]Texas. University. Library. Undergraduate Library, *Annual Report*, 1964–65, p.1.

[67]Interview with Imogene Thompson

[68]Interview with Alexander Moffit.

[69]Texas. University. Library. Undergraduate Library, *Annual Report*, 1963–64, p.4; 1964–65, p.4.

[70]Letter from Imogene Thompson to the author.

[71]Interview with Imogene Thompson.

[72]Interview with Alexander Moffit.

[73]Interview with Jean Cassel.

[74]Texas. University. Library. Undergraduate Library. Reserve Book Collection, *Annual Report,* 1963–64, p.1.

[75]*Ibid.,* 1964–65, p.3.

[76]Interview with Imogene Thompson.

[77]Texas. University. Library. Undergraduate Library. Reserve Book Collection, *Annual Report,* 1963–64, p.[1].

[78]*Ibid.,* 1964–65, p.7–8. Education-Psychology Library books are placed on reserve just like those for any other department library except that 3-day books remain on their shelves instead of being placed on the Undergraduate Library shelves. (Letter from Imogene Thompson to the author.)

[79]Interview with Imogene Thompson.

[80]"The University of Texas Undergraduate Library," p.9.

[81]Texas. University. Library. Undergraduate Library, *Annual Report,* 1963–64, p.3.

[82]*Audio Library,* p.[1].

[83]Texas. University. Library. Undergraduate Library. Audio Library, *Annual Report,* 1963–64, p.3.

[84]Interview with Jean Cassel.

[85]"Tentative Policy for Organization of Materials," p.3.

[86]Texas. University. Library. Undergraduate Library, *Annual Report,* 1959–60, p.5.

[87]Because of a lack of staff time, the main entry cards for Undergraduate Library books were not filed into the union catalog in the Main Library. They were placed in a separate file, which necessitated looking in two places to make sure if the university owns the books. (Interview with Imogene Thompson.)

[88]"Tentative Policy for Organization of Materials," p.3–4.

[89]Texas. University. Library. Undergraduate Library, *Annual Report,* 1962–63, p.1.

[90]Interview with Imogene Thompson.

[91]Interview with Alexander Moffit.

[92]Interview with Imogene Thompson.

[93]Interview with Jean Cassel.

[94]Interview with Imogene Thompson.

[95]Texas. University. Library, *Annual Report,* 1961–62, p.4.

[96]*Ibid.,* 1963–64, p.4.

[97]*Ibid.,* 1964–65, p.4. The Education-Psychology Library books are charged by the Undergraduate Library to avoid duplication of staff and equipment in the building. A combined charging system is considered more economical and less confusing. (Letter from Imogene Thompson to the author.)

[98]Texas. University. Library. Undergraduate Library. Reserve Book Collection, *Annual Report,* 1964–65, p.[1].

[99]Texas. University. Library. Undergraduate Library, *Annual Report,* 1964–65, p.4.

[100]Texas. University. Library. Undergraduate Library. Audio Library, *Annual Report,* 1963–64, p.3.

[101]Texas. University. Library. Undergraduate Library, *Annual Report,* 1963–64, p.1.

[102]*Ibid.,* p.3.

[103]*Ibid.*

[104]Memorandum from Laura Thompson to Alexander Moffit, Jan. 13, 1965 (in the files of the Undergraduate Library).

[105]Texas. University. Library. Undergraduate Library, *Annual Report,* 1963–64, p.3.

[106]*Ibid.,* p.4.

Conclusions

The separately housed undergraduate library was proposed to accomplish several objectives to improve service to the undergraduate student in the large university. These objectives were outlined in the Introduction as follows:

To construct a building with the undergraduate's habits of use in mind

To furnish a collection of carefully selected books containing the titles to which all undergraduates should be exposed as part of their liberal education, as well as to house the reserve book collection

To provide open access to the collection in order to avoid the problems encountered by the student in using a large research collection

To provide services additional to those given in the research library

To attempt to make the library an instructional tool by planning it as a center for instruction in library use to prepare undergraduates for using larger collections

To centralize and simplify services to the undergraduate.

In this concluding chapter, the several libraries will be compared with regard to their individual treatment of these problems, as well as with regard to the reasons for the establishment of each; the buildings; the book collections; services; the staffing of each; and the results in terms of student use. Following these comparisons, an attempt will be made to suggest guidelines, arising out of the experience of these six institutions, that may be helpful for other universities considering the establishment of an undergraduate library.

BACKGROUND

The reasons for establishing undergraduate libraries were strikingly similar, although all of the reasons given above were not subscribed to at each library. Space shortage for books and for readers was a primary consideration at Harvard, Michigan, South Carolina, and Cornell; Harvard, Michigan, Indiana, Cornell, and Texas stressed difficulty of access to books because of closed stacks and scattered facilities. Michigan and Texas wanted to broaden the students' education by encouraging good reading habits. Michigan's decision was also influenced by its commitment to a system of divisional libraries. South Carolina was concerned with providing adequate physical facilities for the undergraduate. At Indiana, the increasing enrollment was a factor in providing more space. At Texas, the undergraduate library was part of an overall accelerated library program.

This should indicate, then, that two reasons—shortage of space for books and/or readers and ease of access—were the prime factors. However, it would be difficult to state that any of the five objectives was not actually a part of the overall plan of each of these universities. For instance, although the Undergraduate Library at Texas was proposed as part of an accelerated library program with emphasis on the program's educational advantages, there was also the need to provide space for readers even if it was not expressly stated. To say that one reason dominated the thought at any one of these institutions would be doing it an injustice. Any new program is motivated by many ideas. The differences are the result of local conditions.

BUILDING

One of the characteristics which was supposed to distinguish the separately housed undergraduate library from a general university library was that the building would be planned with the habits of the undergraduate in mind. The architectural design most favored is a modular building, consisting of large reading areas, some special-purpose rooms, and small reading rooms. The open modular building is more functional and less expensive to build, but it is not the only type of building that makes an effective undergraduate library, as the Uris Library at Cornell illustrates. The modular plan was used at Harvard, Michigan, South Carolina, and Texas, where new buildings were constructed. At Cornell and Indiana, old buildings were adapted to new purposes so that a modular arrangement was not possible.

A central location either in the classroom area or close to the residential area is considered the best location, depending on the pattern of library use. If use is known to be heavier during the day, a central campus location seems more desirable. However, if use is heavier in the evening, a location near the dormitories seems preferable. With the exception of South Carolina, all of the libraries are in a central location. South Carolina considered a location near the dormitory area more suitable to the needs of their students. The new undergraduate library at Indiana (now under construction) is to be near the dormitory area. Besides the educational consideration, the availability of a site has to be considered, although this is not a serious problem unless a central campus location is desired. Unless the dormitories are all in one area, problems are encountered in placing the undergraduate library near the dormitory area.

The interior arrangement of the building should place the reader in proximity to books, but it should not intermingle books and readers because of the distraction caused by persons looking for books. The arrangement of books in the center of the floor with seating on either side has been the favored arrangement. Lamont's interior arrangement was basically one of books in the center with reading areas on either side (South Carolina and Texas use the same basic plan). Such an arrangement forces the student to pass books to reach most of the seats in the building. Michigan arranged its bookstacks in two rows with seating placed between and at both sides. The bookstacks at Michigan have since been rearranged in one stack area in the center of the room with standard 3-foot aisles. The rearrangement seems to be more satisfactory from the viewpoint of maximum space utilization. Because of the physical arrangement of the buildings at Cornell and Indiana, this arrangement could not be utilized. Cornell shelves most of its books in a traditional stack area, while Indiana located the books around the edges of three reading areas.

The question of whether these undergraduate library buildings achieve the aims envisaged for them can only be answered in part. In providing a building that would serve the needs of the undergraduate student, the results at Harvard, Michigan, South Carolina, and Cornell are good. The diversity afforded by the physical nature of the Uris Library differs sharply from the simplicity of the Lamont Library and the undergraduate libraries at Michigan and South Carolina. The Uris Library provides a veritable maze which seems to delight the students. From the viewpoint of the students, the Undergraduate Library at Texas is functional, but from the viewpoint of the staff, the building has shortcomings. The building is not well planned in that related staff functions are scattered. Enclosing the area around the reserve desk would decrease the noise in the first floor reading area. With the exception of Indiana, one error in planning the undergraduate libraries is a lack of sufficient staff work space. Obviously, the volume of work was not anticipated. Staffs increased as the work in the circulation and reserve departments increased. As a result, compromises to convert work space have had to be made. The results have not always been convenient or satisfactory, but sometimes it was all that could be done.

Besides not having enough work space, staff facilities have tended to be too widely scattered over the building, resulting in a waste of staff time. Centralization of these facilities would have resulted in a more efficient operation. This is true in all of the undergraduate libraries except South Carolina and, to some extent, Indiana. At Texas, the problem is especially unfortunate. The Catalog Department is not on the same floor as the card catalog, and the acquisition librarian is on still another floor. Staff lockers are so inconveniently placed that they are not used.

Surprisingly, only in two instances—at Michigan and at Indiana—are the buildings considered much too small. At Indiana, nothing could be done about the size of the building, because an old building (not even a library building) was adapted for use as the undergraduate library. The Undergraduate Library at Indiana provides seating for only about 8 percent of its undergraduates. Indiana is now faced with the problem of adapting the building as the demands on it increase. Little can be done about the physical facilities until the completion of the new library. Because of the experience with the Undergraduate Library in its present quarters, two things were learned about the old building which are being incorporated in the new building. Wide corridors and wide entrances to enable the students to get in and out quickly are considered important to prevent queueing. To help the student identify books new to the library, a new-book room is being placed near the entrance to the new library. In effect, the room is to be a browsing room, although the whole library actually constitutes a browsing collection.

At Michigan, it was known when the building was planned that it was going to be too small, but there was insufficient money to make it larger. When the whole building is given over to the Undergraduate Library, some of the problem will be alleviated. In a state-supported institution where the enrollment is not kept at a constant figure, little can be done to meet the demands that ever increasing enrollments create for seating and books.

Although many of the things that were learned from planning and operating the undergraduate library building were unique to that institution, each library seemed to benefit from the mistakes of its predecessors. This can be seen in two particular instances. The alcoves in the Lamont Library were too small. As it is, they now accommodate one reader. If they had been 3 feet larger, each could easily have seated four readers. South Carolina has the same basic interior arrangement, but the alcoves were made large enough to accommodate five to eight readers. In planning the group study rooms for the Michigan Undergraduate Library, a miscalculation was made about the size. They were made to accommodate six persons, but it was not often that six persons wanted to study together. As a result, two or three persons will use a room, leaving the remainder of the seats unused. When the Undergraduate Library at Texas was built, the group study rooms were made to accommodate four persons, which has proven more satisfactory.

Some of the building features which proved unsatisfactory were not the result of bad planning, but were unavoidable. At Indiana, there were too many entrances and exits; there was no elevator or book lift; the building was badly ventilated; and the physical layout of the building did not permit a satisfactory arrangement of functions. Cornell, where an old building was also used, was faced with some unavoidable limitations. Because of the layout of the building, the circulation desk and the main entrance to the stacks are located in the largest reading room, thereby concentrating the heaviest traffic in one area. To alleviate this problem somewhat, the reserve desk was separated from the circulation desk, which has caused some duplication of effort and staff.

At Michigan, some features, such as the entrance, had to be planned as they are because of the site. The main entrance on the narrow side of the building is undesirable, because a student has to walk through the whole building to get to the back. The entrance would have been more satisfactory on the long axis of the building, but the site did not allow this. The arrangement of the entrance inside the building was well planned, but it had to be altered and made awkward because of changes made by the fire marshall. As it is, students enter to the far right of the entrance and then have to turn back into the lobby. Because the checkout stations had to be relocated to conform to the decisions of a new fire marshall, the lobby is not large enough to disperse the traffic quickly and effectively.

The other mistakes made at the various undergraduate libraries were small things, some of which were easily remedied and some of which cannot be corrected. South Carolina discovered two small faults with its building. First, no provision was made for ventilation when the air conditioning is out of order. Second, carpeting should not have been placed in front of the circulation desk because of the heavy wear.

At Texas, the faults in planning cannot be easily changed. Although Texas planned the group study rooms to be the right size, the typing rooms are too large. The outside book return, which is located on the west side of the building, empties into the office of the reserve librarian. The elevators are so situated that it is inconvenient to move books from the circulation desk to another floor. It is necessary to go from the circulation area through a door into the reserve area, through another door into the reading area, and then through another door into the lobby where the elevators are located. However, most of the insights gained from working in these buildings show that the shortcomings of the buildings are not serious.

As far as furnishings are concerned, certain features have been considered successful in these libraries. Carpeting is preferred because it is quiet and induces an aura of graciousness which the students respect. Only South Carolina installed carpeting when its building was built. Cornell installed carpeting in parts of the library in December, 1965, and Indiana carpeted lobbies and stairways to help diminish noise. Michigan and Texas considered carpeting in planning their libraries but rejected the idea because of the initial cost. The Lamont Library was built before carpeting was seriously considered as a floor covering for libraries.

A minimum of 50 footcandles is sufficient for lighting. Seventy footcandles seems to be the upper limit necessary for good lighting. Each of the libraries meets the minimum requirements. (This information is unavailable for Indiana.)

Variety in seating is desirable. Individual seats should constitute the majority of seating; lounge furniture should constitute only about 5 percent, with the remainder of the seats at tables seating no more than four readers. Round tables have not been considered desirable. Indiana, Cornell, and Texas provided only a small amount of lounge furniture. Indiana and Cornell feature seating at small tables, and Texas uses large divided-top tables. Generally, it has been concluded that students prefer individual seating because of the privacy it affords. The preferred seating is the individual carrel or the divided-top tables which provide the same effect. Lounge furniture is considered less functional because of the lack of writing area and because students tend to make themselves too comfortable. The small amount of lounge furniture at Michigan (only recently reduced), Cornell, Indiana, and Texas seem to bear out this point. Harvard has stated that experience has shown that less lounge furniture would be more efficient. Only at South Carolina is the large amount of lounge furniture not questioned because of student preferences and use of the facilities.

The most functional and economical type of seating is provided by large tables with dividers that seat from four to sixteen persons. The best use is made of available space, allowing more seating in an area without crowding. The least economical, but one of the most popular types of seating, is the group study room accommodating four readers.

Although more individual seating was placed in the Lamont Library than had previously been placed in any library (about 44 percent of the study seats), it is still not enough. If lounge chairs are included as individual seating, each undergraduate library has provided more than half (in fact almost two thirds) of its seating in individual seats. There are two exceptions. Indiana has only a few individual seats. At Texas, the amount depends on whether or not the divided-top tables are considered individual seating.

Some of the librarians advocate light-colored furniture, rather than dark, in order to prevent eyestrain. There is some disagreement on this point, but the facts indicate that eyestrain can be caused by the shift from light to dark surfaces. However, most agree that dark furniture is aesthetically more pleasing than light furniture. Because of its better wearing quality, plastic-upholstered furniture is recommended over that with fabric covering. It is also easier to maintain. Harvard has some leather-covered lounge furniture. Michigan, Indiana, and Cornell have used plastic materials for their chairs and settees. Overall, they have proven satisfactory. South Carolina began with fabric-covered lounge furniture, but the fabric has already begun to wear and is now being replaced with plastic fabrics. Texas has fabric-covered chairs but is not completely satisfied with them, because they become dirty quickly. As additional furniture is added, plastic-covered chairs are being acquired.

BOOK COLLECTION

The undergraduate library was to furnish a collection of carefully selected books to which all undergraduates should be exposed as part of their liberal education; it was also to house the reserve-book collection for undergraduates. One of the first questions about the undergraduate library is the validity of further decentralization of the book collection. Unfortunately, the patterns of research and instruction do not necessarily correspond with book classification or with department or college organization. There are overlapping and constant change in the disciplines and their patterns of research. Decentralization scatters the book collection over the campus and inconveniences students as cross-disciplinary study becomes prevalent. If an undergraduate library means that more books are being removed from existing collections to be segregated for use by undergraduates, then the idea of the undergraduate library is ineffective. However, the book collections of these undergraduate libraries were not taken from existing collections but are largely duplicate collections of books found elsewhere in the university library system. The success of this duplication depends, in part, on the affluence of the institution—the extent to which it can afford to duplicate titles. If it is necessary to transfer materials, other segments of the clientele are inconvenienced at the expense of the undergraduate.

The manner in which the several collections were formed was basically the same. Harvard began by developing criteria for the collection. Using bibliographic sources, local lists, and faculty recommendations, a master card file was compiled and submitted to the faculty for final selection. Michigan compiled a master card file using the Lamont list as a basis and supplementing it with other bibliographic tools, interviews with the faculty, reading lists, etc. Faculty members were hired to work on the project and buying trips undertaken to obtain out-of-print materials. At South Carolina, the collection was selected by the director of libraries, with six bibliographic tools providing the basis for the collection. Indiana began with the Michigan list, consulted with faculty, and made a buying trip for some materials. Cornell began with the Michigan list and a desiderata file compiled by the librarian. The stock of a bookstore was purchased and much of the material added to the collection. Texas also based its collection on the Michigan shelf list. Desiderata lists for materials of local interest were compiled by faculty members.

Progress has been made in serving the liberal education needs of the undergraduates. Harvard indicates that it has succeeded in building a collection which satisfies the needs of its undergraduates. However, this might be questioned since use of the collection has been decreasing. Michigan proposed to meet the needs of the undergraduates in the College of Literature, Science, and the Arts. It feels that it has met the needs of the underclassman in that college, but it makes no real attempt to satisfy the needs of the upperclassman in any schools or colleges of the university. South Carolina recognizes that it has not yet come to the point of satisfying the needs of its undergraduates since the undergraduate library attempts to serve all undergraduates (with the exception of those in professional curricula and those served by department libraries). Indiana made an effort to develop a general collection (below the extensive research level) by purchasing in many areas beyond the confines of the arts college. The collection at Cornell also provides books for exploration, recreation, and stimulation besides those supporting the instructional program. Texas attempts to meet the needs of students enrolled in courses in the College of Arts and Sciences, while also including materials in specialized areas where there is more interest on the layman's level.

To better serve the needs of undergraduates, undergraduate libraries allowed more open access than a general university library usually does. Harvard pioneered in opening the total collection to its clientele, but after one semester, it had to place reserve books in a closed area. The Undergraduate Library at Michigan provides more open access than any other undergraduate library, since most of its reserve books are on the open shelf. South Carolina, Indiana, Cornell, and Texas all provide a like amount of open access—the general collection and some reserve books are on the open shelves. Although some of the libraries experimented with more extensive open access, they found that the students abused the privilege. The demands placed on some books are so heavy that students often panic and steal or hide books, depriving all others of the books' use.

A selective collection seems to be better for most undergraduates. Some students profit from having access to a large research collection, but more undergraduates seem to be confused than helped. A selective collection with open access appears to offer the student opportunities for enrichment, discovery and entertainment, voluntary reading, and required reading. Each undergraduate library provides a selective collection. However, it must be noted that there is no conclusive evidence that the students have actually profited from this except in terms of use of the collection.

The book collection of the undergraduate library should be in a constant state of flux. No particular copy need be a permanent inclusion in the collection, although some titles, which are part of a basic liberal education, should always be there. Some mistakes are made in purchasing and eventually the books have to be removed from the collection. Others lose their relevance or become outdated. The collection should change and grow with the curriculum. Unfortunately, little of this has been accomplished. Only at Cornell and Harvard have weeding programs been carried on. At all the undergraduate libraries, worn-out, missing, or lost books have been withdrawn and replaced when feasible. Most of the collections have changed as they have grown, by emphasizing different areas or collecting in previously neglected subjects.

Most of the undergraduate libraries have an insufficient budget to develop their collection in the most desirable way. However, this is not true everywhere. Harvard considers its book budget sufficient (usually the full amount is not spent) for the needs of its students. South Carolina does not want a larger book budget, because it wants to retain the small, selective character of the collection, although the present collection is not large enough. Texas considers its budget sufficient, but the size of the collection needs to be increased. Until 1965, Michigan considered its budget inadequate. The size of the collection, however, is adequate. Both Indiana and Cornell feel the need for more money and more books. Both are relatively new libraries and have not had the time or the money to build collections in depth or quantity.

Duplication of heavily used reserve titles and general-collection titles is necessary. Indiana, Texas, and Cornell indicate they need more duplication to meet the demands of the students. Harvard and Michigan have liberal duplication policies which meet most needs. South Carolina has purposely limited extensive duplication in order to provide more titles instead of more copies.

Some of the undergraduate libraries have experienced the problem of a few departments buying most of the books and spending more than their "fair share" of the book budget (none of the undergraduate libraries allocate specific amounts of money to academic departments). This has been true at Michigan where four departments purchased 62 percent of all reserve books. South Carolina has experienced this same problem but to a lesser degree. At Indiana, Cornell, and Texas, a few academic departments show more interest than the average department. This interest results in scattered strengths in the collection.

Some miscalculations were made in not providing sufficient periodical files. Ten-year back files, which were usually provided, were not sufficient to meet the needs of the students. Harvard and Michigan did not have a stated cut-off date and provided more extensive holdings. South Carolina provides no periodicals except for current unbound issues. Indiana, Cornell, and Texas followed the ten-year policy with some exceptions: complete runs of important titles were provided, and some holdings began with the date of the library's opening.

Faculty participation aided in building all the undergraduate collections. In no case, however, were the results completely satisfactory because of a lack of interest and enthusiasm. Harvard, Michigan, and Cornell made large-scale attempts to solicit faculty cooperation but the results were uneven. Texas and Indiana did not make such an extensive drive, but, again, the results were mixed. South Carolina received little help from the faculty in developing its collection. Close work with the faculty in continued collection development is advantageous. All of the libraries have achieved this in varying degrees. However, cooperation varies as the faculty changes and as interest in the library rises or wanes. There is too much variation from year to year and school to school to make any valid conclusions.

In most of the undergraduate libraries, the reserve-book collection is an extension of the general collection. These are the books directly supporting the instructional program. The reserve collections at all the undergraduate libraries consist of required reading for undergraduate courses. In addition, some undergraduate libraries (Indiana and Cornell) include supplemental or recommended books as reserve materials.

SERVICES

An important point in considering the establishment of an undergraduate library is the kind of service given to the undergraduate student in the existing library. When the library administration becomes aware of the service the undergraduate is receiving and discovers it is not what it should be, it looks for a way to improve it. Service to the undergraduate is usually influenced by the size of the collection and the nature of the enrollment.

Service to graduate students and faculty necessarily interferes with that to undergraduates. The undergraduate needs a place to sit, a collection to use, and someone to direct his use of the library. The staff of a general library is more oriented to serving research needs than it is to teaching the undergraduate how to use the library, which is the kind of help he needs.

Reference service in an undergraduate library has two distinct characteristics: first, most questions are of a less complicated nature, and second, reference service tends to be in terms of teaching students how to use the library rather than of assisting in bibliographic searching. Each of the undergraduate libraries, with the exception of Lamont and South Carolina, offers similar service both in quality and quantity. The situation at South Carolina is somewhat different in that it does not maintain a reference desk because of the size of the staff. Reference service at the Lamont Library is provided only during the day by a nonprofessional. There has not been much demand for reference service because of the ease with which a student can find what he wants.

The reserve systems used in these undergraduate libraries are similar, with one notable exception. Harvard, South Carolina, Indiana, Cornell, and Texas basically adhere to a closed-reserve collection made up of reserve books not currently being used (a reserve book does not become part of the general collection). South Carolina has been able to prove that reserve books need not exist in great multitudes. By close work with the faculty, closed-reserve books have been reduced to a bare minimum. Only those titles for which there is extensive demand for a short period of time are on closed reserve. Cornell retains most of its reserve collection in a closed-stack arrangement, but some books are placed on open reserve. Indiana also maintains a two-part reserve system. Most of the collection is on closed reserve, but an open-reserve reading room is also provided. At Texas, all reserve books, with the exception of three-day and some "Building Use Only" books, are on closed reserve. The books on the open shelves are placed in their sequential location in each class. The one exception to the basic closed-reserve system is at Michigan. Only a small part of the reserve collection is on closed reserve; most reserved titles are on the open shelves in their sequential location with special markings to indicate they are reserve books. Unfortunately, student abuse has caused the near collapse of the system. Although Michigan's open-reserve system is educationally desirable, there are practical limitations—mainly the hiding and stealing of books made easier with an open reserve system.

For circulation control, South Carolina, Indiana, and Cornell use the McBee Keysort circulation system, which has met the needs of their operations. Michigan and Texas use the system developed at Michigan, which is a two-part form, both parts of which are retained and filed (one by call number and the other by transaction number). In both libraries, thought is being given to another system because of the increased volume of circulation. Lamont uses its own circulation system and considers it suited to its needs.

The special services found in the undergraduate libraries are not actually necessary to the functioning of the library, but they are important for making the undergraduate library something more than a depository for books. Special services are part of the concept of the "cultural center" and part of the distinguishing features of the undergraduate library.

All the undergraduate libraries except South Carolina have special services. South Carolina did not include any because of lack of staff and funds. Harvard, Michigan, Cornell, and Texas have audio facilities. The inclusion of these facilities was usually determined by the availability or the absence of other campus facilities. Indiana is adding audio service to its undergraduate library. South Carolina is the only undergraduate library which does not have typing facilities. Harvard and Indiana provide only space, but Michigan, Cornell, and Texas have rental typewriters. Harvard has a poetry room and a separate collection of modern fiction. Michigan has a student lounge which enables the student to have a cup of coffee without leaving the building, an auditorium or multipurpose room for meetings, and a print study gallery.

The special services differ among the libraries because of different concepts of what an undergraduate library should be, local conditions, and financial considerations. Since there is little agreement on the role of an undergraduate library, various interpretations have produced different effects. Local conditions have played an important part in some features of the undergraduate library. The presence of audio facilities on the campus may exclude their need in the undergraduate library. The same is true for any other feature. Financial considerations also help determine the extent of extra facilities to be located in the undergraduate library. A stringent budget might eliminate some facilities considered useful.

The undergraduate library has provided a means of simplifying and centralizing services that could be concentrated in one place to advantage. Use was simplified by the provision of open stacks and the elimination of unnecessary procedures in obtaining books. The layout of the buildings, interspersing books and readers, added to the ease of use. Centralization was achieved by bringing together books and services in one building and by providing the means whereby the undergraduate could be given more attention and the type of service he needs. The smallness of the undergraduate library also contributes to its simplicity. All of the undergraduate libraries adhered to these principles. South Carolina, however, was unwilling to accept completely the principle of simplification, because it felt that would discourage students from learning how to use a more complex library system.

It is the responsibility of the university not only to teach the student how to use the library but also to teach him what constitutes a good library. Many undergraduates come to college with little library training, and it should be part of their education to get this training at the university. The undergraduate does not easily learn this in the general university library nor is he usually able to get the individual type of service he needs.

There are two views on how students should approach the book collection. One advocates finding the book from the shelf, while the other advocates access through the card catalog. Students usually approach the book collection through the card catalog, because they are seeking a particular title. However, once they go to the shelves, they may find other books equally suited to their purpose. Since the book collection of the undergraduate library serves as the laboratory for the liberal arts student, the library affords the student the opportunity to sample the wealth of knowledge found in books, whether he finds it through the card catalog or by browsing.

The type of instruction in use of the library varies from formal classroom lectures to informal instruction given at the reference desk. Harvard has given instruction only on an individual basis when a student asks for help. At Michigan, the Undergraduate Library is considered a "training library," and the reference librarians are considered teachers instructing students in library use and stimulating them to go beyond required reading. South Carolina considers teaching the student to use the library the weakest point in its operation, simply because there is insufficient staff. Indiana provides instruction in library use through the reference staff and by tours. In conjunction with the English departments at Cornell and at Michigan, library orientation lectures are given to all freshmen each fall. In addition, the reference staff helps individual students in learning how to use the library. Texas also provides classroom instruction in library use, but participation is on a voluntary basis so that most instruction is provided when it is individually requested.

STAFF

The staff serves the student more as teachers than as mere dispensers of facts, and guides the student in his use of the library and his selection of books. The staff must be able to adapt readily to new situations and be flexible enough to meet the constant demands and pressures which manifest themselves. The staff has to be interested in working with people and able to communicate with the undergraduate student. A system of assigning the staff reference duty, book selection, and the responsibility of one area has proven satisfactory at Michigan, Cornell, Indiana, and Texas (at Texas and Indiana most book selection is done by the acquisition librarian).

LIBRARY USE

Throughout this paper it has been asserted that more extensive use is being made of the library. Is this really true or does it just seem that way because enrollments are increasing (Table 39)? Without a comparison of the same figures before the advent of the undergraduate library, the real implication (if there is one) is not evident. In each case, the percent of increase of total book use and attendance has been greater than the percent of increase in enrollment. The increase in total book use has been the most spectacular (Table 39). In the three older undergraduate libraries, it has exceeded 100 percent, while the three other undergraduate libraries should reach or exceed that point in a like period of time.

There are some interesting comparisons in library use. Total book use has increased as follows (for the period the library has been open): Harvard, 123 percent; Michigan, 112 percent; South Carolina, 118 percent; Indiana, 67 percent; Cornell, 26 percent; Texas, 71 percent (Table 39). Attendance (where the figures are available) has not risen as sharply: Michigan, 35 percent; South Carolina, 95 percent; Cornell 6 percent; Texas, 20 percent. These figures seem to indicate that the students who use the library make extensive use of its facilities. The slower rise in attendance may also be attributed to the building's being used to capacity. It seems that attendance has risen faster in the newer libraries than the older ones, which verifies the need that these libraries serve.

Why are more students using the library? One reason is new teaching methods. Many

TABLE 39

COMPARISON OF ENROLLMENT, TOTAL BOOK USE

	HARVARD			MICHIGAN			SOUTH CAROLINA		
	Enroll.[b]	T.B.U.[d]	Attend.[c]	Enroll.	T.B.U.	Attend.	Enroll.	T.B.U.	Attend.
1948–49[a]	5,464	81,766							
1949–50	5,043	151,873							
1950–51	4,649	159,086							
1951–52	4,439	152,798							
1952–53	4,433	148,908							
1953–54	4,356	351,783							
1954–55	4,448	359,284							
1955–56	4,470	336,652							
1956–57	4,463	298,102							
1957–58	4,472	328,270							
1958–59	c	329,549		7,357	481,512	1,457,441			
1959–60	4,542	349,965		7,355	644,956	1,556,227	4,273	30,909	113,01?
1960–61	4,596	368,699		7,669	665,946	1,548,837	4,882	37,799	130,90?
1961–62	4,764	363,299		8,268	713,034	1,731,283	5,163	44,506	147,27?
1962–63	4,728	370,061		8,402	842,670	1,807,896	5,443	53,380	132,74?
1963–64	4,719	317,663		8,779	973,301	1,883,083	5,689	57,431	188,36?
1964–65	4,785	339,170		9,536	1,023,084	1,969,935	6,244	67,451	220,64?

[a]Figures for a partial year—not used in figuring percentages.
[b]Undergraduate enrollment for the fall semester of the academic year.
[c]Figures not available.
[d]Total book use.

instructors are abandoning the lecture and textbook method of instruction and emphasizing independent study. As more instructors adopt the "teaching with books" method, more student use of the library follows.

The real question is which comes first—curriculum changes or an undergraduate library. At some institutions, the nature of the curriculum—more emphasis on honors programs, independent work, etc.—creates a need that cannot always be satisfactorily met in the large university library. In other instances, the presence of an undergraduate library with its expanded facilities may make it possible for instructors to do more "teaching with books" than they had done in the past, because the library situation made such practices impractical. There does not seem to be much doubt—at least among undergraduate librarians and library administrators at institutions where there are undergraduate libraries—that instructors are making more extensive use of the library in their instructional programs.

Undergraduate libraries, however, also serve in large part simply as study halls. Depending on the nature of the parent institution, the amount may vary anywhere from 50 to 90 percent of the undergraduate library's use, depending on how one defines "study hall use" of the library. If it is limited strictly to studying from a student's own books and notes, then the percentage of use would be lower than the figures given above. However, if study hall use includes reading reserve books, the above figures are probably pretty accurate.

Another problem in connection with study hall use is that any one user does not usually come to the library to use it only as a study hall or to use only library materials. His reason in coming may be two-fold, or he may come only to study from his own books but be enticed to use library materials once he is there. This is basically the reason that a study hall "barn" would not suffice as a place to study, because it offers none of the intellectual advantages of a library.

Undergraduate libraries are often used as study halls because in many cases it is the only place where the undergraduate can satisfactorily study. Dormitories and apartments are often crowded and noisy and do not offer good study conditions. Another cause for the high percentage of study hall usage of undergraduate libraries is the increasing

TABLE 39–Continued

AND ATTENDANCE IN THE SIX UNDERGRADUATE LIBRARIES SURVEYED

	INDIANA			CORNELL			TEXAS	
Enroll.[c]	T.B.U.	Attend.[c]	Enroll.	T.B.U.	Attend.	Enroll.	T.B.U.	Attend.
47,361								
144,101		2,902	189,560	705,251				
187,930		3,028	217,306	758,331	8,954	423,475	1,473,048	
241,370		3,069	239,873	752,583	9,746	732,259	1,769,560	

academic pressures placed on students. A third factor is the changing nature of student bodies. Students are now more serious, perhaps because of the keen competition they face to get into college and to remain there.

Use of the library presents a peculiar situation at the Lamont Library. When the building first opened, Harvard undergraduates used the library heavily. But after a few years, general book circulation began to decline, reserve-book use declined, and fewer people seemed to come to the library. At the same time, there was also a reduction in professional staff—from eight professionals in 1949 to two in 1965. There is a definite possibility of a correlation between the reduction in staff and the decline in use of the library, because it seems natural that as service declined, use would decline (of course, the opposite may be true, but the whole pattern of development at other schools seems to contradict this). Another factor affecting use of the Lamont Library is the restriction on Radcliffe girls in using the library. Perhaps it is time to reexamine this policy, because a change would surely increase the use of the library, not only by adding a new clientele but by enticing some Harvard undergraduates back to Lamont.

At Michigan, an instructional program in the use of the library for the undergraduate student would allow the student to make more effective use of the library, but the number of students is so large that no satisfactory solution has been found. South Carolina wants to increase the effectiveness of the library by finding a way to communicate with the students and by giving the student personal help in teaching him to use the library.

Some of the undergraduate libraries have been confronted with another kind of library use—student socializing in the library. Students find they need a break from studying and get it by visiting with other students. If the students do not have a place to go in the library for this purpose, they talk in the reading areas, which is distracting and annoying to the students who are trying to study. When many students are gathered in one place, it is logical that it also serves as a social meeting place. Although some of the undergraduate libraries are faced with this problem—mainly Cornell, Indiana, and Michigan—it apparently does not exist at the others. The library is, of course, a natural meeting place for students. Some students go to the library for the sole purpose of being seen and to see who is there. There is really no way to avoid this, nor is it undesirable for the undergraduate library to serve as a meeting place so long as the social function does not interfere with the real purpose of the library.

Effective use of the library seems to revolve around having enough books and providing service to the student. Without a sufficient book collection, the needs of the undergraduate student cannot be satisfied. But, if there is not a staff to guide the student in his use of the collection, then the needs of the undergraduate are not being met, and the library does not serve its real purpose.

SUMMARY

Now that the establishment of an undergraduate library has succeeded at several institutions, the idea is considered by some as a cure for any library problem that a university library may face. The undergraduate library, however, seems necessary only when the enrollment becomes too heterogeneous to be served in one building and by one staff. When the student body contains many undergraduates and a large percentage of graduate students in addition to a significant faculty group, the distinct service which the undergraduate library affords is a partial answer to the problem. Undergraduate libraries remove the undergraduate from the research library, allowing him better service in his own library, while meeting the needs of the graduate students and faculty members in a more satisfactory way in the research library.

Enrollment at the six institutions which now have undergraduate libraries varied greatly when they opened their undergraduate libraries (Table 39). The total enrollment is not as important, however, as is the percentage of students who are undergraduates. Even so, the figures do not reveal any pattern which other schools might use as a rule of thumb. However, the ratio of graduate students to undergraduates has to be considered. If the enrollment is 90 percent undergraduate, a separate undergraduate library is unnecessary, because the main library is basically an undergraduate library by nature of the enrollment. When graduate students constitute one third to one half of the student body, an undergraduate library is a feasible answer to solving the university's library problem.

Neither is there a definite formula to follow in regard to the size of the main library collection. When a collection reaches a million volumes, few libraries maintain open stacks to provide the undergraduate with access to the collection so that he can make full use of it. When the book collection reaches this point, some sort of division of the library becomes desirable. Whether a vertical division as represented by undergraduate libraries or a horizontal one as reflected in the divisional plan is made depends on many factors. Of course, there is always the opposing viewpoint that the student should be exposed to the total library collection to allow him to select his own books.

The nature of the main library building—its physical layout and structure—helps determine the feasibility of a separate undergraduate library building. If the main library building is one that can be adapted to meet the needs of the undergraduate as well as those of graduate students and faculty, there is no need for a separate undergraduate library. But, if the present building cannot be made to provide for the needs of the undergraduate for seating, access to books, and service, another solution has to be found. Or, if the use to which it is being put makes the building unadaptable to the needs of the undergraduate, it is not desirable to attempt a renovation. The solution may be an undergraduate collection in a separate reading room in one wing of the building or on one floor of the building. It may be as simple as opening the stacks to the undergraduate. But, if the problem is basically one of not enough space for seating due to increasing enrollments, another answer usually has to be found. There is always the possibility of enlarging the building, but it may be easier and less expensive to build a new building.

Although some universities consider the idea of a separate undergraduate library desirable, they reject it because they think the cost of the operation is too high. The undergraduate library is costly in terms of duplication of staff and books, but it is cheap in terms of operation when compared with similar service in a general university library. It is more expensive than offering no special service for the undergraduate, but it is inexpensive in terms of supplying a needed service.

In summary, the feasibility of building a separate undergraduate library varies with the situation at each institution. The size of the student body, the size of the book collection, the kind of service available for the undergraduate student, the building situation, and the curriculum needs are all facets of the problem. Just because Harvard has one, every institution of that size does not necessarily need an undergraduate library. Neither do the undergraduate libraries at Cornell, Michigan, Indiana, Texas, or South Carolina imply any definite trend. In each case, the decision to have an undergraduate library was the answer to a particular problem at a particular institution.

Even though no definitive plan to follow in establishing an undergraduate library has emerged from this study, the fourteen following guidelines are suggested for institutions considering an undergraduate library:

1. Determine the philosophy of library services to be followed.

2. Prepare a written program stating the objectives of library development and translate these objectives into space requirements based upon the size of the student body and the curriculum. Also indicate such factors as type of building, size of staff, kinds of furnishings and equipment, and service functions.

3. Obtain the services of a library consultant.

4. Secure the needed financial support.

5. Select a building site suitable for the students' needs. It is advantageous to be near the main library building because of limitations of the undergraduate library book collection.

6. Decide on the building design (assuming a new, separate building). Choose a design which satisfies current needs but is also flexible enough to provide for future needs (a modular construction is most satisfactory). The size of the building depends on the size and nature of the enrollment to be served. Plan the facilities and services to be contained in the building. Set up the specifications and correlate the functions and their relationships. Plan the traffic patterns for best utilization.

7. Special features of the building should include group study rooms (seating no more than four readers), a special-purpose room or small auditorium (for meetings, classes, movies, etc.) if not available elsewhere, typing facilities, photocopying facilities, a student lounge or informal area where students can gather, talk, and relax.

8. Plan seating for at least 30 percent of the enrollment, with about 75 percent being individual seats (lounge chairs, individual carrels, or tables with egg-crate dividers) and the remainder at tables for four.

9. Choose carpeting for a floor covering, if possible (vinyl or rubber tile is satisfactory but noisy).

10. Provide sufficient work space and office space for the staff and a staff lounge. The offices and work space are best centralized in one area.

11. Begin the development of the book collection by using a basic list (such as that of the University of Michigan Undergraduate Library); expand it in areas of strength and delete materials not considered necessary. The collection

should contain frequently used materials and general reference tools. The collection should contain books, periodicals (complete runs of heavily used titles and limited runs of the remainder—usually about ten-year back files), pamphlets, and audio materials. The collection should contain a basic liberal arts core of books, but it need not be a well-rounded collection. The collection should reflect the curriculum and interests of the students being served. Selection should be based on working needs with little regard to other university library holdings. The collection probably need not exceed 75,000 titles in 200,000 volumes, because it then ceases to be selective in character.

12. Plan public service areas as close to each other as possible, especially circulation and reserve. Provide reference service daily until 10:00 P.M. and on weekends. The circulation system should entail as little work of the patron as possible and allow quick return of books to the shelves. Reserve books should be easily available (as many on open shelves as feasible).

13. Plan for a sufficient number of staff, both professional and nonprofessional. The staff should be responsible for one area, in addition to doing reference work and book selection. Consider a young staff, although this is not necessary.

14. Let use of the library develop according to the character of the student body. Do not try to enforce any stringent rules.

The undergraduate library was created because of a recognition that the undergraduate student body was being neglected due to emphasis on service to graduate students and faculty. It was the intention of those creating these special facilities to produce a new type of library on the university campus, different from the general university library in both collections and services. This study has attempted to outline the development of the several individual libraries and to point out the similarities and differences in their operations. It is the judgment of the present researcher that the undergraduate library has provided a more efficient and satisfactory service to the undergraduate—and has at the same time improved the service of the central library to graduate students and faculty by relieving the central collection of undergraduate service. This method of providing expanded and improved library service has blazed a new path on the frontier of library service—one which many more libraries will eventually follow.

Selected Bibliography

BOOKS AND PAMPHLETS

American Library Association. Library Technology Project. *The Use of Carpeting in Libraries.* Chicago: A.L.A., 1962.

Audio Library of the Undergraduate Library at the University of Texas. Austin: The Undergraduate Library, n.d.

Cornell University. Libraries. *The Central Libraries.* Ithaca, N.Y.: [1962].

────── ────── *Handbook of the Libraries for Graduate Students and Faculty.* 4th ed. Ithaca: Uris Library, 1962.

────── ────── *Basic Library Handbook.* Ithaca: Uris Library, Cornell Univ., 1965.

Harvard University. Library. *Directory, 1949–1964/65.* Cambridge, Mass.

────── ────── *Guide to Lamont Library.* ("Guides to the Harvard Libraries," No. 7. Cambridge: Harvard Univ. Library, 1958.

────── ────── *Lamont Library Handbook.* Cambridge: Harvard College Library, 1949.

Meier, Richard L. *Social Change in Communications-Oriented Institutions.* (Mental Health Research Institute, University of Michigan, Report No. 10.) Ann Arbor: Univ. of Michigan, 1961.

Metcalf, Keyes D. *Planning Academic and Research Library Buildings.* New York: McGraw-Hill, 1965.

────── *Report on the Harvard University Library: A Study of Present and Prospective Problems.* Cambridge: Harvard Univ. Library, 1955.

Michigan. University. Library. Undergraduate Library. *The Undergraduate Library Building of the University of Michigan.* Ann Arbor: Univ. of Michigan Library, 1960.

The Undergraduate and the Library. Bloomington: Indiana Univ. Libraries, 1965.

ARTICLES AND PERIODICALS

Brown, Rollo W. "The Library as a Place of Discovery," *Harvard Alumni Bulletin,* XLVIII (May 11, 1946), 617–20.

Carpenter, Charles A., Jr. "The Lamont Catalog as a Guide to Book Selection," *College and Research Libraries,* XVIII (July, 1957), 267–68+.

Cassel, Jean. "The University of Texas Undergraduate Library Collection," *Texas Library Journal,* XXXIX (Winter, 1963), 123–26.

Elkins, Kimball C. "Foreshadowings of Lamont: Student Proposals in the Nineteenth Century," *Harvard Library Bulletin,* VIII (Winter, 1954), 41–53.

"Harvard's New Library," *Library Journal,* LXXI (Feb. 15, 1946), 288.

Harvard's Open Shelf, 1948–49.

Haviland, Morrison. "The Reference Function of the Lamont Library," *Harvard Library Bulletin,* III (Spring, 1949), 297–99.

Keniston, Roberta. "Circulation Gains at Michigan," *Library Journal,* LXXXIII (Dec. 1, 1958), 3357–59.

────── "The University of Michigan Undergraduate Library," *Michigan Librarian,* XXV (June, 1959), 24–25.

Lovett, Robert W. "The Undergraduate and the Harvard Library, 1877–1937," *Harvard Library Bulletin,* I (Spring, 1947), 221–37.

McAnally, Arthur M. "Library Service to Undergraduates: A Symposium—Introductory Remarks," *College and Research Libraries,* XIV (July, 1953), 266.

McCarthy, Stephen A. "The Cornell Library System," in Cornell University. Libraries. *Cornell Library Conference: Papers Read at the Dedication of the Central Libraries, October 1962.* Ithaca: Cornell Univ. Libraries, 1964.

McNiff, Philip J. "The Charging System of the Lamont Library," *Harvard Library Bul-*

letin, III (Autumn, 1949), 438–40.

—— and Edwin E. Williams. "Lamont Library: The First Year," *Harvard Library Bulletin,* IV (Spring, 1950), 203–12.

Metcalf, Keyes D. "Harvard Faces Its Library Problems," in Conference on the Place of the Library in a University, Harvard University, 1949. *The Place of the Library in a University: A Conference Held at Harvard University, 30–31 March, 1949.* Cambridge: Harvard Univ. Library, 1950.

—— "The Lamont Library: II. Function," *Harvard Library Bulletin,* III (Winter, 1949), 12–30.

—— "To What Extent Must We Segregate?" *College and Research Libraries,* VIII (Oct., 1947), 399–401.

—— "The Undergraduate and the Harvard Library, 1765–1877," *Harvard Library Bulletin,* I (Winter, 1947), 29–51.

—— "The Undergraduate and the Harvard Library, 1937–1947," *Harvard Library Bulletin,* I (Autumn, 1947), 288–305.

Packard, Frederick C., Jr. "Harvard's Vocarium Has Attained Full Stature," *Library Journal,* LXXV (Jan. 15, 1950), 69–74.

[Packard, James] "The Undergraduate Library," *Research News,* XV (May, 1965), [1]–12.

Pautzsch, Richard O. "The Classification Scheme for the Lamont Library," *Harvard Library Bulletin,* IV (Winter, 1950), 126–27.

Quinsey, Robert L. "Undergraduate Library," *California Library Bulletin,* XI (Dec., 1949), 67–68+.

Ransom, Harry H. "Arts and Sciences: The College Library," *Texas Quarterly,* II (Winter, 1959), vii–xii.

Reames, J. Mitchell. "First in the South—Undergraduate Library, University of South Carolina," *South Carolina Librarian,* III (March, 1959), 22–23.

—— "The Undergraduate Library, University of South Carolina," *Southeastern Librarian,* X (Fall, 1960), 130–36.

Shepley, Henry R. "The Lamont Library: I. Design," *Harvard Library Bulletin,* III (Winter, 1949), 5–11.

Shores, Louis. "The Undergraduate and His Library," in *University of Tennessee Library Lectures,* edited by Lanelle Vandiver. No. 11. Knoxville: Univ. of Tennessee, 1960.

Wagman, Frederick H. "Library Service to Undergraduate College Students: The Case for the Separate Undergraduate Library," *College and Research Libraries,* XVII (March, 1956), 150–55.

—— "The Undergraduate Library of the University of Michigan," *College and Research Libraries,* XX (May, 1959), 179–88.

Wilkinson, Billy R. "New out of Old; A Look at Plans for the Undergraduate Library," *Cornell Alumni News,* LXIV (Jan., 1962), 12–13.

Williams, Edwin E. "The Selection of Books for Lamont," *Harvard Library Bulletin,* III (Autumn, 1949), 386–94.

REPORTS

Cornell University. Libraries. *Report of the Director,* 1947/48–1964/65.

—— Uris Library. *Annual Report,* 1962/63–1964/65.

Harvard University. Library. *Annual Report,* 1938/39–1964/65.

Indiana. University. Library. *Library Newsletter,* 1945–1963.

—— —— —— *Report on the Libraries of Indiana University,* 1949/50–1964/65.

—— —— —— Undergraduate Library. *Summary of Library Operations,* 1963/64–1964/65.

Michigan. University. Library. Undergraduate Library, *Annual Report,* 1957/58–1964/65.

South Carolina. University. Library. *Annual Report,* 1957/58–1964/65.

—— —— —— Undergraduate Library. *Annual Report,* 1958/59–1964/65.

Texas. University. Library. *Annual Report,* 1959/60–1964/65.

—— —— —— Undergraduate Library. *Annual Report,* 1959/60–1964/65.

UNPUBLISHED MATERIAL

Cornell University. Libraries, Office files. Ithaca, N.Y.

—— Uris Library. Office files. Ithaca, N.Y.

Faucher, Rose-Grace. "The Undergraduate Library." Talk given at the Library Science Convocation, Ann Arbor, Mich., Sept. 30, 1965.

Hawkins, Jo Ann Walker. "The University of Texas Audio Library." Unpublished Master's thesis, Graduate School of Library Science, Univ. of Texas, 1966.

Indiana. University. Library. *Statement of Program for an Undergraduate Library at Indiana University.* Bloomington: 1952.

———— ———— ———— Undergraduate Library. Office files. Bloomington, Ind.

Lamont (Thomas W.) Papers. Harvard University Archives, Cambridge, Mass.

Metcalf (Keyes D.) Papers. Harvard University Archives, Cambridge, Mass.

Michigan. University. Advisory Committee on the Undergraduate Library. "Program for an Undergraduate Library." Ann Arbor: 1955.

———— ———— Library. Office files. Ann Arbor, Mich.

———— ———— Undergraduate Library. Office files. Ann Arbor, Mich.

Reames, J. Mitchell. "The Undergraduate Library, The University of South Carolina." Speech given at the meeting of the Columbia Library Club, Columbia, S.C., Sept. 24, 1958.

Saidel, Cynthia A. "A Survey of the Lamont Library of Harvard College." Unpublished Master's thesis, School of Library Service, Columbia Univ., 1952.

South Carolina. University. Library. Undergraduate Library. Office files. Columbia, S.C.

Stewart, Rolland C. "Building Undergraduate Library Collections: Questions, Realities, and Prospects." Speech given before the Illinois Library Association, College and Research Section, Chicago, Ill., Oct. 29, 1965.

Taylor, Constance M. "Meeting the Needs of Undergraduates in Large University Libraries: Problems and Attempted Solutions." Unpublished Master's thesis, Graduate School of Library Science, Univ. of Texas, 1956.

Texas. University. Library. Office files. Austin, Texas.

———— ———— ———— Undergraduate Library. Office files. Austin, Texas.

Whitely, Esther R. "Undergraduate Use of the Stack Collection of the Indiana University Library as Indicated by Circulation, April 1959–March 1961." Unpublished Master's thesis, Library School, Indiana Univ., 1962.

OTHER SOURCES

Boston. Public Library. Personal interview with Philip McNiff, Director, Oct. 28, 1965.

Cornell University. Personal interview with Stephen A. McCarthy, Director of University Libraries. Oct. 20, 1965.

———— Personal interview with G. F. Shepherd, Assistant Director for Public Services, Cornell Univ. Libraries, Oct. 20, 1965.

———— Personal interview with Billy Wilkinson, Librarian, Uris Library, Oct. 21, 1965.

Eastern Michigan University. Personal interview with Roberta Keniston, Assistant Librarian, Feb. 22, 1966.

Harvard University. Personal interview with Theodore Alevizos, Librarian, Lamont Library, Oct. 26, 1965.

———— Personal interview with Keyes D. Metcalf, Librarian Emeritus, Oct. 25, 1965.

———— Personal interview with Edwin Williams, Counselor to the Director, Harvard Univ. Library, Oct. 27, 1965.

Indiana. University. Personal interview with Neil S. Boardman, Administrative Assistant, University Libraries, Jan. 13, 1966.

———— ———— Personal interview with Janet Horton, Undergraduate Librarian, Jan. 12, 1966.

———— ———— Personal interview with Robert Miller, Director of Libraries, Jan. 12, 1966.

Michigan. University. Personal interview with Rose-Grace Faucher, Librarian, Undergraduate Library, Oct. 8, 1965.

———— ———— Personal interview with Rolland C. Stewart, Assistant Director for Public Services, Univ. of Michigan Libraries, Dec. 16, 1966.

———— ———— Personal interview with Frederick H. Wagman, Director of the University Libraries, March 10, 1966.

South Carolina. University. Personal interview with Alfred H. Rawlinson, Director of Libraries, Nov. 4, 1965.

———— ———— Personal interview with J. Mitchell Reames, Librarian, Undergraduate Library, Nov. 2, 1965.

Texas. University. Personal interview with Jean Cassel, Assistant Librarian, Undergraduate Library, Dec. 21, 1965.

———— ———— Personal interview with Fred Folmer, Associate Director, the University Library, Dec. 21, 1965.

———— ———— Personal interview with Frances Hudspeth, Associate Director, Humanities Research Center, Dec. 22, 1965.

———— ———— Personal interview with Alexander Moffit, Director, the University Library, Dec. 20, 1965.

———— ———— Personal interview with Imogene Thompson, Librarian, Undergraduate Library, Dec. 21, 1965.

Index

Aalto, Alvar, 12

Academic Center (Texas), 116, 117

Acoustic problems, 100–101, 124

Acquisition of materials: cooperation between faculty and libraries, 44, 70, 71–72, 83, 102, 126, 141, 143

purchasing procedures, 20, 73, 103, 107, 124–125

Activities, nonlibrary, *see* Nonlibrary activities and facilities

Adams, Robert M., 91, 101

Additions, 94

Aesthetics, of furniture, 65, 99

Air conditioning, 32, 79, 140

Aisles: in reading areas, 139; between stacks, 138

Alcoves: 10; reading, 9, 80; seating in, 139

Armchairs, *see* Chairs

Arrangements, *see* Layouts

Art exhibits, *see* Exhibition space

Attendance: 145; Indiana, 90; Lamont, 25; Michigan, 55, 56–57; South Carolina, 75–76; Texas, 133–134; Uris, 109–110, 112

Audio facilities: 144; Indiana, 88; Lamont, 19–20; Michigan, 32, 54; South Carolina, 73; Texas, 120, 125, 130; Uris, 99, 108

Bishop, William W., 29

Blind, facilities for the, 20, 32, 53, 117, 119

Blue Star collection (South Carolina), 70

Boardman, Neil, 83

Bodley, Sir Thomas, 1

Book budget, 103, 105, 125, 127, 142

Book capacity, 17, 63, 124

Book collection

arrangement: Lamont, 17; Michigan, 38; Texas, 127

size: Indiana, 83, 84–85; Lamont, 16, 17; Michigan, 46; South Carolina, 70, 75; Texas, 124, 127; Uris, 103

use: Indiana, 90; Lamont, 23–24; Michigan, 56–57; South Carolina, 75; Texas, 132–134; Uris, 110

Book-return facilities, 10, 140

Book selection: 149–150; Indiana, 83–84; Lamont, 15; Michigan, 43–46; South Carolina, 69–70; Texas, 124–126; Uris, 101–103, 104

Book selection tools: 141; Indiana, 83–84; Lamont, 15; Michigan, 44; South Carolina, 70; Texas, 124–125; Uris, 102

Book stacks, *see* Stacks

Browsing, 20, 54, 139, 145

Buck, Paul, 7, 25

Building costs, *see* Costs

Building design, 65, 118, 149

Building supervision, 76, 131

Card catalog, *see* Catalog

Carpenter, Charles A., Jr., 102, 103, 108

Carpeting, *see* Floor coverings

Carrels

Douglass, 97, 99

individual: Indiana, 81, 82; Lamont, 9, 14; Michigan, 38; South Carolina, 68; Texas, 121–122; Uris, 99–100

Cassel, Jean, 124

Catalog: 3; location, 54, 79, 97; use, 20, 86

Catalog, divided, 20, 130

Cataloging, 20, 130

Central Library (Indiana), 78, 79, 81, 82, 83, 84, 85, 86

Centralization, *see* Services, centralized

Chairs: arm, 122–123; lounge, 12, 14, 38, 43, 65, 82, 99–100, 121–122

Circulation

periods: Indiana, 87; Lamont, 19; South Carolina, 72; Texas, 128; Uris, 106–117

systems: 144; Indiana, 87; Lamont, 19; Michigan, 52; South Carolina, 72; Texas, 128, 129; Uris, 106–117

volume: Indiana, 90; Lamont, 23–24; Michigan, 57–58; South Carolina, 75; Texas, 132; Uris, 110

Classrooms, 98, 107, 130

Clerical staff, 22, 74, 89

Clipping file, 54, 88

College catalogs, 80, 85, 87–88, 107

Color, use of, 12, 43, 99, 117

Columbia University, 2

Conant, James Bryant, 21

Conference rooms, 10, 12, 14, 119, 120, 122

Coolidge, Shepley, Bulfinch & Abbott, 5

Costs, 148

book: Indiana, 85; Lamont, 7; Michigan, 31, 45; South Carolina, 70; Texas, 125, 127; Uris, 103

building: Lamont, 7; Michigan, 31–32; South Carolina, 63, 65; Texas, 117; Uris, 96

Coverings, *see* Floor coverings

Dahl, George L., 117

Dana-Palmer House, 7

Dean, Arthur H., 96

Dewey Decimal Classification, 21, 127
Discarding, *see* Weeding
Divided catalog, *see* Catalog, divided
Divided tables, *see* Tables, divided
Douglass carrel, *see* Carrels, Douglass
Duke University, 2
Duplicates, 15, 148
Duplication: in general collection, 3, 43, 69, 83, 84, 101, 103, 141, 142; for reserve, 46, 48, 71, 86, 90–91, 105, 107, 127, 129, 142

Elevators, 99, 139, 140
Endowments, 7, 104, 117
Enrollment, 145, 146–147, 148
Entrance lobbies, *see* Lobbies
Entrances: location of, 38, 98, 119, 139; number of, 38, 139
Exhibition space, 3, 32, 53, 118–119
Exits: control of, 97; number of, 10, 38, 139

Facilities, nonlibrary, *see* Nonlibrary activities and facilities
Faculty committees, 6, 31, 95
Farnsworth (Dana L.) room (Lamont), 11, 12, 19, 20, 22
Film-preview room (Michigan), 34, 53
Fischler, Barbara, 83
Floor coverings: carpeting, 68–69, 101, 124, 140, 149; cork, 14; hardwood, 82; rubber tile, 68; vinyl tile, 82, 101, 124
Folmer, Fred, 117
Foreign language materials, 18, 48, 101, 125, 126
Forum room (Lamont), 11, 14
Furniture: dark-colored, 65, 99, 141; light-colored, 12, 82, 99, 141; quality and upkeep of, 68, 124, 141

General Education Program (Harvard), 7, 11
General Library (Michigan), 29, 30, 45, 47, 56, 58
Gift books, 15, 103, 125
Gold Star periodicals (Michigan), 43, 47
Goldwin Smith Library (Cornell), 102, 103
Group study rooms, 32, 38, 53, 139, 140, 149

Hanford, Chester, 6
Harvard Collection, 11, 20
Harvard Corporation, 6
Harvard Fund Council, 7
Harvard Yard, 5, 8
Hatcher, Harlan, 29
Houghton Library (Harvard), 7, 9
Hours of opening, 109, 133
Hours of service: professional, 50–51, 74, 109, 131; reference, 50–51
House libraries, 1, 5, 15, 24
Hudspeth, Frances, 117
Humanities Research Center (Texas), 120

Illumination, *see* Lighting
Instruction in library use, *see* Library use, instruction in
Interior arrangement: Indiana, 79–81; Lamont, 7–8, 9–12; Michigan, 32, 38; South Carolina, 65; Texas, 118–120; Uris, 96–99
Internship system, 22
Inventory, 71, 85, 104, 126

James, Henry, 25
James, Thomas, 1
Jessen, Jessen, Millhouse & Greven, 117

Kahn Associated Architects & Engineers, 60
Keniston, Roberta, 55
Kirkland, John T., 1

Lamont, Thomas W., 7,
Lamont *Catalogue*, 44, 45, 102, 125, 141
Lamont Classification scheme, 20–21, 73
Lamont Library (Harvard): background, 5–6; book collection, 15; building, 7–15; financing, 7–18; services, 18–21; staff, 21–23; use, 23–25
Layouts: 139, 144, 148; seating, 65, 138; shelving, 17, 65, 80, 104, 138
Lectures on library use, *see* Library use, instruction in
Lewis, James A., 31
Library of Congress Classification, 108
Library space, increased demand for, 5, 29, 38, 43, 63, 79, 93, 137
Library use
    decline in, 23, 25, 141, 147
    by graduate students, 24–25, 56, 90, 91, 126
    increased: 145; Indiana, 89–90; Lamont, 23; Michigan, 55–56; South Carolina, 75–76; Texas, 132–133; Uris, 109–111
    instruction in: 2, 3, 145, 147; Indiana, 88; Lamont, 21; Michigan, 54; South Carolina, 73–74; Texas, 130–131; Uris, 108
Lighting: 11, 100, 140; fluorescent, 14, 38, 69, 82, 124; luminous ceilings, 38, 124
Lobbies, 10, 32, 79, 97, 118, 120, 140
Lost books, 46, 71
Lounge furniture: 140; Indiana, 82; Lamont, 12, 14; Michigan, 38, 43; South Carolina, 65; Texas, 121; Uris, 99–100
Lyles, Bisset, Carlisle & Wolff, 63

McAnally, Arthur, 1
McBee Keysort system, *see* Circulation systems
McCarthy, Stephen A., 94
McKissick Memorial Library (South Carolina), 63, 75
Meeting facilities, 11, 38, 53, 130
Meier, Richard, 57
Metcalf, Keyes, 3, 5, 7, 63, 94
Mezzanines, 9, 10, 11, 65, 68, 81
Miller, Robert A., 78
Missing books, *see* Lost books
Modular construction, 8, 32, 118, 138, 149
Moffit, Alexander, 117, 124
Multipurpose room (Michigan), 38, 53
Music collections, 47, 105, 125

Newspapers, 71, 119, 126
Noise, 111, 124, 147
Nonbook materials, 11, 19, 47, 54, 88, 104–105, 116, 125
Nonlibrary activities and facilities, 11, 32, 53, 79
Nonprofessional staff, *see* Clerical staff
Norton, Andrews, 1

Odegaard, Charles, 29

Olin, John M., 95
Olin Library (Cornell), 95, 101, 103, 108, 109, 111
Open access to the collection: 142, 148; Indiana, 86–87; Lamont, 18; Michigan, 49; South Carolina, 71–72; Texas, 128; Uris, 105–116
Open-access stacks, *see* Stacks
Orientation, 107–118, 145
Out-of-print books, 45, 52, 83, 84, 103, 125, 141
Outdoor terraces, 120

Pamphlets, 54, 85, 88
Periodical indexes, 71
Periodicals: 143; Indiana, 80, 85; Lamont, 10, 17; Michigan, 46; South Carolina, 70–71; Texas, 118, 119, 125; Uris, 103, 104, 111
Phonograph recordings, 3, 20, 47, 104, 125
Photocopying, 98, 149
Planning period: Indiana, 78–79; Lamont, 5; Michigan, 29–31; South Carolina, 63; Texas, 116–117; Uris, 93–95
Print Study Gallery (Michigan), 32
Processing staff, 15, 20, 43, 44, 74, 103, 130
Professional staff: organization, 21, 106, 131; size, 74, 89, 108, 128; teaching function, 55, 144, 155
Public catalog, *see* Catalog
Publishers' catalogs, 44, 45
Pyetell collection, 102, 103

Radcliffe College, 6, 25
Ranges: direction, 32; spacing, 32; *see also* Shelving
Ransom, Harry H., 116–117
Rawlinson, Alfred, 63, 70
Reading
   areas: location of, 32, 65, 80, 120; types of, 14, 38, 65, 68, 98, 118
   habits, 56, 106, 137
Reading room tables, *see* Tables, reading room
Reames, J. Mitchell, 71
Reference
   collection: Indiana, 86; Lamont, 17–18; Michigan, 47; South Carolina, 71; Texas, 127; Uris, 105
   service: 143; Indiana, 87; Lamont, 18–19; Michigan, 50–51; South Carolina, 72; Texas, 128; Uris, 106
Reserve
   acquisitions for, 20, 71, 86, 107, 127
   closed, 19, 52, 71, 72, 87, 107, 129, 143
   collection: Indiana, 86; Lamont, 18; Michigan, 47–49; South Carolina, 71; Texas, 127–128, 129; Uris, 105, 107
   duplication of books for, *see* Duplication, for reserve
   graduate, 71, 72
   open, 52, 79, 87, 107, 143
   use of: Indiana, 90–91; Lamont, 23–24; Michigan, 57–58; South Carolina, 75; Texas, 132–133; Uris, 111
Rice, Warner G., 29
Round tables, *see* Tables, round
Rush orders, 20, 107
Russell, Donald S., 63

Screens, dividing, 9, 32, 43, 65
Seating
   capacity of: Indiana, 82; Lamont, 14; Michigan, 38; South Carolina, 65; Texas, 122–123; Uris, 99–100

   individual, 9, 14, 38, 68, 81, 82, 99, 121–122, 140; *see also* Carrels
   percentage of required, 149
   types of: Indiana, 82; Lamont, 12, 14; Michigan, 38; South Carolina, 65; Texas, 121; Uris, 99–100
Segregation of the sexes, 6, 25, 147
Selection tools, *see* Book selection tools
Services
   centralized: 2, 144; Indiana, 88; Lamont, 21; Michigan, 54; South Carolina, 73; Texas, 130; Uris, 108
   simplified: 2, 144; Indiana, 88; Lamont, 21; Michigan, 54; South Carolina, 73; Texas, 130; Uris, 108
Shaw, Charles, 15
Shelving: 9; color of, 12, 65; in reading areas, 34, 68, 119; separation of reading areas by, 8, 14, 65, 120
Site selection: 138, 149; Indiana, 79; Lamont, 5; Michigan, 32; South Carolina, 65; Texas, 117–118; Uris, 94
Slanting-top tables, *see* Tables, slanting-top
Smoking areas, 9, 10, 73, 79, 81, 97, 98, 117, 119, 122
Stacks: access to, 18, 49, 71, 105–106, 128; ceiling heights of, 9, 26; free-standing, 9, 11, 32, 80
Staff
   facilities, 10, 97, 120, 138–139
   organization: Indiana, 89; Lamont, 21–22; Michigan, 55; South Carolina, 74; Texas, 131–132; Uris, 109
   size: 150; Indiana, 89; Lamont, 21; Michigan, 55; South Carolina, 74; Texas, 131; Uris, 108
   teaching function, 55, 144, 145
   turnover, 22, 55, 131
   see also Clerical staff *and* Professional staff
Stephan (Ruth) Poetry Center, 120
Stewart, Rolland C., 43, 44, 45, 47
Stone, Edward D., 63
Storage facilities, 9, 63
Student: committees, 6, 31; lounge, 32, 53, 144, 149; socializing, 76
Study: conditions, 111; habits, 126, 133
Study hall use: 146; Indiana, 78, 91; Lamont, 18; Michigan, 30, 58; South Carolina, 65, 74–75; Texas, 133; Uris, 112
Subscription libraries, 1
Supervision of readers, 131

Tables: divided, 99, 121, 140; reading room, 12, 65, 97, 121–122; round, 82, 140; slanting-top, 14, 97, 98, 99
Tapes, 20, 125, 105
Teaching with books, 30, 146
Technical services, *see* Acquisition of materials *and* Cataloging
Test files, 88
Theft, 144
Traffic patterns, 100–111, 140, 149
Typing facilities: 144, 149; Indiana, 81; Lamont, 10; Michigan, 32, 53; South Carolina, 73; Texas, 119, 130, 140; Uris, 98

Undergraduate collections, 2
Undergraduate Library (Indiana): background, 78–79; book collection, 83–87; building, 79–82; services, 87–88; staff, 89; use, 89–91
Undergraduate Library (Michigan): background, 29–31; book collection, 43–49; building, 32–43; financing, 31–32; services, 50–55; staff, 55; use, 55–58

Undergraduate Library (South Carolina): background, 63; book collection, 69–72; building, 63–69; financing, 63; services, 72–74; staff, 74; use, 74–76

Undergraduate Library (Texas): background, 116–117; book collection, 124–128; building, 117–124; financing, 117; services, 128–131; staff, 131–132; use, 132–134

University of California, Los Angeles, 2

University of Chicago, 2

University of Cincinnati, 2

University of Illinois, 2

University of Michigan shelf list, 83, 102, 104, 105, 124, 125, 141

University of New Mexico, 2

University of Tennessee, 2

University of Washington, 2

Uris, Harold D., 96

Uris, Percy, 96

Uris Library (Cornell): background, 93–95; book collection, 101–116; building, 96–101; financing, 95–96; services, 106–118; staff, 108–119; use, 109–112

Vending machines, 32

Vertical file, 54, 88

Vocarium, 20,

Wagman, Frederick H., 29, 30, 31, 117

Warner, Burns, Toan & Lunde, 96

Weeding, 16–17, 46, 85, 104

White (Andrew D.) Library (Cornell), 95, 97, 98

Widener Library (Harvard): space needs, 5; use by undergraduates, 5

Wilkinson, Billy R., 108

Williams, Edwin E., 15, 16

Winchell, Constance, 17

Wood, Frederick C., 94

Woodberry (George Edward) poetry room (Lamont), 11, 19

Work space, 139, 149

Y collection (Texas), 126

Yale University, 2